An Invisible Prison

An Invisible Prison

✦

A true story of survival

Susan Armstrong with C.K. Clarke

iUniverse, Inc.
New York Lincoln Shanghai

An Invisible Prison
A true story of survival

iUniverse books may be ordered through booksellers or by contacting:

iUniverse
2021 Pine Lake Road, Suite 100
Lincoln, NE 68512
www.iuniverse.com
1-800-Authors (1-800-288-4677)

ISBN-13: 978-0-595-38277-4 (pbk)
ISBN-13: 978-0-595-82646-9 (ebk)
ISBN-10: 0-595-38277-0 (pbk)
ISBN-10: 0-595-82646-6 (ebk)

Printed in the United States of America

This book is dedicated to the six people who have helped to
make me who I am today:

My mother and sister, whom I love dearly
My father, who passed away before he could see how far I've come
The man identified in the book as "Rick" for reasons I am unwilling to disclose
Cindy, my best friend, for showing me what it means to be a real person
Finally, my husband and hero, Brian, who treats me like a princess and
makes me feel special

Thank you all.

"Success is to be measured not so much by the position that one has reached in life as by the obstacles which he has overcome while trying to succeed."

Booker T. Washington

Contents

Acknowledgments

Without the assistance of many, this book would not be in existence. A note of thanks goes out to the women who gave me the confidence to publish my story, including Cindy Green, Giselle Kovary, Jennifer Kelly, Shawna Hogan, Michelle Keast, Donna Stirling, Anne Rose, Evi Yannopoulos, and Denise D'Alessandro.

None of this would have happened, however, without Carol Clarke. When I engaged Carol to assist me in writing my story, I already knew she was a good editor, having already worked on a chapter as part of another book I was contributing to. I was unaware, however, that she had spent several years working with adults attending high school for the second time around and were, for every reason, too familiar with failure and defeat. This gave her the understanding necessary to bring my story to life in a very readable way. While I am an eloquent speaker, Carol is equally as eloquent with the written word. Without her work, patience, and encouragement, this book would never have happened. I owe her my gratitude.

Preface

I always felt I was destined to do something great. I don't know what, but something—a paleontologist, an oceanographer, or, at least, a doctor. At one time, I also aspired to be the Charlie Girl in the perfume ad. When it was first released on television, the commercial featured a beautiful businesswoman with a briefcase striding confidently toward an impressive glass office tower. That's the image I really wanted for myself; however, my family was very conservative and very middle class. Ideally, they wanted me to grow up, get married, have children, and be a really good secretary. They weren't dream stealers. They were simply practical people, but I had different plans.

The journey to those glass towers has been a long one. I have made some life-altering choices that created huge obstacles for my stability and success. Some of these choices have had devastating effects on my physical and emotional health, but I have prevailed; it meant my survival. Today, I'm happily married with two wonderful stepsons, a lovely home, and a very successful business. My existence hasn't always been so comfortable.

An Invisible Prison: A True Story of Survival is the first book in a series that traces the story of my journey from disruptive adolescence through recovered adulthood. Its intent is to encourage and inspire anyone who seeks, as I did, self-esteem in all the wrong places.

Because the story you are about to read is true, certain facts and events have been slightly modified. All names have been changed to protect the privacy of each individual involved.

Please remember, personal stories, including mine, can—and do—have happy endings.

1

It was her own fault, I mean, the getting hit by the car thing. I heard the tires screech and the thump of her body hitting the pavement. It was Jessie, bloody and dirty at the curb. Stupid. Yeah, that's what it was, stupid. My friend had been too stupid and vain to wear her glasses, and she had ruined our drinking night at The Ambrose. If she had run across the street when I did, we would have been inside the doors by now, enjoying our first drink of the night. Instead, some lady was racing out of her car, yelling she was a nurse and everyone should stay clear, whatever that meant. For a few minutes, I stood back under the tavern sign, trying to decide if I should just go in by myself or tend to the messy situation on the road. Reluctantly, I joined the growing knot of onlookers. The nurse was in the middle of the scene taking Jessie's pulse, and Jessie was moaning. A cabdriver pulled up and, in a heavy Italian accent, he offered us a free lift to the hospital. He was waving his arms excitedly enough to fly, but I didn't want to go to the hospital. It was Jessie's accident. It was *her* purple bump on her forehead, *her* bloody nose. How could these people get in my way? My evening was being wasted…I should be there…in the tavern.

"Wake up, Jessie! You're just a little shaky. You can make it. Get up! C'mon, let's go!" I begged.

Somebody pulled me away and pushed me into the cab with my limp friend. They rushed us to the hospital. Somebody else called our parents.

All the way home, my parents grilled me, tag-team style.

"What were you doing in the downtown core?"

"Do you know what kind of girls hang around down there?"

"Bikers frequent that bar. What's it called? The one right across where your friend was hit. The Ambrose?" My father shook his head and clucked his tongue as he swung into our driveway. "Bikers!"

Bikers. I was dreamily recalling another ride in the back of my dad's car a year earlier. A big, black Harley-Davidson with polished chrome had hauled up alongside us at a red light. The guy was wearing a patch on the back of his leather jacket: gang colors in black, white, and scarlet red…biker chick clinging to his waist…matching black helmets…wow!

"Answer us when we talk to you, Susan!"

I was startled back into the moment but hadn't lost my position.

"We weren't hanging around the street like you think."

Despite my defensive play of innocence and what I thought was a dynamite alibi, Jessie caused both of us to be grounded. I was so miserable that I complied, but the incident forced me to choose sides. Partying was my priority. I had only gone with Jessie to the emergency room because she needed to memorize my explanation about where she was and how we got there.

"Friends dropped us off, and they forgot us. Yeah, that's how it was. No, we were never there before. We were sort of...lost. Got that? Can you hear me? Lost. Got that, Jessie?"

By fifteen, I had become a very confident liar. My alibis were legendary.

Of course, it hadn't always been that way. My parents had emigrated from Nottingham, England (yes, the home of Robin Hood and Maid Marian), when I was four and my perfect, good-girl sister, Sarah, was two. Mom and Dad were proudly and properly British. They likely felt comfortable in Canada, but my adjustments were far from smooth. I kept my anxiety a secret until I was about seven when I joined Brownies, you know, pre-Girl Scouts. At one of our meetings, while we were busily knotting ropes, a throbbing started to grow inside my head and wouldn't stop. The late afternoon sun poking through the windows hurt my eyes. The other girls were sympathetic, but, because I said I might throw up, they kept their distance. Meanwhile, the entire right side of my head felt like it was about to explode. Brown Owl, the grown-up pack leader, sent me home.

Back in our kitchen, everyone was eating dinner, but I just wanted to lie on my bed. With my Brownie shirt pulled over my face to block out the light, I passed out from the pain. When I woke up, the hurt was gone, but it returned the next day...and the next...and the next. My parents took me to the family physician.

"Migraine," he pronounced. "Adult migraine."

"What would cause such episodes in a seven-year-old?" my mother asked.

As an answer, he ordered an endless round of neurologists and every other specialist or test he expected would help. The migraine headaches lasted about five years. The cause was never discovered, but I suspect it was tension, specifically, the kind found at home.

There was one cardinal sin in our house and it was this: never upset anyone. Above all, you should never hurt someone's feelings! Such a discourtesy was to be avoided at all costs. If you wanted people to like you (and you did want them to, didn't you?), you had to behave in a particular way. There were rules. For instance, you must stand up straight. And your hair mustn't be near your face. It must be tucked around your ears and hanging behind your shoulders.

You had to especially remember this hair rule when you were eating in a restaurant because "You want the waitress to like you, don't you, luv?"

While standing in line for anything, I had to make sure not to fidget or people, including salesclerks, wouldn't approve of me. For instance, if I were waiting in a grocery line with my mother and someone two aisles over dropped her purse, I'd flinch, convinced that it must have somehow been my fault. For years, I wouldn't get into an elevator if there were people already in there because if I got stuck at the back, I would have to ask them to move so I could get off at my floor. That might upset someone. I only got into empty elevators or elevators where I could stand at the front. That way, I was sure I would be able to get off without making anyone angry by asking them to move. Worst of all, I thought everyone behaved this way. I was working so hard to get every stranger to like me, but, truthfully, it didn't matter. No one noticed my efforts anyway.

School caused another outbreak of nerves. I was a smart kid, and I always knew the answers to the teacher's questions. Problem was, when I answered all of the teacher's questions, the teacher liked me but the kids didn't. They called me a browner; it didn't take long for me to figure out that the label had nothing to do with being a Brownie. Yet, if I didn't answer the teacher's questions, then the teacher would get mad (or so I thought) because she knew that I knew the answer. Then she would assume I was being difficult.

I could never win because when you're different, the rules are always contrary to your needs. Even with the greatest care, you could annoy someone, and, if it's your job to please people to gain their approval, they get to decide if you're worthy or not. I was aware that I either had to please or be rejected. Even later, when I rebelled, I felt obliged to worry about it. I *always* felt different. I just didn't fit in.

2

By the time I was eleven, life was mellowing out a bit. Even though the gruesome school tunics my grandmother sent to me from England during the psychedelic 1960s were enough to socially bury me, miraculously, the kids stopped teasing me. I was finally fitting in as a regular Canadian; however, it was not to be.

One morning in January, a lady came to our grade six classroom and distributed tests. I raced through mine and handed it in first. The teacher was pleased. Several days later, the school principal called my parents. It seems that the test indicated that I should be in a "special" class, far from my house. I could walk there, but it would take a half hour or more. I'd have to take a city bus. My parents held some lengthy discussions and I'm sure they asked my opinion, but I don't remember my answer. Mom and Dad always felt that their decision to enroll me in the special class was a bad one. In hindsight, I'm not sure it would have made any difference at all in the outcome of my life. I was signed up in the new "gifted" class for kids like me.

There were twenty nervous kids in that class, mostly girls. All of us were an embarrassing contrast to the rest of the school's normal kids. They knew it, and so did we. This was their neighborhood school, their territory. We were academic freaks, drawn from all over the city to mock them for their standard abilities and their average science fair projects. We were the rhinestones on a beige shirt, attracting all the attention.

It seemed my efforts to please had finally been recognized. I had earned my own privileged seat in juvenile social hell. My confusion was intense. At home, my identity was simply an extension of Sarah's. In public, I was convinced I was inappropriate and had to follow imaginary rules for approval. At school, I was stuck in a pit of misfits. Smart is not the trait that makes you popular. Anxiety became my constant companion.

When Trudy, "the Tower," became my best friend in gifted class, I was grateful. At five and a half feet tall, she stood head and shoulders above the entire class. She wore lots of makeup and had curves in all the places I only dreamed about. She also smoked.

I already knew about cigarettes. Attracted by its cool image, I started smoking at nine. Smoking with Trudy was easy. Since her height gave her the illusion of being much older, she was offered a job in the convenience store downstairs in her apartment building. That meant she had money for smoking and for sharing smokes. In the spring of that year, we tested our maturity together and drank our first beer. In our province at the time, legal drinking age was eighteen. Once again, Trudy's height (and figure) afforded her special privilege. After school, she nonchalantly walked into a beer store at the local mall and, as casually as she could at eleven years old, bought us a six-pack. Drinking the stuff wasn't any big deal. Beer wasn't exactly a taboo for me. My grandparents owned pubs in England, and I had spent summers with them, helping to clear the tables after lunch break. I was already familiar with the sour smell of lagers, ales, and stout and I was well acquainted with the happiness it gave the patrons. My parents smoked, but they drank only the occasional bottle of beer.

I was a drinking natural. In the hot summer months, I was allowed a shandy, which at our house was a mixture of beer and lemonade. When I was sick with a cold or flu, Mom made me feel better with hot orange juice laced with Bell's Scotch. When my parents had parties, Dad would bring me a gin and Wink cocktail while I was in bed. I thought it was grown-up at the time, but now, in hindsight, I assume the drink was to make me sleep.

My first alcohol served without adults present was that day with Trudy on a secluded, grassy hill behind the stores. Just inside the mall was a public wash-room, in case we needed it. Beers, smokes, bathroom, and privacy: the luxury was exhilarating. My poor friend was only halfway through her first beer when she coughed and got sick. Unmoved by Trudy's unfortunate reaction, I was proudly able to carry on. Somewhere into my third bottle, I found myself suddenly numbed, afloat in a heavenly stupor. Miracle of miracles! Those brown bottles held the secret of self-confidence. They handed me a temporary permit to set aside my worries of people pleasing. I didn't have to be quiet, apologetic, or even polite. Suddenly I could be a big, confident *somebody!* Talk about being in a good mood! No wonder people liked this stuff. It was useful.

I drank the rest of the six-pack alone. In the coming years, I would do what-ever I had to do for more and yet more of the same. There was never going to be enough of that wonderful sensation of freedom. Rummaging through our medi-cine cabinet sometimes produced a little something to help me through the end-less days in school. Even a simple cold and allergy medication would give me a small rush or two to take the edge off things while I waited for evening. It became one of my school supplies, an eraser if you will.

At twelve, I also started to like marijuana. It was generously offered by the guys Trudy and I hitched rides with to tour the downtown strip. Pot left me as mellow as warm syrup. And the combination of alcohol and pot produced a very satisfying effect: every evening I was on the street, friends multiplied. Dan the Man, a drug dealer with stringy, black hair assumed the role of my boyfriend. That status was never confirmed, but he did give me some LSD one evening. It was orange double barrel acid, confetti-sized squares of paper imprinted with two orange dots.

Trudy and I tried the stuff early one Friday evening. As instructed, we each placed a paper hit on our tongues, expecting euphoria. An hour later, when nothing happened, we grew impatient. We split another hit and, within minutes, neon signs melted and spilled crayon-bright rivers of color along the pavement. Streetlights erupted in crimson, gold, and emerald fireworks. Unseen sirens blared and wailed.

Thinking that police were converging on us from everywhere, sailing down from buildings and slithering out of sewers, Trudy panicked. She wanted to go home. And I, her Good Samaritan, volunteered to steer her, but my legs had taken a mind of their own. They were twisted as corkscrews, stepping high to mount invisible stairs. The sidewalk, miles below my feet, was contorting in some earthquake agony. I didn't tell her.

Somehow, we made it back to her apartment where her parents were calmly watching television. I had always imagined that Trudy was really the child of her older sister because her parents were in their late sixties. A gentle couple, they suspected nothing. Meanwhile, we struggled to her room. She was a mess, really freaked out, and I did my slow-motion best to settle her down. After what seemed hours, I left her and set out to my own side of the planet, expecting at every corner to be handcuffed and arrested by a tall blue uniform. I imagined it was very late, probably about two o'clock in the morning, but even at that hour, the streets were surprisingly busy. Like a buzzing helicopter, danger stalked me all the way home.

Strangely, my parents were still awake. Treading the hall as carefully as my condition would allow, I concentrated on controlling my every movement. Above me, the ceiling fixture was quietly swaying, a body hanged from a tree in a summer's breeze. When I reached the clock in the kitchen, one of the hands, the little one, was pointing to nine. Only nine o'clock? I could read time…I had just lost my sense of it.

Perhaps if I ate something, I might mutate back to normal.

I found the cupboards and the refrigerator and, with deliberate strokes, placed a bit of cheese on a cracker. At least, I think it was a cracker. It had the suspicious edges of a bottle cap. Worse, it wouldn't hold still. Dad was watching television in the family room. I balanced my snack in both hands and joined him.

"Oh, I've seen this show," I offered by way of conversation. "It's good."

"How could you?" he asked. "It's new. A first-run, made-for-TV movie."

"No," I insisted. "I've already seen this."

"You couldn't have." He studied me as though he were trying to read some fine print between my eyebrows.

Uh oh. I was about to fall off the edge of Earth. I should have been quiet. I should have thought only of chair-sitting and watching actors move sluggishly across the screen.

Happily, I seemed to recall that I had placed a snack on the coffee table as I sat down. Oh, good. Eat. Create a distraction. I reached into outer space, way over to the coffee table at my knees, and stole the cheese from its cracker. That seemed to take a very long time. At last, with a good, wide sweep of my arm, I placed the prize in my mouth. When it touched my tongue, though, I couldn't imagine what it was doing there. Even having a tongue was a surprise. I felt like a dog trying to eat peanut butter, not sure whether to chew or swallow. I'd take a bath, that's what I'd do. At the time, it seemed logical.

It took about thirty-five years to reach the bathroom. The tap poured diamonds that splashed into the tub in liquid glass rainbows, and I climbed into a bouquet. Dozens of orange and green daisies with smiling faces bloomed around me. No good.

I got out and shooed the garden from my skin with a towel. Even though I wasn't tired, I pulled my nightgown on and went to bed. Another long journey and more bewilderment. In my absence, the blankets had grown tough and scratchy as potato sacks. Sleep was impossible. Needing a lullaby, I floated over to my record player and managed to put a Beach Boys album on the turntable. The Boys sang "Good Vibrations" for me, but the good vibrations trailed an echo along my nerve endings and into a rapid spin cycle in my brain, in my brain…in my brain. I couldn't find the kill button even after I turned off the record player.

Finally, terrified enough to wake up Mom, I told her the truth. Her daughter (and I was fairly sure I knew which one) was high on acid. Perhaps, if she wouldn't mind calling an ambulance or something, they'd set the girl right. Instead, she resorted to her standard cure, making a cup of tea. At least she didn't lace it with scotch.

I tried to retrieve a cup, but, since my head seemed to be in my Nana's kitchen in England and the rest of my body was at home, it was difficult for my fingers to find the right cupboard. At last, with the tea cradled on my lap and Mom in a chair, I sat looking out the window in the living room. The birch tree on the lawn, the blue-checkered one, waved at me. Being the polite Alice in Acidland, my light brown hair tucked to the rear of the ears in all refinement, I returned the greeting, cup in hand. The tea flew neatly into a potted plant that drank it up before I could stop it. Poor Mom didn't know what else to do; she simply poured me a refill. She did that repeatedly while we spent the night awaiting either sleep or kidney failure.

At some point, I shuffled back to my room and fell onto my pillow, but its tough, ropy fibers grated my cheeks. Rumor must have spread because Dad appeared.

"Why have you done this to yourself?" He was crying at the edge of my bed.

I could only stare. The dear man had lost so much weight since dinner. He was a skeleton. Protruding from the neck of his oversized pajamas was a skull, and he was talking through its bony teeth. He spoke at length, sobbing all the while behind empty eye sockets. I think he was reciting poetry. Gratefully, I fell asleep.

3

Early the next afternoon, I stuck my arms inside a bathrobe and wobbled toward the kitchen. Breakfast was full of accusations.

"I hope you're proud, young lady. Look what you've done to yourself!"

"Do you know how dangerous those drugs are? What were you thinking?"

"You didn't learn that kind of disrespect from us!"

Break here long enough for me to picture both parents strapped and screaming in a rocket ship that crashes on the moon. I didn't really want them dead. I merely wanted them to evaporate on the spot.

"I'm really sorry."

My throat was raspy and dry. The room was spinning. I wanted to run outside. "It was a stupid kid's thing," I croaked. "I'll never do it again!" Did they believe me? Was I excused yet? I was strangling in a near-death experience, trying to breathe through my guilt. Why couldn't they hurry up and disappear?

"Sure, that's it. Just make light of it. You always do, Susan."

Would they never quit? I hated them. "No, I mean it. I'll never, ever experiment again. I promise."

For effect, I placed my hand over my heart, which was banging mechanically in my chest. We volleyed the same words around for an hour. Attack, apology. Attack, agreement. My tactics were firm. I said I wouldn't do it again, but they didn't get it. Their anger, their whining, and their helplessness built a thick wall of resentment between us. I was determined not to be broken.

"I've learned my lesson," I offered once more, buttering toast with jittery hands.

An exchange of looks, a fingering of teaspoons. Twin sighs. "We are worried about you."

"Yes, I know. I'm quite fine now. Really." Quietly, my stomach heaved.

"If you're going out today, you'd better be home by teatime." (British thing: dinner.)

I had better. What could they do anyway? Ground me? Slap me with a curfew? Keep me inside?

They had already tried that. My mother had stood in my way when I tried to break out; I had simply brushed by her and left.

They had no further ammunition in their arsenal. I changed my clothes and stalked out.

That same evening, whether for spite, bravado, or in despair, I did another hit. After that, I avoided acid for many years. My absolute darkest nightmare was founded in those stories of people who spend the rest of their lives in mental institutions, the ones who never returned from their last trip.

Partly because of the acid thing (And was bad acid my fault?), Trudy and my other three friends, Dana, Lisa, and Rachel, dropped me. I had been away all summer in England, vacationing with my grandparents. When I returned, I expected my friends would be excited to see me. I was mistaken.

"We need to talk to you." The four of them, with sour looks on their faces, led me to our usual bench at the mall.

"What's up?" I asked cheerfully. See? I am happy. Don't say anything scary. I'm keeping a light mood here.

"We don't want to hang around with you anymore." This, from Trudy in her new, softer image without her usual midnight blue eyeliner.

"I...uh...what? You what?"

Lisa's turn. "We just don't want you to be with us anymore."

"That's it?"

"Yeah."

"Pretty much."

"We decided."

Panic. "But...why?"

No response.

"Please, I need to know *why*!" (Rescue me! Say we're friends. Help me! I'm dying here!)

Nothing. That dial tone you hear when someone hangs up on you.

Whispering, already ashamed of whatever they had chosen to accuse me of, I begged them. "Was it something I said?"

"Not really," offered Dana. The other three exchanged quick glances of approval with each other for her vague answer. Dana was not compelling anyone to offer the truth.

"Was it something I did?"

I didn't really need to ask. I was already clueing into what had happened. They had been able to develop it over the past few weeks, detailing it with colorful gossip from supposed friends until they had their perfect story: Sue sailing around town in a van filled with degenerates, doing drugs, drinking, and who knew what else. Well, it wasn't hard to guess. All of them knew about the day with the spiked Coke when I had fought my way out of being raped in the back of a van. The guys must have bragged a different story. Was that the version they heard? Then again, who would believe that Sue would have refused a spiked drink?

"I'm not a slut."

Offended, they arched carefully penciled eyebrows. "Nobody said you were."

"I'm not. I'm still a…"

Sharp half smiles all around. They didn't believe me.

"We have to go." Obviously they hadn't worked out this little drama to a clean ending; I was supposed to take the hint and be smart enough to leave. But I didn't. I waited, hoping they would change their minds.

"Yeah…well…maybe it's best…you should…like, you know. Go now?"

And so it was concluded. They turned their backs to me and made their way out of the mall. And that's when I met Jessie.

Days later, I had to pluck up the courage to return to the mall. With nothing to lose, I approached two strangers. Bumming a light was a ploy we often used to meet guys. I had never used the line to meet other girls.

"You have a light?" I asked Jessie, the skinny one.

"Yep," she said and produced a purple Bic while her friend watched.

I lit up and took a long drag to calm myself and asked which schools they went to. I handed back the lighter and soon we were deep into playing "Who do you know that I know?"

Within minutes, I was being invited to a party that night. Did I want to go? Why, yes I did! You betcha!

For the rest of the afternoon, I strolled around the mall with them. As luck would have it, during one of our laps, I spied my former friends several store-fronts ahead of us. I had to dive between a couple with a stroller and some old guy with a walker to make the chance meeting happen, but Dana, Lisa, Rachel, and Trudy deserved to hear the news. They stood gawking as I jerked my head toward my new best friends.

"Sorry I can't stay and talk," I said, breathless with intrigue and tension. "Jessie and Eve and me are getting ready for a party tonight. Something pretty big!"

"Oh?" They stretched their necks to see who I was talking about, silently checked with each other, and the response fell to Dana. I pretended not to notice her narrowed, suspicious eyes.

"Hmm, that's nice. Well, it was good seeing you again, Sue," she said.

"Uh, likewise. Well, see ya around!"

The party, as it turned out, was at a run-down apartment. When I arrived, the volume was on full tilt to a Led Zeppelin album loud enough to vibrate the walls, yet nobody was the least concerned. I guess that immediately discounted their need to be liked by neighbors or, for that matter, anyone within earshot. I was in awe.

Jessie was bleached-blonde cool. Not quite fifteen, she had a regular boyfriend. Despite her pencil-thin arms and legs, she had large breasts. A guy magnet, she was taken, but that gave me her leftovers.

"Wanna drink?" she asked, the perfect hostess in cutoff jean shorts and bare feet.

"Yeah!"

The bathtub was filled with beer and ice, and I was in heaven.

Remarkably, Jessie didn't drink; she preferred pot. To our mutual delight, we were two sides of the same coin. She got high while I got drunk. In the coming weeks, we'd both skip classes to meet for drinks and smoking up. She introduced me to her friends and I introduced her to mine. Together, we started a tradition. From Monday to Thursday, we'd hitchhike uptown and back, looking for joyrides with guys who had pot and beer. On Fridays and Saturdays, we'd hitchhike again. This time, we went to the bar called The Ambrose. Because Jessie was tall, they let her in and I'd follow willingly behind. Once inside, we'd only need enough money to buy our first draught. As I recall, that was thirty-three cents. Invariably, some guy (or guys) would spring for the rest of the evening.

That was our happy pattern until the car accident and the race to the hospital with the Italian cabbie. Oh, afterward we were nagged, lectured, warned, and grounded, but it didn't matter a bit. A week later, we were once again hitching a ride in the downtown strip of our town. Jessie had combed her bangs over the yellow-blue bump on her head and plastered on an extra scoop of makeup and a good smear of pink lipstick. Eventually, a black Cutlass pulled up. The driver was about seventeen and alone.

"Ride?"

"Sure!" We jumped into the front seat and introduced ourselves. Our host for the ride didn't ask where we were going. He didn't have to. The pattern was understood. We would drive around for a while and just get acquainted. Soon we were at his hangout, a midtown fast-food joint. He had friends there, guys who impressed us because they had their own apartments and their own muscle cars with deafening stereo speakers and awesome bass control. Within the hour, we were part of a convoy of flashy cars wheeling onto a strip of beach on a nearby lake. Trunks flew open and beer cases were hauled out and carried to food-stained picnic tables. The air smelled of fish, but, in the last rays of a summer sunset, with the music pumping Aerosmith and April Wine, we were in paradise.

Spontaneous partying became a regular thing. A few of the guys had bachelor apartments located over a store, the kind with a bare-floor living and sleeping area, a hot plate, and a cramped bathroom with rust-stained fixtures. Sometimes we'd start at one of their places before patronizing the Ukrainian halls where we could slow dance and drink more beer. Alcohol was the standard of our evenings. How could anything be wrong with so many happy faces, mine being the happiest?

Jessie, as you may recall, preferred drugs to my alcohol high, but we both did pot. One careless night after the car accident, we got caught. We were at her kitchen table, and we hadn't expected Jessie's mother to be back so soon from shopping. We told her the crumbly stuff on the paper napkin was oregano and that we were going to play a trick on a friend and pretend it was real grass.

"Oregano, eh?" She looked amused.

"Yeah, spaghetti spice. Funny, eh?"

"Very." She wedged herself between us. "Then you won't mind if I smoke it."

What could we say? "No, it's real. Send us to jail now."

"Oregano?" Jessie's eyes grew wide. "You'd smoke *oregano?*" We glanced at each other with surprise and nervous giggles. "Sure, if you want to."

Horrified, we watched while Jessie's mom smoked our joint. She busted us. Took everything we had and gave us a lecture.

Interestingly, years later, after her divorce from Jessie's father, we discovered she had always smoked pot. She knew exactly what she was doing when she scooped our stash.

4

It was late one school night when I wobbled up the driveway, waved a wild good-bye to Jessie and a carload of friends, and passed an unfamiliar dark vehicle in our driveway. Company calling. Dripping boots in the hallway. Voices. I tracked them downstairs to the family room where my parents and two strangers—a man and a woman—greeted me.

"Susan, these people are here to take you away." My father glanced hard at my mother as though to silence a change of heart.

"*Away*? Why?" I hung back in the doorway, close to the bottom of the staircase.

Four adults were in our family room, two of them from the Juvenile Detention Center, and all of them were fixed on my every action. The strangers stood pillar straight, shoulder to shoulder. My parents were paired opposite them. I searched from one to the other for an answer and finally looked my father straight in the eye. He'd save me.

"What? Did I do something *wrong*?" (I was careful not to get too close in case they caught a whiff of the alcohol on my breath.)

My father stared at the ground and swallowed hard. "We don't know what to do with you anymore."

"*Where are you sending me?*"

The man spoke up. "A juvenile facility," he said.

"Facility!" I knew what that meant: group home, counseling, and *curfews*.

"I don't need that!"

"You can get help there," the lady said. Unlike my parents, the visitors were calm, deliberate, and lacking facial expressions. The man nodded. He had somber brown eyes and big hands, and he scared the hell out of me.

"Help? For *what*?" I was ready to bolt even though I knew it would be useless. The adrenaline and alcohol coursing through my system would prevent that from happening. Fight: can't. Flight: wouldn't get far. Trapped.

"Susan, you are fifteen years old. You have taken bad drugs. You are drinking." My father's lost gaze turned in my mother's direction.

"And the problem with your grades," she added, miserably.

"My grades? I'm passing. There's no prob…"

"Fifty-one percent average on your report card, Susan. You've missed nearly a third of your classes. We just don't know what to do with you anymore."

My father had already said that. Is this all they *had?* Suddenly, my mother's face caved and she searched her pockets for clean tissue. Voice quaking, she resumed by dragging up the next item on their prepared list of offenses.

"That time…that time…*I tried.*"

So, she must have told them, the authorities, about how I almost knocked her over that time she tried to ground me. They looked away, waiting for my own parents to condemn me.

My father took over, but not as I had expected. "Susan, before you know it, you'll be just like that friend of yours, that runaway, living like common filth on the street."

True. One of my friends was a known and chronic runaway, but I rose to her defense.

"And that's just why Amber ran," I protested. "She…she…her parents drove her to it. They didn't *care!*"

It was the parents' fault, it always is; surely they could handle that much logic.

My father's face flushed. He was getting frustrated. No one else moved a muscle while he exposed an ancient fear shared by fathers everywhere. "My daughter, running around from bed to bed."

"I *never!*"

He was deaf to my protests. "No man wants to marry a *tramp*, Susan!"

My name, next to that word. And from my own father's mouth. I braced myself against the doorframe.

"You don't understand. I'm not doing that. I'm still a…" Four pairs of eyes, suddenly alert, fixed on me. Embarrassed, I found myself unable to complete the sentence or prevent what was happening. I was being sent to juvenile hall, a detention center for loose girls, the kind who disappoint their parents.

"I'll be good," I pleaded. "I'll change. Just tell me what you want me to do!"

A small, efficient cough came from the male detention officer. He was transmitting a danger signal to my dad.

"Careful," it said. "You could lose it here."

Everyone was still standing. *Why was everyone still standing?*

I lifted my arms from my sides in a gesture of surrender, of mercy. I blinked, threatening real tears, and was able to massage a few fake ones past my mascara, hoping it would smear and run, all the more pathetic.

"Pleeease, Dad!" I was panicking.

My mother blew wetly into a tissue.

"And look what you've done to your mother!" My father's disgust with me hurt worse than the threat of juvenile hall. All I had ever wanted was for him to be proud of me, but that didn't look like it was going to happen. Instead, I was disgusting.

I looked desperately from one parent to the other, thinking of the twenty friends I had just left and how I didn't want to name them; some of them were already known criminals. They wouldn't *like* my going away. They wouldn't *like* anyone to ask me stuff.

"Whatever you say!" I whimpered. "Anything! I really want to try…this time." Then desperately, I said, "I love you!"

The visitors leaned forward, worried. They knew they were losing.

Dad ran his hand through his hair and gave that familiar sigh. He finally spoke the quieting words I longed to hear. "I guess we have to give her the benefit of the doubt."

I brightened. The game had turned.

"Mr. Armstrong, are you very sure about this?"

"Susan," Dad implored, "will you promise?"

"Yes!" (Hurray! I won.) "I will be good!"

The lady picked up her briefcase. She looked tired. The man shook his head. The adults clustered and exchanged words I couldn't hear. They shook hands, the thank-you, good-bye kind. I backed up to let them pass, my whole demeanor grave with humility. No one hugged me. Good. Did they catch my scent?

I'd play the dutiful daughter until my sixteenth birthday when I could legally quit school and become a free agent. Sixteen was less than a year away. Until that magic moment, I could cope.

I spent the next several months trying to behave so that the authorities wouldn't take me away, and the next twenty-five years trying to prove my father wrong about no man wanting to marry me. Ironically, when I finally did marry a good man, he wasn't able to witness it. He passed away five years before that happened. As for his fears about my reputation at fifteen, I really was still a virgin.

5

My year of being good passed with few consequences. The family was pleased that I was settling down and gave me the space of forgiveness. In turn, I walked an artificial path of acceptable teen behavior. Patiently, stealthily, I was biding time.

On the evening of December 1, my sixteenth birthday, a gentle snow began falling while we had our family dinner. I was going to meet Jessie at seven o'clock, and I couldn't wait. A scream of joy was mounting inside of me. Sixteen and free! I had made it!

At six thirty, the phone rang. It was Jessie. For some reason, she didn't want to walk and meet me halfway to our fast-food hangout at Mickey's as we usually did. Instead, she asked if she could meet me there. She hedged about the reason, but I suspected the truth must have had something to do with her new boyfriend, Kane. Controlling, and combative, he was obsessed with her whereabouts. I hated him. I hated his pimply face and his long, frizzy hair. I hated his superior attitude. Until Kane, Jessie and I were never far apart. If one of us had a date, without a question, the other would tag along. It didn't happen with this guy, though. I also couldn't stomach any of his friends for a double date.

Kane drove Jessie to Mickey's. I was waiting for the red light to change when, from the opposite side of the street, I saw Jessie climb out of his car trying to juggle what looked like a hatbox. She slammed the door with her hip, and he skidded away through the slush. Only a minute behind her, I stamped through the doors, kicking my wet boots. When I looked up, there were all my friends crowded into booths. They were grinning like crazy, there to surprise me. Jessie, barely out of her coat, flipped open the box to reveal a strawberry cake with wavy, pink icing. "Happy Birthday, Sue" was spelled out in red sugar sprinkles. She had baked it herself.

Even my old friends, Dana, Lisa, Rachel, and Trudy, had agreed to come. It was a wonderful, momentous evening. I had sixteen candles and twenty-four friends to celebrate my independence.

Two weeks later, Jessie had another surprise for me, except this one wasn't so joyous. She was shivering and flicking cigarette ashes on an icy patch of pavement. Her eyes were sad, her head hung low, and she wouldn't look at me. Jessie was pregnant. Like me, she had just turned sixteen. I felt a twinge of guilt. I had recently become friends with another girl named Holly, who was in my grade eleven class, but, in my estimation, she was high society. Her nails were carefully manicured, and on her finger was a whopping diamond birthstone ring that her father had given her for her birthday. Everything about Holly translated sophistication to me. She lived in a gorgeous apartment with her divorced mother, whom she called by her first name. She had an en suite bathroom. Most wonderful of all, she owned a car.

My mother was very disapproving of the friendship.

"Out of your class, Susan," she nagged. "You can't keep up with that kind of money." Can if I want. Watch me. I believed that money bought class. If you stood close enough, you'd get some, too. With Holly, I imagined myself in the presence of a celebrity. It didn't take long to abandon Jessie to her pregnancy and Kane.

Since Holly's having a car allowed entertainment farther away from home, we tracked all the weekend events at bars that featured bands. Every Thursday night, we'd scour the entertainment section of the newspaper to choose our destination. Disco was coming in, and we made sure to dress the part. No more hitchhiking. Forget the T-shirts and slum image. The new Sue whipped up a three-piece suit on her sewing machine, bought a satin blouse, and learned how to paint her nails.

Had I been superstitious, I would have avoided the Black Cat lounge. During one of our weekend outings, Holly and I found a club called The Hilltop. It was a fifty-minute drive from where we lived, but it was a big step up in excitement. The Hilltop was very large, a T-shape configuration, and in their Black Cat lounge, disco bands and comedians performed on a regular basis. My friend and I were cute, we were nicely attired, and we were admitted. Chins held high, we strode elegantly to the lounge. We always arrived early to get good seats on the balcony section against the railing, the best place for viewing and for being viewed. Ladylike and grown-up with skirts smoothed and legs crossed, we sipped Martini & Rossi sweet vermouth on the rocks with lemon. The smoke from our cigarettes rose delicately from poised hands, alternately raised, then gracefully reaching for the glass ashtray (yes, *glass*, not those tin things with the bar's name stamped on the bottom). One must try not to think about poor Jessie back at Mickey's in her jeans and her predicament. I was in grown-up land being eyed by guys in suits. Very nice suits.

One special evening, the waiter set down four draft beers and pointed to two guys across the lounge who nodded. We tried to look demure and thankful, but under the table, Holly was excitedly kicking my shin with the pointed toe of her shoe. What next? I stole a look and choked.

"Psst, Holly! Those guys are still looking this way." I gasped. "No! Don't look! I'll tell you when. Oh, they're coming over here." I could hardly believe it. "Oh God, I could just die. Shh, shh! Just act natural."

(Try not to drool!)

Randy, who was tall, black, strong, and suave, approached Holly. The other one, lethal with cologne, was Shane. He was shorter than his buddy and slimmer, but he was interested in me! Imagine! Jeez! How I could replay this to Jessie! What could I tell her *first?* That he's employed at one of the local steel mills! He's older, maybe nineteen. Oh, and Jessie, you're not going to believe my luck! He said he owned a motorcycle. Really! A Triumph. I met his friends, but, for some reason, they all seemed to be somehow related. Whatever. Get this. They *all* rode bikes! He asked me to dance, and he talked to me, told me everything about himself but, now here's the really romantic part…are you ready? He never left the table. We drank the evening away.

I could have told the tale to Jessie, but I didn't. My life was really moving now, much faster than she could appreciate anyway.

6

Before he immigrated to Canada, my father owned a motorcycle, a 1942 Indian bike with a suicide shift, that is, a hand shift on the gas tank instead of the standard foot shift. My mother eventually made him sell it because he liked to drag it into the kitchen to fix it.

Shane had a motorcycle, but, probably because seeing me slung on the back was not his idea of a bike accessory, Dad disapproved. If my mother had spoken up, I'm sure she would have reminded me that my new boyfriend was beneath me or everyday riffraff, but she held her tongue. After all, the guy had a steady job at the steel mill and sent me roses on my birthday. He lived at home in his parents' tiny house and paid room and board. He had to. His parents were supporting his younger sister, who was still in high school, and an older sister, who had left her abusive husband, again. Two other children, young adults, had already moved out. On Sundays, Shane's parents must have enjoyed celebrating that semi-accomplishment because right after High Mass, they'd come home, plop a major-sized bottle of rye on the kitchen table, and drink…and fight…and drink. It was a holy ritual.

Holly and I maintained our own religious observations, making a pilgrimage to The Hilltop every night of the week. Even though I considered Shane as my first real boyfriend, he always arrived late and only stayed for one beer. The benefit to his having a large circle of friends was that in his absence they bought drinks for me.

Shane's lateness meant he was either at work or working on his motorcycle. I considered him a workaholic, and his lateness annoyed me. When he was supposed to pick me up at home, I'd be tapping away the minutes into hours with my fingertips on the closest tabletop. Worst of all, my mother would also be keeping vigil at the window, nattering about the lateness and giving advice about guys who were chronically late. Oh, he'd call and say it would be twenty more minutes, which would turn into forty, but eventually he'd show up. I never said much about it because part of me still clung to that fear of displeasing. If I challenged him, he might not want to be my boyfriend anymore.

One evening, while my mother was pacing at the window and maintaining surveillance for me while I silently fumed, she shrieked.

"A hearse has just pulled into our driveway! What is a *hearse* doing in our driveway? Surely, there must be some mistake. And even so…what a dreadful omen!"

Shane was summoning me with the horn. I grabbed my purse and sprinted out before my mother could catch up. She was still taking great gasps of breath and squawking when I slammed the door behind me.

Shane wasn't much of a talker, so we rode in silence. I assumed he was repairing the hearse for someone and had borrowed it for the evening. I didn't care. It was transportation and for me, it was a first. I had never been in such a creepy vehicle. The interior was plain and grim, but behind our heads, drawn the length of the seat, were dark red, velvet drapes. They were split in the middle, I imagined, so you could peek behind every once in a while to check to see if the coffin was still there. I didn't snoop, but I heard scratching and rustling sounds.

"Shane, did you hear that?"

"What?"

"There's something *back there.*"

"Oh, now, don't go getting goofy on me. There's nothing there."

Silly girl. Just be quiet, I thought. Don't be one of those airheads who likes to play girly, helpless games. Get a grip.

But there *were* noises. Animal sounds. I tried ignoring them and focusing on our destination, but as Shane turned a corner, I caught sight of something reaching from behind. It was a human hand. I couldn't help it. I screamed.

Shane laughed like a lunatic. His friend Al stuck his head out from behind the drapes, howling with laughter. Their prank had scared me almost out of my mind.

"Oh, I love you guys!" I roared. "That was so funny. It was! It really was! You're such jokers!"

(Okay, they were morons.)

Shane got the hearse again for our only real date. He took me to see *Orca the Killer Whale* at a drive-in movie and parked in the back row to get started on my next first. I was a virgin. Shane was very patient, but making out was limited. I knew I'd have to get in the mood or lose him, but neither the limo of death we were thrashing around in nor the close-up of the whale's eyeball watching us from the movie screen did anything to enhance the moment. When the closing credits floated up the screen, I was still a virgin.

7

Dawn and Lana were sisters who lived in an apartment very close to Shane's place. Sometimes Shane was late or didn't show up at all because Dawn was "having problems." According to Shane, the girls were merely his good friends. He was glad to be able to help, especially with Dawn. Did I mention? She had *problems*.

During this phase of Shane's amateur crisis intervention counseling, my drinking increased dramatically. The more I drank, the more I felt I needed my bar buddies; yet as much as I needed them, I distanced myself from them with my unpredictable behavior. The cycle of being different and needing to fit in was still ruling my emotions. I presumed everyone else drank as much as I did, but I was wrong. How was I to know anyway? I had become a blackout drinker.

Take for instance the stab wound on the back of my leg. I don't remember how it got there, but it was there when I woke up one morning.

Intoxication was my identity. Many mornings, my father would be on his way out to work and find me passed out inside the back door, boots and coat still on, and my purse clutched in hand. Would I make it to class that day? Doubtful. Grade twelve? Who cared about that? Certainly not me.

I dismissed everyone's concerns. My friends tried heart-to-heart talks.

"You're so pretty."

"You're such a nice person."

"Why do you do this to yourself?"

Denial became an automatic defense. I went about my business, pretending nothing was wrong, yet being a drunk was like having a pointy growth sticking out of my head: it gave me a pitiful image, and it got in the way of everything. Shane dumped me just after our second camping trip. I never asked why because I was afraid to hear what I knew already: I wasn't good enough.

For our first camping trip in Shane's funky orange two-person tent, I lied to my parents, telling them I was going to Holly's place for the weekend. That was partly true. I was going to the campsite with Holly where we planned to meet fifteen other friends, and where I'd be sharing a tent with Shane.

When I met Shane at the site, he had already set up his tent. It wasn't a regular campsite, just a couple acres of brush, but it was perfect for our needs. Camping was a first with Shane. I had never done it before, and I was excited. From the minute I burst from the car, I was ready for fun. One of the guys was totally drunk, leaping around in yellow underwear with saggy elastic legs. Great! I wouldn't be the first to get shitfaced! And I must have been (shitfaced, that is) because there are a lot of things I can't remember. At breakfast, someone asked about my leg.

"My leg?" Huh! It was all bandaged up.

"Oh, it's fine," I insisted, hoping for clues to find out what had happened.

That's the thing about being a blackout drinker. You become a detective, searching for clues for how the bruises or cuts occurred. The most I learned about the injury was that it was a stab wound. Go figure. What a party!

For the second camping trip, we went to a real campground with another couple for the long holiday weekend in May. That Friday afternoon, I skipped classes to meet Shane and his friends, Andrew and Bernice, at a donut shop. They were working adults, an engaged couple with their own cars. Bernice was very attractive. She neither needed—nor wore—makeup and was impeccably groomed, right down to the shine in her long, dark hair. Even while Shane was introducing me, I could feel his awkwardness and their sorry surprise. What was Shane doing with this pale, skinny high school kid?

The four of us took one car, crammed with camping gear. For me, the trip was excruciating. The conversation in the car eluded me. I couldn't keep up with adult topics. I needed a beer. I really needed a beer. When we arrived at the site, I was expected to help. Used to being a child, a tagalong, and the chick that guys bought drinks for, I had no idea what to do. This was all too tedious and way too boring. And boring meant I wanted to get drunk and nobody else did. Weren't there any drinks around? How could people waste so much time playing with tent poles? *What about a beer?*

Finally, and not until the camp was set up—tent poles just so, guide wires snug, sleeping bags rolled out, all lah-dee-dah and the whole thing—did someone bring out beer. I drained mine before I noticed that Bernice, seated as gracefully as anyone could be on a log, was sipping a glass of wine. I excused myself and got up "to go to the bathroom."

Somehow, as luck would have it, I found a campsite filled with drunken, beer-guzzling party animals and I gratefully joined them. Vaguely, I remember waking up in the dark. Moonlight was just barely peeking through the clouds, and I was lying next to some guy passed out on his back, snoring. I saw the outline of their cooler and crawled my way over fallen bodies to grab a couple beers. Then shoe-less, I set out on a zigzag trip through the park to find Shane.

I have to cut now to the next morning, because, well, you know, blackout.

Andrew's station wagon was all packed.

"We're leaving? But, we just got here! Hey, don't be mad! I got lost! I couldn't find my way back, that's all!"

We left the campground and headed home in stony silence.

Around noon, Andrew pulled into a go-cart racetrack with a burger stand out front. All of us got out, but Shane pushed me back inside and told me to stay there. In the car next to ours was a large dog. It sniffed at the space cracked for him at the top of the side window, bared its yellow dog teeth at me, and barked. I jumped to the opposite side of the station wagon and sat motionless.

In a while, Shane came back and asked for the twenty dollars my mother had given me for the trip. I handed it over, and he disappeared again. The people parked next to us returned with their burgers and a treat for the dog. They backed out and pulled away.

After about an hour, Shane stalked into view, yanked open the door, and sat down. He stared straight ahead, watching Andrew and Bernice approach, hand in hand.

I was in tears.

"You were gone a long time, Shane."

He didn't respond.

"I was worried. Where were you?"

He kept his eyes fixed ahead. His jaw was clenched.

"I was on the go-carts," he snarled. "You gotta problem with that?"

"No."

"Good. Now, just shut up." He was angry, hurt, and ashamed in front of his friends for his stupid girlfriend. The scenario was becoming my signature: get drunk, be stupid.

Four days passed, and I hadn't heard from Shane. As usual, I was carrying on at the bar. On that fourth evening, I was sitting with a friend who was babbling away about her job when I spotted a familiar figure behind her. Shane had just walked in with Dawn, that is, crisis management Dawn. He waved to his friends, and she laughed aloud when both their arms flew up together to reveal their fingers entwined.

Within seconds, Shane spotted me and steered Dawn back outside. By this time, my friend had tuned into the little drama and began to cry.

"What are you crying for? He's *my* boyfriend." I tried to be casual, delicately picking a fleck of tobacco from my tongue. Without caring, I noticed my nails were chipped.

"I'm crying for you," she sniffed, wiping her eyes on a napkin.

I refused to join her. I didn't want anyone to feel sorry for me, set me apart, or make me different again. "Hey," I pushed her arm and managed a smile. "So, Shane and I split up. More freedom for me, right?"

Being dumped removed my false sense of stability, which in turn left me as an anxious free spirit. To compensate, Holly and I adopted some of Shane's female friends from the lounge to be our party pals. We'd buy a load of beer at the bar and haul it off to a hotel room to drink. One night, among others, someone invited us to an after-the-bar party. What the hell. It was at another hotel right on the way home. Still early. Only midnight…Let's go!

Nobody told us it was going to be dull. It was just a bunch of losers sitting around talking. No drugs. No cute guys. Not much to drink. This was their idea of a *party*? Now what? Let's go see what's behind the building. Ooh, looks like a farm. It *is* a farm. Horses! Wow.

"Anybody wanna ride a horse?"

Didn't matter we were in high heels. Didn't matter it had just rained. The girls were going to ride horses. Anybody ever do this before? Never? Even funnier. If we were too drunk to walk, then we'd ride, right? All right!

I climbed the fence first, teetered over the other side, and landed in a puddle of barn muck. Three others plopped down beside me. Oops. Pretty squishy here.

"Where's my goddamn shoe?"

None of us could help ourselves. We started laughing, first quietly, and then in loud snorts.

"Shhh!"

"You shut up!"

"No, you!"

"Jesus, you stink, or what?"

"Horseshit. That's my middle name."

We were howling now, almost in convulsions we were laughing so hard.

"Here's your shoe. Now jus' be quiet!"

"Hmm, not my goddamn shoe. It don't fit."

"Hey, if the shoe don't fit, fuck it!"

Four intoxicated girls, standing in manure, were nearly peeing with laughter. One broke free and sprinted into the field.

"We don't need shoes!" she shouted. "We're gonna ride *anyway*…fuckin' bareback!"

Three intoxicated girls, left standing ankle deep in manure, squinted into the darkness as the fourth ran toward the horses. Two of us struggled to pull each other from the muck, while the other decided to remove her panty hose so she wouldn't get them dirty. She sang country and western tunes while she peeled them down her legs. When they were securely tied around her waist, she had a revelation.

"Hey, cowgirls!" she shouted, despite the fact we were right beside her. "Somebody's gonna see us in our white tops, eh? So, let's take 'em *off!*" Grabbing both sides of her blouse, she ripped it open, buttons popping off everywhere, then twirled it over her head on one finger. "Whoo, whoo! Whoo!"

"Jeez, she's right. Look at all the cars on the highway over there. The cops might drive by!"

Clever conspirators, snickering and stumbling in the dark, we took off our tops and rolled up our skirts to prepare ourselves for riding.

Four muddy girls in brief skirts, who were drunk, shoeless, and topless, chased horses in a dark, wet field. Three were wearing panty hose. One was barefoot. Not one of them, however, could recall how she got home that night.

Nor could the farmer explain the next morning why one of his horses had a white lace push-up bra, size 32A, dangling from its ears.

8

Poor Sarah. Poor, good student Sarah. She shut herself in her room and studied while the entire household revolved around my antics. My parents were perpetually caught up in arguing about what to do with the likes of me. In turn, I saw the tight facial muscles, felt the silent treatment, and heard the chronic battles. All of which only proved to me that I was living with people who couldn't behave themselves. *They* were the source of the problem; of that, I was sure.

My parents frantically channeled all their energies into my salvation. By default, Sarah was left to her own devices. I saw her as odd, the obedient child. Back then, she looked up to me as an adventurer. My favorite occupation at home was thrilling her with stories: "Tales of Party Sue and Her Untamed Friends." Naturally, I left out the most incriminating details in case she told my parents.

I got most of the money. At allowance time, the old equality game was a bust. I had to complain and sweet-talk, but in the end, I always won a better portion than Sarah. Because I still sewed, my dad even replaced my sewing machine as a bonus birthday gift, six months after the date. "Tough love" was not in my parents' vocabulary. They were trying to rehabilitate me with bribes.

Graduation was a relief. After being constantly reminded that I owed my clothes, food, shelter, and, indeed, life itself to my parents, at least I stuck it out to finish high school. Mind you, I earned the bare minimum of credits with the lowest of marks, but I could get a job and earn my own cash. Post secondary education wasn't an option, or at least it had never been discussed. I assumed that girls who attended university in the 1970s weren't the norm anyway, never mind that I had neither the ambition to apply nor the grades to be accepted. I wanted independence, my own money, and the ability to call the shots.

The government was running a program called OCAP, a specialized career-assistance program for unemployed youth. My aunt had called my mother to tell her that my cousin Caryn had applied. Would Sue like to try as well? Why yes! As it turned out, I was accepted and Caryn was not. I was quite smug about the victory, but my cousin was not an at-risk candidate floundering into welfare. I was.

Finally, I was a grown-up. During all of those early years, I had a recurring fantasy that when adulthood finally reached out its big, strong hand, I would be safe. At the OCAP orientation session, I was told that my assignment would be at a local college campus not too far from where I lived with my parents. It was a trade campus for high school dropouts and people who, for various reasons, couldn't find employment. Yes, I'd fit in exceedingly well. I could relate to the clientele. In fact, I would fit in too well.

My placement was in the guidance office. The position included switchboard relief, but that was the treat. The major portion of the day was passed under the supervision of a pastor or reverend of some sort, an unsmiling, wrinkly old man who burdened me with mindless filing. I was relegated to a small, airless room with a great pile of papers and was told to cross-check names. Now, mind you, this was before the age of computers. Thousands of names had to be checked manually. Apparently, the name of anyone who had ever taken a course at the college was in those lists. My job was to sift through every file and record how many semesters each person had attended the college in the last five years. Banished were my delusions of being a real secretary answering phones, typing letters, and sashaying over to the file cabinets, perhaps catching the latest gossip around some water cooler. What was this crap?

At least I had the weekends. On Fridays, I'd leave directly after work to party. I'd be gone for the entire weekend. That's because there was always an after-bar event available. The next morning, I'd feel so bad, I'd have to have another drink to feel normal again and then…well, you know the rest. At least I was fairly safe. I had a protective string of friends who would see that I wasn't taken advantage of and who made sure I landed where I was headed. Even Shane would take his turn at the bar, seeing to my well-being. As a blackout drinker, the first order of the day was always piecing together the evidence of my conduct the previous night. First of all, I had to ensure I had all of my clothing and hadn't lost any at the bar or a house party along the way. Only then did I search my purse for standard contents, including house key, ID, and wallet. I'd count the money to see what was left. Before I dressed, there was the body check for cuts and bruises. That would be my first indicator of whether I'd have to listen carefully to conversation. If something ridiculous or awful had happened, I'd have to conclude that it involved me.

And always, I felt worthless. My friends were ditching me, my family was causing me headaches, and everyone else was just being hypercritical or paranoid. What do you do when the laughter stops? What do you do when your popularity starts to look more like tolerance, or worse, contempt? Clearly, I needed a fresh start. But, where could I go? I spread out a map of Canada and picked a place. I only had two months to complete my work assignment. After that, I could leave home.

When my parents asked, I had a destination already chosen.

"Kapuskasing," I told them.

I thought it had a cool ring to it. Never mind that it was situated in the backwoods of Northern Ontario.

To my surprise, my mother thought that was a good idea.

9

I was going back to England. My mother had suggested it as an alternative to my road map quick-pick. I agreed it was probably as good a place as any, even though I suspected her motives were selfish. She had wanted to move back for quite a while. Undoubtedly, I'd serve as a convenient excuse. There were also plenty of relatives there who could watch over me, but whatever my mother had told them, I'm quite sure they were not ready for me. You'd think 3,500 miles was a good distance to begin a new life, except no one pointed out that I was taking my problems with me. My mother's sister, Beth, and her husband, James, offered to put me up temporarily, not that they had enough room. Both of their daughters were already sharing a small bedroom. Nevertheless, I was anxious to leave.

Finally, when I was settled in the village of Arnold with Aunt Beth, Uncle James, and my cousins, I had a chance to prove myself as an adult. After all, I had rid myself of my biggest barrier: my parents. Finally, here was the freedom I had so desperately wanted. Halfway around the world from my family, I was aiming for a geographic cure. What I didn't know was that I could run, sail, fly, or leap, but distance cures nothing. I was still packing the problem of self. Imagining I was making a completely fresh start, I took myself job hunting. Within a few days of my arrival, I was on a double-decker bus, making my way to the employment center in downtown Nottingham.

The job board was huge, row upon row of jobs, but after careful consideration I decided on a secretarial position at a barrister and solicitor firm in downtown Nottingham at Simms, Weber, and Son. My interview was with Henry Weber.

Weber: Do you dicta-type, Miss Armstrong?

Me: (*Dicta-type? What's that?*) No, but I type eighty words a minute on the keyboard, and, as I'm a very fast learner, I'm sure I could learn, Mr. Weber.

Weber: Yes. I see. The position does involve some typing. However, may I assume you are familiar with using a plug switchboard?

Me: (*Think fast! Plug switchboard? Oh, right. That old-fashioned switchboard operation. Lily Tomlin on* Laugh-In. *Ernestine and her "one ringy-dingy." That's the setup.*)Yes, sir. I've been trained with Bell Canada telephone service on their system, and I'm very efficient at it.

(*Translation: I was good at losing and cutting off both in and out calls.*)

Weber: (*Writing something.*) Ah, Bell Canada. Fine company, I daresay. (*Folding his hands before him on the desk, he gives me a concerned look.*) If I may ask, Miss Armstrong, a twofold question..."

Me: (*So fire away and quit stalling.*) Of course.

Weber: Why have you returned to England, and just how long do you plan to stay?

Me: (*Whoa, hard questions.*) I do love England and realized in my visits to my Nana and Grandpa that I wanted to return. Of course, my mother and father will miss me terribly, but they wish me well. And since I've completed my secondary school diploma, I'm certain the move will prove to be permanent. (*There, that should get him.*)

I had two interviews. I became so good at the answers I invented that I began believing them myself. I got the job.

I was now the foreigner, the Canadian girl. Once again, I was different, even in my own birth country. The office didn't provide much camaraderie to relieve my isolation as the outsider. After Mr. Weber hired me, we seldom spoke. As a lowly clerk, the occasional highlight of my day was leaving my closet of an office to relieve Emily, the young girl on switchboard. One afternoon, I was just finishing paging someone when Emily breezed in after her lunch. I had been saving an off-color story for her that I had heard that morning on the bus. It only took a minute to tell her and we both had a good giggle, that is, until I noticed I had left the toggle switch on the microphone in the on position. I had inadvertently broadcast my dirty joke to the entire office staff. As I returned to my desk, clerks all the way down the hall turned in their chairs to see the rude Canadian girl.

You didn't have to be Sherlock Holmes to figure out who told the joke. I was the only one with a Canadian accent. I didn't think it could be possible, but, after that, the staff became even more distant and the job more stressful. Frankly, I hated it. I didn't make enough money to keep up with room and board for my aunt, let alone save enough for a place of my own. I needed an extra job, and the most logical place to find an extra job on the weekends and nights was at a pub. It was England, after all. There were plenty of establishments to choose from.

One evening after work, I strolled down the main road in Arnold. There were three pubs in view, two to the left and one to the right. For no particular reason, I chose the one on the right. It was called the Unicorn, and it looked pretty big. I stood outside, systematically checking my watch and straining to see down the road, pretending I was waiting for someone. I finally worked up the nerve to go inside, but, as I touched the doorknob, someone called my name. Impossible. To my surprise, when I looked up, a guy was approaching me, waving and smiling. Morgan! What a coincidence. I hadn't seen him since I was fourteen when we dated briefly during one of my summer visits. I was thrilled to see someone I knew.

Morgan and I sat in the Unicorn, drinking and catching up. His parents had kicked him out, which suited him fine. He was existing on the dole (the public welfare system), and was quite proud of living in what he called "me own li'tle digs," a tent in his uncle's backyard. That's where I came out of my first blackout in England. I recall waking up with an urgent need to pee and did, right behind the tent on his uncle's back lawn. During my overnight absence, my aunt and uncle had morphed into my mother and father. Oh, there were different words, but it was the same lecture. They were "terribly annoyed" with my escapades.

"Why ever would you do such a thing, Susan?"

"I don't know." My eternal answer.

"The lad's a right lush."

"James!"

"It's the truth, Beth. A right lush, that one. You didn't let him borrow money, did you now, Susan? A quid or two?"

"No, uh. No, definitely not." Well, maybe…then again, I couldn't remember. Oh God, here we go again! Had I really left home?

I made it to work that day, hung over and sick. It took another week before I recovered enough from a few more rounds with Morgan before I nailed down a second job at one of the pubs on the main road in Arnold. The manager actually hired me because I was Canadian, thus a novelty. My nickname became "Canada." Patrons dropped in to meet the foreign girl from the land of beavers and polar bears. They stayed to raise a glass to her colonial accent. Basically, I was good for business.

Morgan lost interest after one night when he passed out drunk on our lawn. Uncle James was livid, as though I had invited the guy to do that.

"What will the neighbors think?" he ranted.

What did I care? I was hardly ever there to notice because I was usually out clubbing all night with Emily, until I met Derek.

Derek was a lagger. No, not a laggard, a lazy good for nothing; he was a pipe fitter. He and his buddies had been in a couple times before and always bought a drink for me with each of their rounds. Each took his turn buying. This particular Saturday, they were into their third round when I reported to the designated payer what he owed. Instead of digging into his pockets, he grabbed his beer from the bar and turned his back to me. I expected he'd pay up shortly, so I put in some time to serve some of the regulars.

"It's not my round," he said when I returned. "I'm not about to pay." And he turned around again.

Off I went to serve more patrons. Back I went to collect.

"It's not my round," he insisted. "I'm not paying."

I had had enough. This time, I stood behind the bar with one arm firmly locked on a hip.

"Oh, really? Well, if you're not paying, you're not drinking *either*."

He turned away from me. Furious, I picked up what was left of his beer and poured it over his head. It took but a second to realize what I'd done before I retreated on the double to the back room, the guys' raucous laughter trailing after me. I straightened my collar, smoothed my hair, ignored the knot in my stomach, and returned to face the challenge.

"Well?" some voice said from within my own body. "Are you ready to pay up yet?"

My delinquent patron was mopping his head with a bar rag.

"No, I told you," he said, chuckling. "It's not my round."

Before I could react, he reached out for my hand and said, "Name's Derek. Wha'cher doing tonight, luv? Would ya like to go out wi' me?"

Flabbergasted, I agreed. Surely with such a sense of humor, he had to be worth *something*. He still didn't pay though. One of the others held out the cash to me, declaring the show was a ripper and well worth the few quid. Everyone was still laughing.

Once again, all was right with my small world. I had a new boyfriend.

10

Being someone's girlfriend was the ticket to fitting in. Since he drank way more than I did, it made my drinking acceptable. And since his company suited my needs, I was determined to maintain my role as Derek's girl.

My work started to suffer. Every night I'd be blasted, dropping into bed after three in the morning. I wasn't old enough to legally drink, but at thirty-three Derek was. I told him I was twenty. There were other problems. Not only was he the father of a ten-year-old son, he was also an itinerant worker. How would I keep a hold on this guy? His job in Nottingham was nearly concluded. He'd move on to another good contract. Why would he stay with me?

One night at his flat (we were both drunk, no surprise there) we had a terrible fight. It was a long, extended series of accusations and recriminations. My insecurity translated into an entire library of bitter one-liners, the "you don't care" and "you always" and "you never" kind. For whatever reason, at the time I was very naked, but in high drama I declared I was leaving. Nobody was going to abandon me and get away with it! I yanked on my boots and stomped to the door. As a last thought, I grabbed my coat, my lovely black leather coat that so perfectly matched my tall boots, and prepared to exit. Derek stopped me. That's all I wanted anyway, his assurance. We made up as most couples do. By morning, we had struck an agreement. He'd finish his job in Nottingham, and, when he left the next week, I'd go with him.

When they heard I was leaving, Aunt Beth and Uncle James disguised their relief very well.

"Susan, we've loved having you, but we do understand. It's time to follow your heart. You'll call your parents then? About your move?"

"Oh, yes."

"Then what about your position?"

"Oh, that's all taken care of. I've already given notice." Never did. In essence, my aunt and uncle quit by proxy for me when Mr. Weber showed up at the door a few days later.

Derek took me to a town called Redcar on the North Sea, which during the summer was a sunny, seaside resort crowded with happy tourists. In the cold winds of late October, it was dismal, yet afforded plenty of empty rooming houses eager to offer us lodging for two pound, fifty pence a night. We settled for one with clean but worn linoleum floors. It also had a bed and a small table and chairs. The loo, with a big, old tub, was right down the hall. Each morning, we were provided with breakfast. Derek would go off to work and I'd stay home, such as it was. At eighteen, I was a kept woman.

The first day in Redcar set the tone for the duration. After checking in with his boss, Derek returned for me and we made our way to a pub at the end of the pier. It sat over the water with a full view of endlessly dark and angry waves. The other patrons stared; it wasn't proper for a woman—young or old—to drink pints, so Derek ordered two half-pints for me. I drank the same amount anyway. It just cost more. When some of Derek's friends teamed up with us, we headed to the downtown streets, determined to find a nightclub. Instead, we encountered a man walking his dog. When the dog started to bark, Derek kicked it. After some loud exchange of colorful words with the dog's owner, my darling man was surrounded by several police constables and arrested for common drunkenness. They hauled him off in handcuffs to sober up in a jail cell.

I had finally outsmarted myself. By having it all my way, I had managed to move in with a drunk who was fifteen years my senior. I was penniless in a strange town, so I quite naturally set off to continue drinking with Derek's friends, men I didn't know. Ahh, the freedom of being delusional! The joy of no self-esteem! Lucky me! I could access courage in a fresh keg at the next pub with Derek's friends. After an hour, they were getting seriously drunk, and even I knew I was in danger. Making my excuses to go to the loo, I slipped out into the street and found the police station. No luck there. They wouldn't release Derek and "didn't know" when they would. Suspecting I might be arrested too, just for good measure, I returned to the rooming house, keyless. It was two o'clock in the morning. The landlady was not very happy about being awakened by several rings on the front doorbell.

"Where's Derek?" she asked.

"Oh...uh...he won't be coming back tonight."

I pulled the crying face of a jilted lover and raced up to the room. I wondered what she would have done had I revealed that he was in jail? Kicked us out? Told me I was a bad person? Either would have crushed me.

Morning hadn't yet dawned when I was awakened by what sounded like rain or hail hitting the windowpanes. When I looked out, Derek was staring back at me with one hand wrapped around a drainpipe. With the other, he was tapping the glass.

I don't recall why I just didn't open the stupid window and let him fall inside. Instead, I fumbled my way downstairs to unlock the front door and helped him up the creaking stairs back to our room. Considering our shared condition, it was fortunate we didn't tumble backward down the steps, piss-eyed Jack and his drunken Jill. Once again, I fell asleep, only to dream I was drifting on the ocean, a very warm ocean. But that was Derek's fault. His bladder had given up waiting for his brain to respond and released a tidal wave onto our mattress. I was livid. In one night, he had been arrested, jeopardized our living arrangements, and caused me to lie soaking in his urine.

Instead of leaving (How could I without money?), I helped him strip the linens the next morning and haul everything to the local Laundromat where we washed and dried the stinking evidence. His simpleton assistant, I made the bed and then we skipped out to find other living quarters. I was far too ashamed to face our landlady.

11

The peace I so desperately craved still eluded me. I did have the freedom of adulthood; still, I continued to feel I was walking on eggshells. It started that first night in Redcar when I called my parents from a public phone booth. I told them that I was moving in with a guy I had just met. I said it out of spite. It was a way to send a message that I was now able to make my own decisions.

In response, they lectured. Oh, how they lectured! From more than 3,000 miles away, they warned and argued and fussed.

"If eternal misery ever needed a permit, Susan, yours is pre-approved." Apparently, I had found their promised slippery slope and was going down, hand in hand, with wilful self-destruction. They were both "so very disappointed with my moral choices."

I had created the rules. Why couldn't I ever win these games of misery?

On my side of the world, I simply held the receiver away from my head and told myself I didn't care. Then again, there was that knot in my stomach, the size of a football and growing. My whole body was so wracked with stress that I walked hunched over as an old woman. Where was the clinic where they could hook me up to an alcohol intravenous to restore my confidence?

Our next landlady was a kindly woman with ruddy Scottish cheeks and red hair. Every morning, she made me a good, big breakfast of bacon, stewed tomatoes, eggs, and potatoes and hovered over me while I ate it.

The accommodations were plain and affordable. Ours was a clean, spacious room with a bay window overlooking the North Sea. I should have been enjoying some sort of domestic bliss, but we were in a boarding house with a shared bathroom and no television set. And what was there to do while Derek was working? When crossword puzzles and walking along the docks were exhausted, I began to mope.

The days wore on. Derek felt the brunt of my desperate hours without him. When he appeared at the end of the day, I'd leap on him, grateful as a lonely dog who had been waiting all day for his owner's return. One night he was late. I sat close to the window waiting…and waiting. Every sound in the hallway put me on high alert. Now what? Was he sick of me? Had he left town? Each minute that ticked away pushed me further into panic and worry. Suddenly, I heard the lock. Derek! Thank God. Look! He had news, see? He'd found "a regular place" for us. A new rooming house with a larger room "with cookin' and all." It had a coin-operated television set, a common room for all the boarders, and one more surprise: he had bought me a radio/cassette player. He felt the "right proper" provider.

Hold on a second. "Cooking?" Now just where would I have picked up that little skill? Oh well. Now's not the time to break the news about that. I should just be happy.

"That's great, Derek!"

I turned on my best wide-eyed enthusiasm and gave him a hug for insurance. If he found out I couldn't cook, I'd definitely be homeless in a strange country. I'd die in one of my fantasy scenes, probably drunk. I kept hugging him until he laughingly pushed me away. He fancied my pleasure was due to his manly initiative and was proud.

Cooking? Me? You might as well try to teach a fish how to ride a bicycle. I was wondering how I could learn before Derek found out, but I wasn't quick enough. Our first evening in the new digs, Derek came home with a dreaded paper package from the butcher shop. He untied the string and laid aside the brown paper to reveal a stack of pink pork chops.

"Oh," he said, rubbing his palms together. "Gonna be just like me mum used to make!"

The trembling started around my knees and worked its way up to my tongue before I could spit out how clueless I was in the kitchen. I turned, resigned to pack my clothes, only to hear Derek laugh.

"Want me to teach you then?"

Did I! Whew! For a few magic evenings, I was grateful and happy. Derek shopped for the groceries and cooked, which enabled some home time for us. He bought me a promise ring, something to keep on my finger to remind me of our life together. Poor, idiotic me had finally become someone's little woman.

The joy lasted as long as Derek was home. While he was at work, I was bored to death. A coin (ten pence) got me an hour's worth of television. I had three stations to choose from. Restless, I'd eventually walk to the corner for bottles of beer. I smuggled them back to the room where I'd spend my time listening to Rod Stewart, the only cassette tape we owned. I drank, I sang sad songs along with Rod, and I mourned the loss of a dream.

Now that I was a grown-up, I longed to be a real person with all the regular trappings, including a doorbell, closets, and a white picket fence. I was starting to wonder if that would ever happen for me. After all, if I knew one thing for sure, I wasn't good enough, not for my parents, or Derek, or, for that matter, anything. That message had come through loud and clear.

Redcar was a tourist town. There were no office jobs. I'd have to go elsewhere to find employment. That left Middlesborough and, according to the telephone book, the Alfred Marx Employment Agency located there. I got dressed up, took the train, and completed all the agency's requisite tests. Within days, I had a job on switchboard at Barclays Bank. The assignment was successful. I worked hard and kept to myself, and everyone was pleased. Soon, I was offered two weeks of work in a law office in Stockton, which was a little farther away. The commute was long and exhausting. At the end of the second week when the assignment was up, I quit.

Meanwhile, Derek was secretly house hunting. He came home one evening with keys to a rented house and the car he had just bought. Yes! My life had received a stamp of approval! I was going to be a homemaker with an address to call my own. Visions of our happy little household consumed my thoughts. Rainbows would arc on our doorstep. Each sun-alive morning, bluebirds would twitter while I'd kiss Derek off to his job. Every night, he'd come home to a wonderful table.

"Please? Could we see it now, Derek. Could we? Just drive by. Please? Oh please?"

"Oh, Aw-right. Let's be off, then."

As we drove along a quiet residential street in North Redcar, I suddenly understood why Derek had bought a car. The neighborhood was quite a stretch to the downtown area, and it wasn't readily accessible by bus. Ah well, there was a small grocery shop around the corner. Yes, that was good.

I wondered how soon I could play house. Next week? Yes? Cool. In preparation, I rushed out to buy a mop, two pots, and a large envelope of some exotic incense.

The first full day at home saw me going off to the shops to buy groceries. That night, Derek came home to a fish dinner with mashed potatoes, cabbage salad, and peas coated in a nice, not too lumpy, white sauce. And naturally, we had beer. After his meal, he lit a cigarette, slid back his chair, and announced he was going to "fix the electric."

I accompanied him to the front hallway where he snooped around until he found the power box under the stairs.

"Ya see this wheel, darlin'?" Manly and knowing, he was demonstrating his knowledge with all things mechanical. "It measures how much electric we use."

I couldn't see any problem, but asked stupidly anyway. "It's broken?"

As though in answer, he took a good drag on his cigarette and jammed the butt against it. "Yeah, *now* i' is!" The meter wheel stopped dead.

I freaked. So much for being real people. We were nothing more than criminals, poised to go straight to jail for vandalism and theft. At first, Derek laughed off my rage of disappointment.

"Think we're gonna be pulled in by the coppers and dragged down to the local nick for a quid's worth of electric? Aren't you the one?"

"Take it out, Derek! I won't have it. You'll ruin everything!"

"Ah, bollocks! Leave it."

"They'll find out!" I was so panicked that I became both of my parents at once. "You'll see…*it's only a matter of time!*"

"Time, eh? Well, *clock this*! It stays!"

And so ended the first fight in our new house. He never did remove the cigarette butt. I worried about it the whole time we lived there.

12

Derek tried seven things to make me happy:

One. He risked his life teaching me to drive. Up to that point in my life, I had relied on others, mostly men, to chauffeur me around. They drove the vehicles; they picked me up and took me places. That was the system. Half of me resisted the idea of a driver's license and that sort of responsibility. The other half was fairly intoxicated by day's end and didn't care. Then again, after having a few drinks himself, Derek was hardly fit to teach me to drive. Now let's add two more ingredients to the driving fiasco:

(a) The English drive on the wrong side of the street.

(b) Derek's car had manual transmission. Who in her right mind really wants to be shifting gears this way and that through residential streets?

We began late one night in a deserted shopping plaza. With Derek shouting orders, I released the clutch too soon and the engine stalled. He barked something about "easin' the bloomin' clutch" as if he hadn't said it at least fifty times already. His attitude was grating on my patience, but I tried again. With a tight grip on the key, I turned it in the ignition until something under the hood (the bonnet) screamed. Derek yelped in unison with the engine.

I had had enough.

"You expect me to keep trying?" I said. "Fine then, *just watch me!*"

Here we go! Lurch into first, grind into second, and kick down on the accelerator. Slam into third and jerk the steering wheel to make a hard right turn. Screech to a stop within a hair of the Safeway Grocery Mart's front window. Near accident.

Crikey!

Your fault, Derek!

Oh, givvus a bloody break, woman!

End of driving episode.

Two. He bought a sewing machine for me. I took myself to the local sewing shop. There, among the housewives, I chose a pattern and two lengths of fabric. Over the next few days, I whipped up a pair of brown corduroy pants and a yellow, flowered shirt, daisies, I think; they looked more like fried eggs. And that was the end of that.

Where would I model my home fashion ensemble anyway? Nowhere.

Three. He brought another couple home. And where did he dig them up? Adele and Herman were old enough to be my parents and were twice as boring.

Thanks, but no thanks.

Four. He asked me to see a doctor. In midwinter, Redcar was cold and damp. It had all the charm of mildew. Pretty soon, I was spending the mornings in bed. When I woke to rain clouds, I'd roll over again just to block the rhythm of more rain chink-chinking at the windows. Eventually, I'd stay in bed until just before Derek's arrival when I'd manage to get dressed, stumble downstairs to greet him, and wait for pub time. The day finally came when I hadn't eaten or bathed in a week. Actually, I hadn't done anything. There was no purpose in it. Derek hoisted me to the tub, encouraged me to wash, and brought me a cup of tea. That's when he mentioned the doctor again.

I went the next day. The diagnosis was clinical depression. I was given a prescription for some tiny, green, triangular tablets, which reminded me of spaceships. That suited me well. I was an alien anyway, a long way from home and stranded on a planet of puddles.

Five. He made sure I took my medication. Before long, I started feeling better. I did want to please the guy. My alternative was to go back to my parents, so even though I still spent most of my days in bed, I'd feed and groom myself just before he arrived home.

Six. He told me I was beautiful. I didn't believe him because of a stranger whose comments had struck a low chord in me. He was only a pub patron drinking at the bar, but his tongue was loose enough from the drink to remark, "Y' know, y' might be quite pretty an' all…if you wanted to…"

I'd never met him before. Who was this idiotic, self-appointed ego-basher? I rushed to the restroom to check the mirror at all angles. He was right. I wasn't pretty. I used to be, but it was gone. Worse still, I didn't know how to fix it. I had done my hair as best I could and applied extra makeup over the dark circles under my eyes.

How had this aging thing happened?

The comment bothered me enough to complain to Derek. He set down his pint, gave me a long stare, and then finally said, "Don't pay the arsehole no mind, Sue. Regular Lady freaking Godiva. Tha's you!"

He turned back to the bar, satisfied he had said the right thing, but his compliment gave me little comfort. That week, I started venturing out during the day. I got my hair cut. Still, the "could be pretty" comment lingered. I wanted to go home.

Seven. He bought me a ticket. Since I was homesick, I reasoned that a vacation in Canada would restore me and cause this awful depression to vanish. Derek agreed. When he got paid that Friday, he came home with an airplane ticket for me.

Hooray! I could visit my family.

It left us without any money for the rest of the week, but he was hopeful. I, on the other hand, was jubilant. I was going home. The following Friday, he had another ticket in hand. He'd come with me! And wasn't that just "smashin'"? Was I as excited as he was? "Very! Absolutely!" *Not.*

I wanted to see my family and friends. I honestly didn't want him to tag along to find out about the real me, that worthless fake lurking in the shadows back there in Canada.

Could I risk his discovering my troubled past? What if he quit talking about marriage? What if he wanted his ring back? Whatever. It looked like we were both going to Canada anyway.

It was early in March, and it would still be cold back home. I dug out my best sweaters and my cherished leather coat, which I had bought with my very first Canadian paycheck. For days, I packed and repacked, my excitement at a fever pitch. Emily, my friend from the legal office, would be meeting us in Nottingham on the first leg of our journey. From there, we'd have only a four-hour drive the next day to Heathrow Airport in London. We checked into the Savoy Hotel and connected with her in the lobby. She was very excited to see us.

Fueled on antidepressants, I agreed to go pub-crawling. What a mistake! Sometime during the night, I woke up in the hotel bed to find Derek on one side of me and Emily on the other. I was comforted by the support, but I was nervous about going home the next day. I needed another drink to stabilize my nerves, so I fumbled my way into the hallway, where I quickly became lost. By chance, I came across a fellow drunk at the elevator who invited me back to his room for a drink.

Sure! Why the hell not?

It was what I was looking for anyway, and a drinking buddy was always welcome. Of course, as soon as my drink was poured, my new buddy decided that was license to grope me. I kneed him off me (he was a weakling) and I flew into the hall. I credited the escape to self-preservation, but I found my way back to my own room.

I came to at ten fifteen the next morning. Our flight was scheduled to leave Heathrow at two that afternoon, yet neither Derek nor I had set an alarm clock nor asked for a wake-up call. Emily had already left, probably gripped by regret in the cold light of dawn for whatever she feared had occurred. I knew I'd just lost another friend. As for Derek and me, we'd obviously never make our flight in time. I was sick, hung over, and hysterical. He immediately tried setting things right by throwing things into our suitcases.

"No time for a mug a' tea, Sue. We're leggin' it outta here."

"We'll never make it!"

"Never mind. We've just overlaid a bit. We'll make it!"

"No, no. We won't!"

I was crying inconsolably, a slobbering wreck. I wanted to believe him and tried to help, but he had to push and yank me to the car. We hadn't stopped to brush our teeth.

"We have to brush our teeth, Derek!"

We also didn't pause to check out.

The drive to London was a panicky blur. Crying, I kept checking my watch the entire way. As we neared the airport, I actually started to believe we might make it. Derek screeched up in front of the departures lounge, dumped the bags on a cart, and grabbed me by the wrist. We bolted to the check-in counter, my legs in shaky strides behind him. Good news. The flight had been delayed by thirty minutes. We were in time to make it to the plane, but it was too late for me. I couldn't calm myself. The mix of adrenaline, alcohol, and antidepressants had me wired. I couldn't stop worrying about the car.

What would happen to the car?

It had been left in a no-parking zone with the keys in the ignition. Derek kept urging me to calm down, assuring me everything would be all right, but I couldn't stop obsessing. As soon as we climbed into the air, I ordered a beer and a scotch.

They tell me I was a raving lunatic by the time we landed in Canada. The flight attendants apparently had to remove me from the plane in a wheelchair. I have to believe it because I can't remember that part. What I do recall though is coming out of my blackout in customs. The officials were searching our luggage.

I was yelling, "You can't do this to me. I'm a Canadian! I have rights, you idiots!"

I could hear my own voice but was having a hard time understanding what I was saying or why I was saying it. Mercifully, my social self that governed common sense took over and abruptly shut my mouth. Now I was really frightened.

Had I lied to the customs officials?

I was a landed immigrant, not a Canadian citizen.

Stupid girl, I was provoking the very people who upheld the rules governing my fate. I couldn't understand why I was being so obnoxious.

After profuse apologies on my part, I was rolled, still in the wheelchair, into the arrivals lounge and released into the waiting arms of my extremely stressed and embarrassed parents. They must have had chapter and verse lectures prepared for such an occasion because they immediately launched into them and continued for more than an hour down the highway. At home, the message was only slightly more subtle. My mother had made up two single beds for us in my old room, one on each wall.

Two weeks into our Canadian holiday, I ran out of antidepressants. To say the least, the visit was not going well. Derek was being remarkably tolerant, but I was a land mine. Step on me, even lightly, and I'd blow. We tried double-dating with my old friend Holly and her new fiancé, Joe, but I couldn't even sit through the movie. We had to leave. I needed more pills.

The family doctor was happy to help treat my depression. He provided me with "anxiety relief" in the form of a temporary prescription, but there were side effects. My hands trembled. My legs cramped. I couldn't sleep. He prescribed another round of medication, capsules to counteract the reaction to the new antidepressant. See? Everything would be just fine. Control the nerves, manage the medicine, take the dosage according to instruction, and then go out and drink. Couldn't hurt, and it might help. I had been drinking since I started taking the prescription back in Redcar and no one—not the doctor or chemist in England or the pharmacist in Canada—had mentioned the danger of mixing alcohol and antidepressants. The side effects would soon become obvious anyway.

Where I lived, there was often a last blast of winter with a snowstorm in March. One evening, I stepped off a bus into a winter wonderland of knee-deep white snow. Clean and fresh under the streetlights, the snow lay glittering like crushed glass. I marveled at Mother Nature's thoughtfulness because waiting for me at the bus stop were wonderful ice sculptures: Arctic foxes, snowshoe hares, and polar bears. I longed to stop and touch them, but I had to hurry home for dinner. During dessert, I was recalling what I had seen at the bus stop when I suddenly had to stand and pour my entire cup of tea into a soup bowl to douse the raging fire. That same night, I dressed myself in the yellow, flowered blouse I'd made in Redcar, and then topped it with a blue plaid shirt. In that ensemble, I made my way to the basement to do laundry. It was three o'clock in the morning. This is all hearsay of course. I don't remember any of it.

The next morning, my parents escorted me to the local hospital and signed me into the psychiatric ward. The doctors determined my hallucinations were caused by substance abuse, that is, mixing prescription drugs and alcohol, but you probably guessed that.

When you are substance abuser, you know your fate. If you use long and heavily enough, you'll end up in one of three places: a psychiatric ward, a jail, or a coffin. Well, one down and two to go. I had achieved my first milestone. And I was still only nineteen.

13

The attending psychiatrist made his diagnosis, and it was a label I would not accept. I may have been wild and disruptive, but I didn't think I was schizophrenic. Scared, strapped to a bed, and alone, I began screaming. A man was peeking into the porthole window to my room. Everyone came running. A search party was launched. I swear I saw him, but they claim I didn't.

What if they were wrong?

Because I was strapped down, he could sneak into my bed and molest me.

Jessie? Where was Jessie? I called repeatedly for my old friend.

I was in a dark room of some sort. Its only features were a door with a viewing window and a stiff, kitchen-like chair beside me.

Help! Jessie would help me. Get Jessie!

My parents, who were ready to do anything for me, looked her up and found her living with Kane and their little boy. They drove over to her apartment to try to explain my cries for her and my illness, hoping she would come to visit and calm me down. Apparently, she did. I have no memory of her being there. After all, I was crazy.

When the psychotic episode subsided, they moved me to a dormitory-style room I had to share with another girl. I hated it, absolutely loathed it.

Get me out of here! What do you mean, I have to participate in activities? Bowling? That's too stupid for me. If I didn't bowl on my own time, why would I do it in a *hospital?*

I wasn't that nuts. My protest took the form of a hunger strike. More recruits were sent to care for me. An aunt who lived nearby came to coax me to eat.

Everyone seemed to be watching me without having a clue how to help. The doctors and nurses were efficiently detached. They took notes, checked my pulse rate, scribbled on charts, and left. Yet fortune was still my friend, and it sent me a guardian angel. Jessie's mother just happened to be a social worker and a counselor in the psychiatric ward at that hospital.

Yes, Jessie's mom, the one who had smoked our joint all those years before, was influential.

"There must be something else wrong," she told the psychiatrist.

She'd known me for years and schizophrenia didn't seem to fit my behavior pattern. Something she said must have clicked with the right department. Within days, I was released on condition that I see a psychiatrist regularly.

"Okay! Sure! Oh yes," I assured them heartily. "I'll make an appointment immediately."

With that, I was free to go. Somebody let me bum a quarter. I ran down the hall and called a friend from my days at the bar. She agreed to pick me up at the hospital. I threw on my clothes, said my farewells, and within two hours I was partying in someone's town house.

Ah! That's better!

Drinking beer, smoking pot, and partying in old circles. I was an adult, and my treatment of choice was to quit taking the antidepressants.

And what happened to Derek? My mother said he stayed with them until it was time to go back to England. They took him to the airport to catch his flight home. I never heard from him again.

A week after my release from hospital, my father drove me to the psychiatrist's office for my initial appointment. His office was quiet and unattractive.

"How are you doing?" asked the good doctor.

"Fine."

"What's been happening in your life?"

"Nothing."

That's the way the interview ran. I didn't have any intention of talking to this guy. He'd just call someone, the hospital or my parents, and report anything I divulged. I was sure of it. Besides, I was perfectly well. I didn't need anybody's help. To satisfy my parents, I made an appointment for the following week; I just didn't keep it. My sole concern was to earn money. I would need it to support myself.

14

My baby sister, Sarah, had grown up. When I left for England, she was a skinny kid with stringy, dark hair and outdated glasses with cat's eye frames. Without makeup, her face was quite ordinary. She was clueless about fashion. In my absence, she had blossomed into a stunning seventeen-year-old. Her hair was permed and stylish. Her clothes were sharp and trendy. She wore contact lenses and makeup. A car was parked in the driveway, a Toyota Celica. It was hers. All those years, while I had been spending money as fast as I had earned it, Sarah had saved all her part-time earnings and studied hard at school. Her success served to show me up as even more of a loser.

One day, my mother came home from work with some news. An English-style pub called the Brass Door was opening downtown. They were hiring. Wasn't I a likely candidate to be hired?

Why, yes!

I headed downtown to put in an application.

Fortunately (dumb luck often did seemingly trail me), the owners' ambitions exceeded their knowledge. They had invested a great deal of money in the project but failed to realize that pumping an unpasteurized British beer through flash coolers ruined its stability and taste.

During my interview, they asked if I knew how to pour an English pint.

Well, duh!

After I offered an historical description of the British brewing process that dated back to the eighth century and the need to keep the beer at sixty-three degrees Fahrenheit or thirty-eight degrees centigrade, I was hired. The brew also had to be drawn from a cool cellar up to the bar, but I saved that tidbit as insurance, just in case I needed to reestablish my credibility with them. Their setting was right though. They had refurbished a grand, old Victorian-era bank building. It was ornate and rich with atmosphere and scary stories. Legend had it that, during one of a number of bank robberies, someone had been shot and his ghost roamed the hallways. You'd have to check that out for yourself. The whole time I was there, I never encountered him. My own ghosts kept me haunted enough.

A week later, cleanly attired in my regulation black skirt and beige shirt, I was ready for my first shift. Of the four other workers, two were older women and two were gay males. All of them were helpful on the job. After work, all of us went to the downtown bars, including gay bars and biker bars. I'd wake up in an assortment of strange situations. Once in a while, I wouldn't even leave after my shift. I just stayed to drink with the customers. It goes without saying that they picked up the tab. After a while, I had to find somewhere else to drink or follow the newly instituted one-only drink policy for after-hours employees. My personal drinking style had something to do with establishing that rule. One of my bosses told me straight out that I was a sloppy drunk. I'd spill drinks, fall down, the usual.

Then there was this silly broken finger thing. It was so funny. I had slammed it in a car door and hadn't noticed. The next day, I was pretty hung over. The finger seemed somehow connected to some of the pain, so after a while I had to leave work to take the finger and myself to the hospital for an X ray.

No, that's not the part my friends found so funny. That part came a week or so later when the blackened nail fell off while I was pouring drinks.

Oops. Sure hope it fell on the floor because no one mentioned finding it in their mug. I was having a good time; what was wrong with everyone else? Sober, I was all responsibility. I even covered management duties. My boss didn't have any sense of humor, however, when I reeked of last night's booze and tossed back another drink just to get started on my shift. Other than that, it was a perfect job. I'd sleep half the day, work at night, make a load of cash, drink for free, and then start all over the next day. Who could ask for anything more?

One of the girls at work was looking for a roommate and asked if I were interested. Absolutely!

Anything to get out of my parents' house. We found an apartment in a triplex in an older part of the city. The neighborhood came complete with hookers trolling every corner. It was close to work, and the rent was affordable. Each of us gave the landlord a fifty-dollar deposit and left happy about our new place. But about a week before the move-in date, my intended roommate announced she was going to live with her boyfriend. Since I couldn't afford the apartment on my own, we'd both lose our deposits. I was furious, but I was afraid to tell her so. Being irate would only prove me a bad person, so I never said a word about it. I never forgave her either.

My mother, always desperate to set things right, manipulated another opportunity for me. My cousin Caryn, who was two weeks my elder, had just lost her roommate. Caryn and I had hung out a bit when we were teens, smoking, drinking, and taking aspirin mixed with Coke for a buzz; we had done all the exciting adolescent milestones together. Her apartment had two bedrooms, one and a half bathrooms, a big living and dining area, a small galley kitchen, and a balcony. It was located a mere three blocks from where I worked. The only problem was that her former roommate had taken most of the furniture. Never mind. We'd manage. We had a television, and we each owned a bed. Neighbors of my parents donated a vacuum cleaner. I'd never use it, but it was a nice offer.

I like to consider this period of my life as a "normal" interlude. I guess that was a matter of opinion. Waking up with my feet in the bathroom and my head in the bedroom was, in my estimation, normal. Caryn evidently didn't think so.

15

A few months after I moved in with Caryn, she moved out to join her boyfriend. Along with her meager furniture, she had taken a companionship I had come to rely on. For the first couple weeks after she left, I aimlessly wandered the empty apartment. My job dissolved. The Brass Door closed over financial difficulties, meaning the entire staff was unemployed. A biker friend came to my rescue with a position at another bar. That job lasted one whole week before I arrived one evening for my shift to find padlocks on the doors and angry employees hanging around outside.

Now what?

The answer came in the form of a newspaper ad. Right down the road from Gilbert's, one of my old, reliable drinking haunts, a new country and western bar and restaurant complex called RoundUp was about to open. I was hired as a waitress for the restaurant and bar on the main floor. For the time being, I was happy. I had new friends at work, and, at home in the empty apartment, I began to appreciate my privacy. I could party and come home to pass out anywhere I pleased, which I did on many nights, except for the night I woke up to find something touching my leg.

What time is it? Where am I? What is *that*?

It felt like a warm hand, steadily working its way toward my thigh. Someone was in the pitch-dark room with me.

Was it night terrors? A demented dream?

I screamed and bolted upright. The hand evaporated from my leg, but where was the intruder? Why hadn't I heard the door to my apartment close? Was he still lurking close by, waiting in some black corner? My every breath was painful. Whoever had touched me was probably still in the apartment.

I flew to every light switch in the place and checked the bathroom, the closets, and even the kitchen cupboards. The door chain was locked and motionless, but the sliding balcony door was open. On the balcony, a plant had been knocked over.

Who could have entered that way?

I lived on the twentieth floor! Could it have been the guy next door? I barely knew him, but had he climbed around the panel on the shared balcony and fondled me in my sleep?

Was that possible?

At six o'clock in the morning, I called my parents.

"It's your lifestyle, Susan. Men see you as a target. Don't you know how reckless you're behaving? It just keeps getting you into trouble now, doesn't it? It's time. You really have to…"

Enough of that. I turned on the television and managed to distract myself until later in the day when I went out and found Chase, my current boyfriend, in a pool hall. He and his friend Enzo returned to the apartment with me to check things out. They combed the place, as I had already done at least five times, and found nothing unusual. We left and went out to a local coffee shop where we met with Kim, one of Enzo's collection of girlfriends. Enzo was what people called a real player. He was smooth, street-smart, and gorgeous. Kim took me back to her place for the night, just to help me calm down, and I was surprised by her respectable home life. She lived with her parents and had a good job that required nice clothes. She was kind, soft-spoken, and mannerly. I wondered if she knew her boyfriend already lived with someone else. Enzo treated her like a princess and, foolishly, she idolized him. Despite that, I envied her.

Who would want to marry me?

Derek did once, but that was finished. That night at Kim's, I think I buried a dream: marriage was out of the question. How could a screwup like me have a decent life or raise good, responsible kids when I destroyed every chance offered me? It was too late for happiness, at least that kind.

Only a matter of a few weeks later, Chase and I broke up and I started the new job at RoundUp. The mystery of my bedroom invader was never solved, even though, much later, my suspect, the next-door neighbor, met with an accident with a baseball bat. He had to take off six weeks from work to recover from it.

I went about my job in tall cowboy boots, jeans, Western shirt, and a dorky plastic cowboy hat. Behind the uniform, I was living the Patsy Cline "Falling to Pieces" lyrics. Without Chase, I believed my life was over, never to be loved again. Mentally, I was sending myself flowers. In my happier moments, I befriended some of the other waitresses at work. The place was filled with activity. It eventually swept me up with its energy. Working next to my old haunt at Gilbert's and trooping over there after work with a half-dozen girlfriends from RoundUp began to energize me. It took a few biker parties, the sounds of a few dozen roaring motorcycles, and several cases of beer, but I was back on my Snakes and Ladders game of life. Climb up. Slide down. Climb up…

Slide down, Sue. Step into the shower. Enjoy the splash of warm water and the lovely slippery foam of that scented body wash. Nice. I was feeling better. The boyfriend blues were disappearing. Life was good. But as I passed my hand across my chest and over my left breast, I felt a lump.

Oh no, I thought. Not again. I had already been through that scare the year before. My golden rule of "don't think, don't feel" had gotten me through that. The scare had started at a pool party while I was changing out of my bathing suit and my hand brushed against my left breast. I was sure I felt something. I raised my arm, tapped the fingers of my right hand over the spot again, and lost my mind. Given all the alcohol I had consumed that afternoon, I shouldn't have been able to feel anything, but that pea-sized lump was enough to make me hysterical. There must have been some scrambling outside the bathroom door to find a volunteer because eventually, one of the girls burst in as though she had been pushed. I didn't even know her, and I didn't care. I just needed someone to tell me I was wrong. Uncomfortable, she pressed the spot I pointed out with her nicely manicured forefinger and quickly retracted it. Yes, there was something there, all right.

"Check again! Please!"

She poked once more.

"Something. Yeah, it's hard, like a ball bearing or something."

She withdrew her finger and held it close to her shoulder. Concerned, blood-shot eyes stared into mine.

By early evening at the hospital, after an eternity of waiting, the on-call doctor said it was probably just a common cyst. I should see my family doctor. I went home and got drunk all over again. The next day, I was in my own doctor's office, listening to a diagnosis of fibrocystic breast disease. It wasn't cancer, and it didn't necessarily mean I was going to get cancer. I relaxed and nearly forgot about the whole threat *until that day in the shower*. The "little marble" was back, and it had swelled to the size of walnut.

A month later saw me on a hospital gurney, prepped for surgery. Someone was asking me to sign papers for a mastectomy. I refused. The nurse handed me two sedative pills and explained that the papers were simply a precaution.

"If the surgeon found a malignancy, you wouldn't want the lump to simply be left there to grow, would you?"

"No, I would not."

"Then sign," she said.

I closed my eyes and repeated the rule. "Don't think, don't feel." I did this until deep anesthesia released me from my fear.

A drugged mind can hold a fear and wait for conscious thought. It can force a waking hand, newly released from being strapped down in surgery, to creep across a tightly bandaged torso to search for a breast. The mind can do this before it can command eyelids to open or even help a mouth search for words. It can also release a primitive cry to answer the flatness of the bandages under the sensing fingers. And that cry can sear the air in a hospital recovery room. It sent a nurse running.

"No, no, dear. Take your hand away. You're fine."

"Naughh, naughh…" I couldn't shape words to explain.

She understood what I needed to hear. "Your breasts are both still there." There was a smile in her voice. "You just don't have very big ones."

She was reassuring me and patting my hand back to my side. Still, I knew my fate was breast cancer. Barely on the edge of consciousness, I was convinced of my clairvoyance; I would lose a breast, maybe both, to cancer. One day, I would die of it.

"Now," said the nurse while she smoothed the sheets, "just relax. There was only a lump, and it's all gone. Be a good girl and don't disturb the bandages. I'll be right back."

"Good girl?" Something like a laugh surfaced through the pain, but the nice nurse soon returned with an injection.

Ah, Demerol. I sighed deeply and fell asleep.

Two days later, I left the hospital, determined to put the cancer fears behind me. I wouldn't even think about cancer again. No, I would not.

The determination to shut down my feelings lasted about a day and a half until it was time to unwrap my bandages and step into the shower. I was afraid of what I'd see. I was very afraid.

What if the nurse had lied? I hadn't confided in anyone, not even my friends at work. Sober, one doesn't talk about private parts to other people; it's too personal. I simply told everyone I had a problem with my shoulder. They believed me, but the success of my lie left me vulnerable and lonely.

One careful layer at a time, I peeled the gauze from around my ribs, unhooking the pins at the edges and letting the stained, white bandages fall to the bathroom floor. The mirror was impartial. It would deliver the truth. Still, I was unprepared for what it revealed when the last strip was pulled away.

What was this? Some sick joke? What happened?

From collarbone to waist, and halfway around my back, stretched an angry purple bruise. Slashed into the side of my blackened breast was a long, red wound. Suddenly, against all of my plans and without any warning, I was soaked in tears. They dripped off my jaw and chin, scattering in salty streams down my ruined breast. Nobody at the hospital, nobody in a white gown and stethoscope, had prepared me for what to feel. There wasn't any support group for this moment in my life. There wasn't any therapeutic touch or gentle words. No one could offer me a tissue and whisper, "I'm here for you."

I cried the whole afternoon. When I could cry no more and when my breath stopped coming in spasms, I called my dad. He would know what to say. Somehow, I felt that my dad was the only person on the planet I could call for just the right words in the right tone. I was wrong. We were both embarrassed. Curled up at the end of the couch, with the receiver pressed to my ear, I refolded my bathrobe across my chest with my free hand and drew a pillow against myself. I listened intently to his every syllable. His words faltered and were not what either of us wanted them to be, but all was not lost. Just the sound of his voice was a comfort. It helped me cope.

"The doctor, Sue. The surgeon. Tell your surgeon. You're upset…too many bruises. You should report it to him."

I believe he meant well. When I hung up, I thought about it long enough to make up my own mind. I would not call the surgeon; neither would I brood about it and be miserable.

Instead, I went back to work. I really couldn't offer much physical labor because I had to keep the elastic bandage in place. The movements of my arm had to be kept to a minimum, especially as it was in a sling. I couldn't lift or carry, but I could help with small food items and I could clean tables. My colleagues were very impressed with my energy after the "shoulder" surgery and provided plenty of sympathy. I especially enjoyed the free drinks, yet the bruising still bothered me. I had never seen bruises that color or size before on anyone. After a week, I decided to share my concern.

On the first Sunday after my operation, I was socializing at a house party where one of the guests was a nurse. It didn't matter whether she was a veterinary nurse, a nurse in training, or a nurse on a soap opera. Once I had downed enough courage, I cornered her. After all, I didn't want to bother my doctor. He was busy, and I rationalized it probably wasn't all that urgent anyway. After the nurse and I slipped into the bathroom though, and I removed my shirt and bandage, she gasped. I kept my panic in check and waited until she offered some medical words. After a closer inspection of the wound and some "hmms" and "uh-huhs," she declared that everything seemed fine. I was so relieved! There wasn't any need to look silly in the doctor's office. An intoxicated nurse, whom I had never seen before, had declared I was fine.

I could get on with my life and forget about the whole horrible episode.

16

My boss at RoundUp had a volatile personality. Depending on the day, he drank as much as I did and, amazingly, sometimes more. This made for an interesting relationship between the two of us. Our first clash was over the plastic cowboy hats the staff was made to endure.

I felt foolish in the thing and hated the hat head that came with it. (Biker chick helmet-head, however, was quite acceptable in my estimation. Cowboy hats that flattened my long hair were not.) After my shift, I'd have to bring along a curling iron and spend a very long time in the restroom redoing my hair. The process was beginning to get to me. I decided to ask if I could stop wearing the hat, but it was essential to catch "boss man" in a good mood. Actually, he had two moods: drunk and hung over. Drunk was easygoing, near silly. Hung over was edgy and sullen. I felt I had chosen the better of the two opportunities when I approached his smiling self.

"No way," he laughed. "Keep the hat." That ended the conversation.

I tried testing his eggshell personality a second time, knowing that a wrong move could invite an explosive tirade. He was angry I tried again, angry I hadn't respected the fact that this was his place and he could dictate the dress code. Yet in an instant, his mood swung to flirtatious. Everyone else had to wear a hat. I alone could go without if (and here he gave me a sly smile), *if* I would curl my pretty hair every day. I dropped the issue. The guy was sleaze. A married sleaze.

Our next run-in was over his "upgrading" our uniforms. We were to wear brown, fringed mini dresses with plunging necklines and so-called sassy underwear to peek out at the hem. He announced the plan at a meeting and produced an outfit for me to model for the others. The sassy underwear was a pair of bulky, old-fashioned bloomers, but even more ridiculous was the neckline.

Was I supposed to bend forward to wait on a table and give a good peep show of my scar tissue at the same time?

"I'm not wearing this thing!" I said, and the other girls nodded in agreement. The costume must have come from one of his adolescent dreams. I was a damned good waitress. Say what you want about my lifestyle, my biker friends, or anything else, but I was organized and loyal to my job. Both staff and customers liked me. Because I was fast and efficient, I was making five dollars an hour when other waitresses were being paid two dollars and sixty-five cents for the same time. I threatened to quit.

"Fine," he snarled. "Go ahead!"

"Suits me! This is my last week."

It wasn't. We didn't speak for two days, but he relented because there was no one capable enough to replace me. I was also promoted to supervisor, meaning I could ditch the uniform and wear jeans. I still had to wear the hat though. I couldn't get rid of the hat. Because I hated being set apart by being different, the supervisor title began wearing thin. I took to wearing the stupid uniform anyway. Strangely enough, as old staff quit and a succession of new people came on board, the uniform was shelved. The damned hat remained.

The boss's alcoholic personality invited fights with everyone on the floor, including his wife and business partner. Upstairs at the bar, brawls were frequent, enough to justify hiring two big-ass bikers as bouncers. After hours, he'd invite that staff and the bouncers down for a few drinks. Of course, always hanging around for the last drop, I'd also appear. I'd even stay after the regular staff went home and served drinks for the card games that went on between the bouncers and the owners. I was playacting the nice person. My sole motive was free drinks.

One afternoon when I was dragging my sorry self out of bed after one of those all-night drinking and card parties, I found I could barely walk. I rubbed my backside, wondering why it hurt so much.

Maybe I had slept wrong.

I limped into the bathroom to look in the mirror and found the bruised outline of a heel mark pressed into the muscle.

How had that happened?

Surely, if it hurt so much, I'd have to remember. Ever the detective, I'd have to sort through clues. It would be too obvious to simply admit I was a blackout drinker who expected others to remember my antics. I got dressed and went to work.

When I arrived, the boss was sitting in a shadowy corner, obviously hung over, but nursing a fresh drink. He watched my approach and caught the limp. His face was pale; its only outstanding features were his two, red-rimmed puffy eyes.

"You all right?" he asked, not a little sheepishly. But then, one must allow for his being drunk at four in the afternoon.

"Sure," I lied. I was aching like I had been run over by a truck. "Why do you ask?"

"Just checking. It was late when we left. That's all."

The bouncers were no help for information. They, healthier looking than either of us, knew about last night and weren't telling. As the shift wore on, snippets of the evening began surfacing anyway. Over the next few days, I was able to retrieve some of the images. The first recollection was sunrise, and the second, leaving the place alone.

Whew! At least I hadn't gone home with anyone.

Next, there was a sense, an image of my fighting with boss man. And then, it became clear he had booted me out on the pavement. That explained the imprint on my behind. That also explained his reluctance to yell at me for being drunk: I had been assaulted. Needless to say, I didn't press charges.

After that night, the guy skidded rapidly into his own hell. His wife left him, and his partner took over the bar. It was too bad, though. In a strange way, I liked him. I empathized with him, probably because he was as screwed up as I was, a trait that was steadily becoming the link I sought in other people.

The bar began attracting bikers who were older and seasoned in the lifestyle. Most of them already knew the bouncers upstairs. Members of the "brotherhood," they had ridden with each other for years and all of them oozed of knuckle-crushing domination. A glance from any of them could crumble cement. Poor dumb me. I was infatuated with their celebrity. These guys were aggressive, raunchy, hard-drinking party animals, which, for me, was instant attraction. At closing time, when they all traveled from our bar to another location, I was hitching a ride with the first offer.

It was at one of those after-hours black leather affairs where I met Ted. He was fifteen years older, divorced, and, at the end of the night, he wanted to drive me home. I was hoping it would be on his Harley with the screaming red-and-orange flames detailed across the tank, but Ted offered me a ride in his van. Now, most intelligent young women would hesitate somewhat if they considered the risks involved. They wouldn't be miles from home at four o'clock in the morning and shit-faced drunk, either. I considered myself intuitive; I saw his decent side. Why, he didn't even care that I lived all the way across town. He was still willing to drive me home at that late hour. I had recently lost my apartment for lack of a roommate to share the rent, so I had gone to live once again with my parents. That was safe, wasn't it? I was living with my parents; I was a nice girl, and bad things don't happen to nice girls.

"Oh, gee," I gushed. "I really appreciate the lift."

And he appreciated giving it. Life sometimes holds wonderful surprises. Ted was one of them. Not only did he escort me home in the most efficient and direct way, we also sat in his van for a long time in front of my house, just talking. He was studying at college to be a machinist while he was sharing rent with two others guys in a house. Here was a guy who owned a van *and* a bike, and he was working toward a noble career. The guy had stability. That was enough for me. Dad would love him. Even my mother would approve because Susan's new man had a *future.* Within a week, we were dating. To top off the good news, Ted didn't drink, well, at least not as much as I did.

In the town where I lived, there was no shortage of motorcycle clubs, and they were all quite popular with the police. Every biker seemed to have some connection with one of them, including Ted.

Ted's biker club partied at a farm property belonging to another club. These guys drank and rode hard. Their parties were announced by a procession of Harley-Davidsons thundering down unpaved country roads and coming to a majestic halt in some pasture. Lean more closely into the clouds of dust, and you'll see me clinging to Ted's waist, thrilled with the excitement of being a bona fide biker chick. Look again. That's me in the center of the crowd on the farm, spending beer tickets into the evening and socializing with staggering, cursing drunks, some of them naked. It shouldn't seem like status, but that's how I saw it. For years, I had aspired to being someone's ol' lady. I reasoned I had the best of both worlds: reckless abandon because of the clubs and stability because of Ted's job.

Okay, I know what you're thinking about the stability part. Was I crazy? But listen to this. As it turned out, Ted was really a teddy bear. He treated me like a lady. It's true. We had been going out for nearly a month before he asked if I'd like to stay at his place for the night. He asked. He was even nervous I might not want to sleep with him. I had a choice. Without a second thought, I went with him.

Before I continue with the rest of this bizarre Cinderella tale and how, because I finally got my way, I lived happily ever after as the Motorcycle Princess, let me add another dimension to the plot. Allow me to introduce Runt, the vertically challenged biker. You understand, of course, that he wasn't vertically challenged because he was always lying down on the job. That would be silly. No, among the gigantic brutes he hung out with, Runt, at five feet ten, was considered a midget. Even smaller were his morals.

I was drawn to him. Surprisingly, his lack of moral fiber caused me some (not a lot, but some) inner conflict. On one hand, I'm five foot three, a perfect height next to his. He was cute, a free spirit, and a member of Ted's motorcycle club. He was also unattached. It seemed that one fine day, he had left his girlfriend at home to get a pack of cigarettes and rode halfway across Canada to get them. He had been gone for three years. I thought the story was hilarious.

On the other hand (and this was where the inner conflict came in), Ted and I were living together on the main floor of a two-story house in midtown. We had moved in with his single bed, my couch and coffee table, and my mom's old curtains. Ted had graduated and found a full-time job. We were a domestic couple. And Runt was Ted's best friend.

What to do? Well, let's solve the problem. Meet Runt at the bar after work and have a drink. Ask Runt how Ted could be a big, bad biker and yet be so meek and mild. Runt, glad I confided in him for the answer, had been wondering why a girl like me would want someone as unexciting as Ted. If bikers were students, Ted was the class nerd. Runt insisted I should find someone with more "energy" to take me out partying instead of sitting at home enduring the plain life with his friend.

Why, what a good idea! Where should I start?

We could go back to Runt's place. He was sharing digs with Big Bob just a couple of streets over from where Ted and I lived. Good plan. Here we go: twenty-something girl going home with a thirty-something biker to meet his scary forty-something biker roommate who owned a tattoo parlor. Charming. The word "drink" cast its magic and we were there.

Oh my! Oh, oh…yes! That night made Ted's missionary position seem even duller. Runt, by comparison, was much more inventive and enduring. We rolled around in his unmade bed, exploring every fantasy until we fell back exhausted, wearing only our satisfied grins. But then, guilt, my near-constant companion, yanked us both out of the sheets.

Who would get blamed for this one? The new girlfriend? The best friend of twenty years?

There was going to be trouble. We had one more beer together while he played "Free Bird" by Lynyrd Skynyrd on the stereo, just for me. He told me I was someone special who should look beyond Ted. I should think about it.

On the walk home to Ted, I couldn't think of anything else but cheating with Runt. The experience was a confused and misdirected girl's idea of romance: all sweet words and passionate embraces. I was desirable. He had told me so.

What did Ted have to offer that was exciting? Nothing. He was reliable, stable, and about as stimulating as stale gum.

I felt chronically remorseful, but I'd get used to it. Over the next two years, I got a lot of guilty practice with Runt. Ted never knew, even at Runt's celebration party when he was initiated into his new biker club. That night would prove to be a close call.

17

When Ted and I got to the party at the farm, everything was fine. The music was pounding and the booze was flowing free. He went off to drink with a couple guys in the field, but not before forbidding me to be alone with Runt or his new friends: they were members of one of the "big two" clubs. That made them dangerous. Specifically, I wasn't to go near the clubhouse alone.

"I promise."

(Yeah, yeah, whatever). You'd think I had my yappy parents in tow.

Ted didn't have any idea that I was considered Runt's "Girlfriend Number Two," which provided me special designation for protection. All the guys in the new club covered for us. Runt's other girlfriend (aka "Girl of the Week") was there, so I waited until he was by himself before we spoke. You'd expect the conversation would be breathless and filled with intrigue. It wasn't.

"I need to pee!"

Legs crossed firmly under my beer-sloshy bladder, I was really requesting to use the bathroom in the clubhouse. Club rule stated I had to use the field, but I just couldn't manage it. Oh, I'd had tried many times, but I always fell down in the process, pants around my ankles, peeing on my shoes. It was just too improper for a girl of my delicate breeding. Amused, Runt produced a key. The house was off-limits for everyone else except me. Wasn't I privileged?

I really must have had to go because I risked Ted's anger. Anger and rejection were still my primary fears.

What if Ted kicked me out of the house? I'd have nowhere to go, and my entire homeless panic reaction with its "dead in the gutter" ending would become a reality.

Forget that. Nature dictates: bathroom first, gutter later.

Once I had relieved myself, I headed for the back door, but Runt was lying in wait.

The next thing I knew we were both covered with straw and reeking with something gross smelling and muddy.

Strange. Had we gone out?

It was like sleeping through an entire movie segment. Was this intermission? I did have a vague recollection of being upstairs in a bedroom and looking out the window to see Runt lurching out of the barn and heading toward the house. I must have come downstairs because, the next thing I knew, we were standing in the kitchen, both of us filthy enough to be condemned by the Board of Health.

What in hell had happened to us? And why were four guys, all belonging to Runt's new club, lined up against the kitchen counters falling over each other laughing?

One of them was Big Bob, who seldom spoke, but that night his face was bright pink from trying to catch his breath. Neither of us knew why. They had to tell us.

As the story goes, Runt and I had been in the barn. As a matter of fact, there were witnesses to our rolling around in the wet stalls. Because we were making so much noise, some of the partygoers thought animals were mating in there. They were right. That's when our four protectors stepped in. They guarded the barn until we passed out. They left Runt there. I was carried back to the clubhouse and put in an upstairs bedroom to recover. Embarrassed, Runt and I listened to the story while the smell of manure rose up between us.

I needed a beer. It took a shower and a few more bottles to help me sort out the facts. What had I learned this evening? Lessons in loyalty? The evils of alcohol? Not exactly. Runt had gambled his friendship with Ted to have his way with me, while his friends respected me enough to protect my interests. Why would I give up such validation? I must be truly worthy.

My motto had cemented itself in my mind. "Don't think, don't feel. Just drown it with alcohol." After all, if feeling and thinking got me into so much trouble, what was left to worry about?

18

I was a sloppy, embarrassing drunk. Or so I was told. As far as I was concerned, drinking was a priority and that excluded opinions about it. When I wasn't drinking, the reality of who I had become was too great to bear; therefore, drinking and ignoring advice about it was my best choice. I knew it, but did I want to *admit* that I wasn't a real person, that I used a refrigerator almost exclusively for chilling beer, that I couldn't maintain a solid relationship? When I was sober, I hated myself. Drink was my only escape.

After my boss lost his share of RoundUp and his partner stepped in, new rules were posted. A cover charge was instituted, a measure intended to keep out the riffraff, me included. All employees were instructed to leave the premises as soon as their shifts were finished. There would be no more free drinks for me upstairs, no more sloppy, embarrassing, drunken Sue with her head thrown back, draining the last drop at the bottom of the bottle, at least not at RoundUp. If I stayed, it wouldn't be long before I was fired. Since being fired would be one of those "bad person" moments I couldn't face, I had to quit. Shortly after the new rules went into effect, I hung up my plastic cowgirl hat for the last time.

In the first few weeks after RoundUp, I took a job at one of those shabby hotels where old men with sunken faces and shaky hands drank six-ounce drafts all day. They seldom tipped. I moved on. Another new restaurant called the Copper Kettle was opening. It was in the mall, which meant it would be busy and the tips would be good. Another perk of the location was that it was right on a bus route. I applied and got a waitress job. Naturally, I had issues with the uniform, but I did like the staff, and it didn't take long to find a new drinking buddy. They were getting younger. Margot was a high school kid, and I was her bad influence. We started hanging out at Gilbert's and even at RoundUp (despite the cover charge) until all hours of the night. Of course, when I got home myself, there was always a fight with Ted waiting for me. He had big problems with my dragging Margot along to drink with his friends. (Obviously, some of them were reporting my escapades to him.) Some nights, I didn't want to go home to the hassle. It was better to stay in malfunction mode, anywhere else. That included Runt's biker clubhouse. One of those evenings became especially memorable.

What a big shot I was showing Margot my special underworld! On the exterior, the clubhouse was like me, perfectly ordinary looking in a nice way. The interior, however, was a large, hollowed-out space dedicated to drinking and loud, lewd socializing. Of course, Runt was in attendance. Ted wasn't. I already knew he had been invited to party that night, but he had passed on the offer. Margot and I had booked off work early just to be there. Ted thought I had to work a late shift. The clubhouse was merely an old cottage, fenced off with chain link, but its guarded doors made two giggly girls feel glamorous and exclusive. Once inside, I climbed on a barstool, animated and chatty, while I parked Margot beside me. I had been there at least fifty times before, but she was in awe.

At the back doors (for break-in protection) was a railroad tie secured by an iron plate. The plate was screwed into the floor, and you had to step over it on the way to and from the bathroom. I had performed that minor athletic move on many occasions, but when I wanted to appear especially sophisticated for my friend that night, I caught my toe and tripped. Everyone thought the sight of Sue clowning around on the floor with her short skirt flipped up over her bikini panties and her legs (toothpicks in their leather fashion boots) sticking up in separate directions was just hilarious. Large hands hoisted me up and steered me back to my place at the bar. Margot and I enjoyed the wide attention and continued drinking well into the night. Hours later, on a television set in a corner, early morning cartoons flickered to life.

"Aw, closing time already?" Margot blinked and yawned.

"Yeah, it's five o'clock. Okay, let's go!" I said.

I was anxious to leave. Despite the large amount of alcohol in my system, I could feel one of my ankles throbbing. When I stepped down from my stool, I hit the ground like a felled tree. For more than one reason, I couldn't stand upright. One of the bikers (such helpful guys), whipped out a switchblade and sliced my boot, top to sole. Inside, we found a swollen, purple band where my ankle should have been. Because I couldn't walk and Margot was far too drunk to drive (she had lost her keys as well), one of the guys carted me out fireman-style over his shoulder and put me in a cab. To add to my predicament, the cabbie was a woman. She didn't look strong enough to carry me from the cab to my door, and she wasn't. We had to struggle out of the cab, but she let me lean on her while I fished out my keys. With my hand on her shoulder and her arm around my waist, I hopped to the porch. She left the motor running. I gathered she hadn't intended to stay and nurse me back to health.

"You okay there, kiddo?"

"Oh yeah, sure. I'll be fine." Relieved from duty, she swung her cab back out of the driveway and disappeared.

Early morning joggers would have wondered about the weirdo in one boot and one bare leg, kneeling before the doorknob as if in prayer. They would have been able to watch for several minutes as I tried catching the swaying keyhole. One try...two tries...on the third attempt, the door creaked open. Resolving to appear sober and knowing I couldn't walk, I lowered myself to my hands and knees. Imagining myself to be quiet as a mouse (there were a few of those around), I crawled stealthily through the living room and down the hall.

"Where have you been?"

The sudden booming voice coming straight at me caused my hands to fly out in surrender. Ted leaped out of bed to find me stretched out on the carpet, crying my eyes out. Maybe it was hysterical surprise; I had been caught in mid guilt.

"Oh, I fell! I fell! I hurt my ankle!"

"Liar! I didn't hear no fall!"

"No, no. At work! I fell...in the parking lot!" (More sobs. Rolling motions. Simulated agony.)

"Why didn't you come home then?"

"Ohh...ow, ow! Margot took me to her place to put ice on it, and I fell asleep!"

Hey, wow that's believable, but just for good measure..."And she didn't want to wake me up! Please, don't be mad at me!" (Moan here. Blink eyes. Go for Academy Award.)

He scooped me into his arms, *Gone with the Wind* style. His face suddenly gentle and his voice sympathetic and protective, he carried me to the couch and inspected the damaged ankle. He wasn't angry at all. Now that was some neat little tactic I had to file away for future use. *Pain brings sympathy.* Foolish me. I had always tried to win acceptance by pretending strength. This helplessness thing was something new, and obviously very effective.

"We're going to the hospital with this, Sue. You really done a job on it."

With a great sigh of relief, I draped my arms around his thick neck.

"Whatever you say, Ted. *I love you!*"

19

"What! Two weeks!"

"Yes. Two weeks. Keep the ankle elevated and iced." The intern glanced up at Ted. "When the swelling subsides enough, we can put a cast on it."

"Is it broken?" Ted stepped up to the X ray in a lighted panel on the wall. He looked frazzled. I felt sorry for him.

"No." The intern used his pen as a pointer and tapped at some stuff I didn't care to look at. "See here? She's torn the ligaments and tendons around the ankle."

He kept addressing himself to Ted, who was frowning and shaking his head at the screen as if it were asking questions. I reached out from the examining table for the list of instructions, although I was more eager to snatch the prescription for heavy-duty painkillers. My ankle was swollen to three times its normal size. The rest of my leg, from toes to knee, was rapidly becoming a vibrant shade of purple. If I couldn't walk, I couldn't work.

How was I going to pay my share of the bills? What if I slipped into another valley of depression like that awful winter in Redcar? Two whole weeks of boredom! What would I do with the time? Voices in my head protested all the way home.

Misery, you are about to meet your company. I didn't have to worry about the boredom as long as we had mice in the house. The thought of their nesting on my sedated body while I slept kept me awake. Meanwhile, I grew restless waiting for my cast because it would mean a refill for pain pills. Every day was filled with anticipation. How much longer now? Finally, the big day arrived when I got my walking cast. It would take about seventy-two hours to harden and then, liberation! I could return to work!

My family ethic was, "If you're too sick to go to school, you can't go out to play." Well, I wasn't sick. I was just walking funny, that's all. Besides, I really needed to go find a party or at least a few drinks.

The sympathy thing played out very well indeed. After thumping up the steps of the bus (with the plaster barely dry) and back down and then working through a shift or two feeling my leg swelling again under the cast, even strangers showed me respect. Somehow I managed to juggle heavy trays and keep up with the pace. It must have been impressive because the tips were gigantic.

The plaster cast managed to survive for several weeks, even enduring the night I walked twelve blocks to the all-night convenience store to get a box of antacid. Well, I didn't want to wake Ted, now did I? I had to keep a bank of sympathy and that would be a withdrawal I wouldn't risk. The whole way, my gut was grinding with pain.

What in heck was it? Gas?

Let's buy three different types of antacid medication to settle things down. It's two o'clock in the stupid morning. Just buy the stuff already and hobble home.

Three hours later, the pain was more than I could stand. I was forced to wake Ted. Of course, he was upset I hadn't done that already. Once again, he accurately diagnosed an emergency. By 5:30 in the morning, he loaded me with my plaster-encased leg into the van and we made our way through the darkness back to the hospital.

The pain was shooting between my hip bones. No one wanted to offer a firm diagnosis. It might be my ovaries. Best send this girl to Henderson, the cancer hospital. Give her something for the pain.

"Oh, I am dying! This is it! But, wait. Gee, this is nice...the painkillers are kicking in. Everything is kind of...*fluffy.*"

I woke to find myself in a hospital recovery room with a nurse at my side. She told me that I'd have to stay where I was for another couple of days because the emergency team doctors had removed my appendix.

It wasn't cancer? Yippee! May I have a larger dose of narcotics, please?

Within the week, I was back at the job. The weight of the cast and the tightness of the incision forced me to limp along, hunched over my tray. It was the Christmas season: gently falling snow, everyone was happy, and then there was Sue, the poor, little cripple. Next to me, *A Christmas Carol's* Tiny Tim could have been a poster boy for good health. All the customers stared and were amazed.

"Check out that waitress, man. Ever pitiful, eh?"

"Looks like somebody dug her up from a graveyard."

"Shaddup! Whaddya you? The Grinch? Lookit how she has to walk, you jackass! It's like nearly freakin' Christmas! We should be nice to people like her."

And you think my tips were good before! All through the holiday season, my apron weighed me down with goodwill of the best kind, silver coins and folding money.

A year passed. Ted and I were still together in our turbulent relationship, arguing over my drinking, having changes of heart, and reconciling. We'd have fights where I'd be hollering and swearing so loud the neighbors could hear, and Ted would be trying to hold me down to prevent my hurting either one of us. I'd spend the night with my parents and return to him, always wondering why he was so foolish to put up with me. Would I ever be able to live normally and be welcomed among real people? The idea was tempting, but I had long lost the rules of fitting in with regular people. From wild child to wild, tattooed adult, I was damaged goods. Who'd be willing to get involved with that? No one with a sane mind. I had to stay where I was considered acceptable.

Even so, there is something absurd about the female psyche that causes even biker chicks to want to play at being the blushing bride. I was still maintaining my secret relationship with Runt, even though somewhere along the line, he had proposed to his live-in girlfriend. She was about to become "Mrs. Runt." Not that the marriage would have interfered with my relationship with the guy. It would have merely heightened the guilt for a while. I was used to sharing him with other girls, but on the occasion of their Tupperware bridal party, I was feeling very abandoned. To compensate, I had to arrive late, in a cloud of perfume and alcohol, looking for the grand entrance.

My first flamboyant act of the evening was to fall straight over the threshold. So funny! What a showstopper! If I couldn't be carried through the doorway in a white dress with a bouquet clutched in one hand, a bottle in the other, then, hey, just taking a free fall onto the carpet would do. Obviously, this was some sort of corny Jack and Jill deal because Runt was there, albeit hiding out in the kitchen. After scooping myself up and loudly greeting all the guests, I made my way, cute and flashy, straight into his arms. He pushed me away, but the game was on; I needed consoling. The little girl in me hated the attention going on in the other room, and I had to prove that my needs were of primary importance. Yes, I had the man's attention. I even got his fiancée's attention when she walked in to find us kissing and pawing in the pantry. I believe there was a lot of noise, followed by my hasty departure. At any rate, I came out of my blackout in the lobby of their apartment building and found, to my astonishment, blood pouring from the back of my head.

Help! I had to get help, but the lobby was vacant. All of this blood, and nobody saw or heard anything? Okay, pick myself up…stagger into the elevator…stand bashing at the apartment door until the bride-to-be opened it, just a crack.

"You can't come in," she snarled.

"I'm really hurt. I'm bleeding! Please!"

At the sound of my voice, Runt appeared and pulled the door wide.

"What in the hell happened?"

"Her head's bleeding," the fiancée reported, "an' the blood's getting all over the goddamn rug."

She stalked out of the room to get a towel. The guests backed up while Runt set me down on a mat and started to call a cab.

"Who was it?" he called from the phone table.

"Dunno," I said, mopping my head. "Stupid kids. They pushed me into the glass door trying to steal my purse. The window part's all smashed out." Truthfully, I didn't know what had happened to me and I was too ashamed to admit it.

Even though I should have gone straight to the hospital, I instructed the cabbie to take me home. I just hoped I hadn't messed up the backseat of the cab too much. My real worry was Ted. He'd be mad at me. The needy side of my personality couldn't handle that. Like a sneaky child, I hid my bloody jeans in the laundry hamper and then tried washing the shirt. With Ted still dead asleep in the bedroom, I leaned against the kitchen sink rinsing, rinsing...red water...run the tap again...detergent...more rinsing. At last, when the last trace of blood was gone, I flopped into bed, my head pounding.

When Ted found me the next morning lying on a blood stained pillow, he freaked. I hated the idea of his taking me to emergency yet again.

"No, no. I'm fine! And no, I can't identify the muggers. Leave me alone. I gotta go to work."

(Must calm Ted down. Must make my freaking head stop hurting so much!) I was woozy way past the usual hangover. By the lunch shift, when the room was still spinning and I could no longer focus, I knew I had to get to a hospital.

The on-call doctor suspected I had a concussion. Why hadn't I come sooner?

Why indeed. Was it because I was too proud to admit I was drunk again? That I'd let myself down again?

The head wound, because of my neglect, was beyond stitches. I retold my thug story. Shouldn't I file a police report? Oh no. I couldn't remember enough for any kind of description. And gee, my front tooth is loose and hurting. (Can we stop talking now?)

I was told to go home and rest. Yes, I had done quite a job on the tooth. Be sure to see a dentist. Yes, by all means, I would do that as soon as I could get rid of the fog in my brain. Yes, ma'am...you betcha. I would endure a dentist jackhammering in my mouth. As tough as I longed to be, within hours, the pain forced me into a dentist's chair.

The night had been very expensive. The dentist's bill for pegging my tooth, the root canal, and the prescription medication combined with the lost work time was an enormous drain on my wallet. My nervous system was shot. I couldn't stop thinking that I had done something really wrong. Any day now, police would show up and charge me with who knows what, but definitely for the broken lobby door. As for the blow to my self-esteem, it just reinforced what I already knew: I was a loser.

20

Joey was an old friend of Runt's. What I found curious was Runt's eagerness to set me up with him. I wondered if he had grown weary of trying to convince me to leave Ted and gone ahead to find someone for me. Maybe he had just grown tired of me.

Apparently, Joey was waiting for me to call, which I did. I lied as usual to Ted, telling him I had been invited to a jewelry party. I drove to the baseball field where Joey was playing.

A first date at a baseball game? What was Runt thinking?

This Joey guy did little else except play baseball. He did smoke weed all day though. Then again, he didn't drink. This setup was either a ploy to get me to stop drinking or Joey was a wonderful solution to rid both Runt and Ted of the job of being my babysitter. Right from the start, my relationship with Joey was platonic and remained that way. We never even kissed. He'd call me over and I, always grateful to be needed, would haul over a case of beer to sit and watch him inhale numerous joints. I suspected he dealt drugs; at night, he had good parties and during the day, he was jobless.

Our association with each other was so unexciting, I never imagined his apartment would be the location for rape. I should have expected something to happen. Because of the way I regularly passed out at parties, some opportunist would eventually follow me into the bedroom. One night, while Joey's place was rocking with noise and people and no one missed me, I woke to find myself half-naked on Joey's bed. A large man was on top of me, fully engaged in trying to satisfy himself. The music was so loud it drowned my screams. I tried to move, but my legs were painfully forced apart under his weight. My skinny thighs were pinned aside by his tree trunk legs.

He kept calling me, "Baby! Oh, baby!" as though our intimacy was something usual, or, for that matter, consensual.

When he tried to flip me on my stomach, possibly to violate me again, or to push my face into the pillow to smother me, I gained a small advantage of space, enough to fight back. Untroubled by my small fists, he simply got off the bed, zipped up his pants, and returned to the party as nonchalantly as though he had just been to the bathroom.

As soon as I could find my clothes, I managed to climb out onto the fire escape and, from there, staggered as quickly as I could down to the street. Disoriented, I tried to pick out where I was. None of the street names made sense. I walked until I found something familiar, a name, some building, anything. After a few blocks, I paused to check my purse. My cigarettes were there and so were my keys and wallet, but every dollar had been taken. I had no money, no means of getting home to Ted. After wandering several more blocks, I stuck out my thumb and hitchhiked. Thankfully, somebody picked me up.

I woke the next morning to the rumble of Ted's van pulling out of the driveway. As soon as I was conscious, the word "rape" began plaguing me with all of its ugly meanings: disease, pregnancy, and the belief I had invited it. Bathing and showering were not enough. As much as I scrubbed, I couldn't wash the revulsion from my skin.

Could Ted make things right? Would he love me and protect me even though I had done this horrible thing?

No, I couldn't risk it. I couldn't tell him about this awful thing that had happened to me. My secret was evil. I decided to keep it to myself. It was just one more padlock on the door of the invisible prison that housed my self-hatred. I was beginning to wonder if anyone would ever let me out.

Two nights after the rape, I was drinking with a big group of friends at Gilbert's. There was plenty of beer and lots of laughter and a feeling of security returned to me. I began to relax. During the course of the evening, I was weaving my way through the crowd on my way to the restroom, calling out to friends along the way when a large hand clamped my arm.

"Hey, girl!" The voice was deep and sleazy.

Still on edge from my attack at Joey's, I spun around and came face to face with my rapist.

"Hey, baby! Doncha go runnin' away. You was a real fine time for me the other night, darlin'!" His smile framed badly decayed front teeth.

My stomach tightened. I twisted under his grip on my elbow. He tried pulling me closer. "We should be doin' that again, real soon. Whatcha say?"

I wrenched my arm free and ran to the bathroom, locked myself in a stall and threw up. Here? He's here in my sanctuary? This can't be happening.

Both sides of my mind, the intelligent and the reckless, battled it out. Reason told me to stay put for a while. It was a big bar. The animal would eventually give up and find another victim. Recklessness won out. I decided to walk boldly back to my table and pretend, the best I could, that nothing had happened.

Within minutes, he was pulling up a chair to sit with us, familiar, oozing with friendly charm. He addressed me by name. The others must have thought I had lost my mind when I stood up and tipped the table on him. Every drink on the table splashed on his fancy suit. When he yelled out in angry surprise, I ran, bolting past patrons, knocking them sideways, past waiters juggling trays, down the hall, out the front door, straight out to the parking lot and into the backseat of a parked squad car. Two startled police officers turned to hear me blurt out the whole story, breathless and frantic. The officers exchanged glances. I thought I noticed a flicker of amusement: *the bimbo gets rough sex, so what's new?*

"Sorry, miss," they said, "you should have reported this incident when it occurred. It's too late now."

Too late? Two nights was *too late*?

They weren't interested in the fact that I had been sexually assaulted and my assailant was just inside the building right beside us, the one I had just come flying out of?

Now what?

I thanked them and walked back to the bar, moving just quickly enough to avoid their getting any second thoughts about arresting me. (Even my imagination perpetually felt guilty.) I had to go back inside. I wanted my things. Besides, my friends were probably wondering what had happened to me. The doorman escorted me directly to my table and back to the door where I quickly called a cab and went home.

That was a sleepless night. My table-tipping antics would have enraged my rapist. If the police wouldn't help me, I'd have to find someone who would. I called Runt. He didn't rush over. It took him two hours, but he did come and he did listen to my story, all of it, from the night at the party to that previous evening's encounter. Runt told me the guy was notorious for his sexual attacks; he had already done prison time for the same thing. That's when I really started to panic. What else would he do to me if he caught me again?

A few weeks later, as I was weaving through a crowd at Gilbert's, I nearly touched shoulders with my rapist. He never turned in my direction or acknowledged my presence. While I stood shocked at his ignoring me, he hobbled by on crutches. His idea that he had a right to violate women had been tested at a recent party. Another girl, a much bigger girl, had managed to subdue him with a beer bottle until her friends answered her screams. This time, each of his knees took a hammer blow before he could zip up.

Sometime later, I read that he was caught attacking yet another young woman. He had moved his predatory arena to a different province, but this time, his punishment didn't leave any room for repeat behavior. Someone shot him. Apparently he died instantly.

21

I encouraged Ted to move. In the darkest corners of my mind, that strange and persistent little voice was still telling me to be normal. I truly wanted to participate in all that a "real" existence meant, including having a respectable relationship. I thought a new address would help. Without knowing my desperation, Ted agreed to look for a new place. He was making good money and together we could afford better living space. After a short time hunting, we found something in a nicer area of the city.

We signed the lease for a two-story town house in a fairly new complex. Compared to the other place we shared with rats and nothing except beer and salami in the refrigerator, this was heaven. It was walking distance from my friend Margot's and right on a bus route. Ted was really happy to have a garage to store his Harley. I was proud of having a doorbell and a foyer that led to a real living and dining room, not just structures of my wishful thinking. Our move was celebrated with buying a new bed. We had been sleeping together on a twin-sized mattress; we felt luxurious buying a double. We arrived in suburbia as Mr. and Mrs. Normal, blending in perfectly with other humans. Mom did the family thing by pitching in with curtains, and I bought a kitchen table and chairs.

The new place was twice the size of the old one, which always means twice as much cleaning. I hate cleaning, so it wasn't long before the place was a mess. Ted, an old-school kind of guy, expected the domestic chores to be mine.

"Ten minutes a day, Sue," he'd say. "You only have to spend ten minutes a day picking up. Then the place wouldn't get like this, and you wouldn't have to spend all day at it."

I resented every minute I spent doing domestic chores. I paid half the rent. Ted made a lot more than I did, which left him cash at the end of the month. Fairness told me he should be doing half the housework.

I started getting restless. My sidekick Margot went back to school and the Copper Kettle wasn't doing that well. Time to move on to another job. Wouldn't you know it! I found one in the neighborhood we had just left, all the way on the other side of town. Would I ever get it right?

Flannigan's was a great place. Even though I had to commute an hour on the bus or fork out twenty bucks for cab fare, I didn't mind. The tips were good, and the place was always busy. On weekends, it was transformed from a restaurant to a really hopping nightclub with a line waiting to get in. Once the disk jockey arrived, the place boiled over with music and dancing. I worked as many hours as I could.

Margot was going to college, but she was glad to come in as a hostess to pick up some extra cash. How I admired her. She went to school, she partied without getting drunk, and the whole time I knew her, she only had two boyfriends. Even so, on some nights, we'd go to a new bar down the street called The Track and play a game we called "pick a guy, any guy." It involved randomly choosing some target male and daring the other to flirt with him until he asked her to go home. At that point in the game, we'd refuse. The conquest involved enjoying the rounds of drinks bought by the target. We thought ourselves invincible and very, very funny, but even though I enjoyed Margot's friendship, her presence was a reminder that I was a screw-up. I wanted to be like Margot, fun but normal at the same time. Instead, I put all my energy into being a good waitress. In the beginning, management liked me; in the beginning, it was mutual. Inevitably, I was bound to break someone's social rules. It was just that when I was drunk, I was oblivious. Shock and embarrassment for me always came as a delayed reaction when someone had to point out my misdemeanors. For my indiscretions with the attractive, young busboy, the surprise arrived with his innocent question.

"So, how was I last night?"

"What do you mean...how was *what*?" I answered with rising fear. I knew the answer almost as soon as I spoke.

"You know..." His cheeks flushed a little and he lowered his voice, not low enough however to block out the revelation to the entire kitchen staff. "C'mon, you know...it was my first time."

First time? First *time!* Oh no! Oh, surely this kid couldn't *mean*...and yet he did...and what did that make me? A pervert. I had corrupted a minor when all I had needed was a quick fix. This baby boy thought I was sincere.

"Yeah...uh, you were fine," I lied. I honestly couldn't remember. "But, you know this can't happen again, don't you?" I scolded in a motherly way. He nodded his beautiful, blond head. Without understanding, he agreed.

Of course it happened again.

I believed my life would go on that way forever. It would swing from being outright dull to thrilling self-indulgence and back again. Ted shouldered more of the finances, I made it home most nights, and I was expecting years of the same pattern. Little did I know I was standing on the edge of a major cliff. I was about to fall so far and so deep that nothing could have prepared me for the experience. If a fortuneteller could have described it to me, I would never have believed it. I thought I had seen everything. As it turned out, "everything" was about to occur.

22

In the middle of the main room at Flannigan's was an elevated bar. Constructed like a cell in a beehive, it was six sided. On that memorable Thursday night, it was buzzing.

At first because I was serving a table, I didn't notice him, but when I passed the bar on my way to the kitchen, I happened to look up and was instantly infatuated. He had big, hard muscles, a moustache and beard, and he was drinking beer with his buddy. I wanted him. My every move became a strategy to include him in my line of vision. Several times I passed him closely, feeling his presence, memorizing the strawberry blond whiskers in his beard, his well-worn black leather jacket, faded Levi's, and the pale gold of his long hair.

All I could focus on was *him,* and all I needed him to do was look at *me.* Surely he'd instantly recognize that we were meant to be together and, in response, pull me to his chest with one arm and press his mouth to mine in deep, sensual passion. I'd drop my tray and melt into his arms. Hey, and why not? I needed and deserved it. Runt had deserted me. The illicit encounter with the busboy had left me feeling empty. Ted was boring. His missionary-only sex position was boring. No sex during the daylight hours was boring, especially since I worked nights and he worked days. That meant there was no sex. But now, this gorgeous Tarzan was in my nightclub jungle, and I wanted a little dangerous excitement with him. Ted's concentrated stability on the job kept my parents happy, but a part of me was always restless. I couldn't imagine being a permanent couple with anyone. Are there regulations for surviving marriage? Is there some balance between hysteria and boredom? Since monogamy couldn't fill all the gaps in my emotional needs, I had affairs.

For a mere second, I turned to a customer. When I glanced back, Tarzan had vanished. Fortunately, he had left behind a link. His buddy was still there, a little farther along the bar, but alone.

With that familiar knot already forming in my stomach, I approached him. "What happened to your friend?" I asked.

"He went to meet his girlfriend." Grinning enthusiastically, he added, "My name's Gary." Oops, he had the wrong idea already. His eyes were confident. They said, Whoever you are, chick, you're really flirting with me, aren't you?

"Well, Gary…" and here I began to drown in desperation, resisting the impulse to grab his shirt and shout directly into his face. Instead, I smiled coyly. "You tell him I wanna meet him. Don't worry. It's just…physical. It won't get in the way of his girlfriend."

If Gary had been disappointed, he didn't show it.

"Sure," he said. "But you gotta bring somebody for me."

It was agreed. We negotiated a meeting for the next week at the bar. It would be Gary, my friend Cassie, me, and Rick, the person who would quickly recognize my need to please in exchange for acceptance.

Even though Cassie and I both knew what we were going out for, we were nervous. We steadied ourselves for our double date by being already primed with a few drinks. Opening introductions consisted of a couple rounds of beer followed by Rick and Gary escorting us back to their place, conveniently, right across the street. It was one of those bachelor rent-by-the-week flophouses: hot plate, black vinyl couch shoved against a cinder block wall, a bare mattress, and an indoor/outdoor carpet that had the odor and dark stains of what looked like motor oil. Stacks of *Easy Rider* magazines and empty beer cases leaned on each other for support. Next to the grimy toilet was a drum of an industrial-strength cleaning solution. It was being used to wash dishes, presumably in the bathroom sink.

My heart sank, but I was facing what I had asked for, and I got it…several times. In the morning, I woke to find myself alone and sprawled awkwardly across the plastic couch. I still bear rug-burn scars. They are reminders of that night, the first of many episodes with Rick, my soul mate, whose needs were as alternately calm and chaotic as my own. That night, I left Ted.

23

Weeks later, Ted was begging me to return "home" to him.

"Marry me," he said.

He was that desperate?

"I've been wrong," he said sadly. "I should take better care of you, pay all of the bills, and uhh...keep you safe." He clasped his big, thick hands between his knees and stared mournfully at the floor.

Good old Mom, trying to look wise and capable, did the only thing she could. She served us tea in flowered china mugs.

"No, Ted. What would be the use?" There. I had said it. The relationship was dead. After all, I was totally into Rick. I had even moved my small collection of clothes out of Ted's place, the one he mistakenly called our home, and put them into my parents' closets. It was over between us. Rick was now my one true love.

Ted, aware of my mother's presence, lowered his voice to a whisper. "The guy's no good, Sue." Then, in a normal voice, he said, "C'mon back, an' I'll do some of the housework."

Oh yeah, sure he will.

"I'll take care of you, Sue."

He had already said that. *Leave it alone, Ted. It's too late.* "Sorry, no."

Mom dabbed her eyes and sniffled her way out of the room. Ted was her last hope to keep me away from Rick. She saw Rick's spell over me, and it worried her. Without another word, Ted got up and walked slowly up the basement steps.

I sat on the pullout couch in my parents' downstairs family room and day-dreamed about Rick.

How could I have been so lucky to find the one spirit in this universe who validated my own existence?

We shared the same astrological sign, Sagittarius, the heavenly archer. I liked the very same things he did. Even though we had met in Canada, we had both been born a mere two years and six days apart in Nottingham, England. Our parents even came over to Canada the same year. This was meant to be. Rick and I were one and the same.

In the months to come, every blow, every bruise he delivered was a reminder of his dedication to my need to feel accepted, and apparently I did need the beatings because somehow I was always wrong. Right from the beginning, I spent as much time with him as I could. We'd pass a full day in bed reading his *Easy Rider* magazines together and making love. As tortured soul mates, we drank a lot, and often. I adored him. Even though I was head-over-heels in love, others saw the relationship differently.

Runt's face was tight with anger when I met him at the bar and shared my news.

"He's a drifter, Sue, he's no good. Get outta there, fast."

No, no. Rick and I were meant to be together. Runt was merely jealous.

Rick's girlfriend was another hassle. Poor thing, she thought Rick was hers. I had only been living with Rick and his buddy Gary a few weeks when I had to deal with her delusions. It was the first Saturday night that Rick had failed to come home, and I suspected that some other girl might be responsible. Of course, he explained he had been out all night drinking with friends. I totally understood and forgave him.

Hey, that happens, right?

Just seeing him again after twenty-four hours was reason enough to be grateful and happy. I abandoned the "other girl" nonsense.

But the competition appeared the very next Saturday night when I didn't see him at the bar. After work, I sprinted across the road to our place, but he wasn't there. Once again, I spent the night at my parents' house, worrying and drinking the night away. In the morning, I borrowed Mom's car and drove back to the studio apartment. I found Gary repairing his beat-up motorcycle on the living room carpet.

"Gary, where's Rick?

"Dunno. Hand me that wrench, will ya?"

"He didn't come home last night?"

"Nope. Want a beer? Get me one too, eh."

I stayed. We fixed Gary's bike and drank. I wanted to be there when Rick walked in.

He arrived with a fresh case of beer and *her*. Surprisingly, he was quite relaxed about our meeting. She was not. In fact, his comfortable attitude assured me there was no wrongdoing. He even demonstrated his true feelings by trusting me to "take her across the street" to the bar because she was upset. Eager to prove how cool I was and anxious to get the scoop on this chick, I agreed. We found a corner booth where I encouraged her to whine about her relationship with Rick. She talked. I listened and nodded, playing the sympathetic sister. She was a stripper. Every Saturday, Rick showed up right after she collected her $600 paycheck. He'd spend the night and then leave with half of her cash. Her gripe was that, despite her loyalty and devotion, he never paid any attention to her.

I shook my head sadly and urged her on. After a couple hours, many complaints, and several beers, I asked why she didn't leave him. Or rather, I suggested she'd be better off without him. (After all, I had been sent on this assignment to get rid of her.) She was offended at my suggestion. Dump him? Dump *Rick*? Naturally, she loved him. Well, she'd have to get over it. This lowlife was mine. I deserved to have him, to shell out my money from my earnings to bargain for his attentions. Didn't she get it? What a dumb broad! He was just using her.

When I returned to Rick, he was only too eager to confess that he had let her think they were having a relationship. He had led her on, just for the money. She wasn't all that pretty anyway, and didn't even have a great body. He was willing to let her go for me. *For me*! I was flattered for all eternity.

I am all he needs!

The thought stroked me, nurtured me, and reassured me that the world was finally spinning in the right direction. Our two broken personalities and desperate souls were going to be together forever or, at least, whenever he wasn't looking in other directions.

Rick believed his every need should be met. He felt it was his right as a man. When he strode into the bar where I worked and slipped behind the counter to hide a couple of bottles under his jacket, he saw it as being owed to him. As punishment for his thefts, I was only given lunch shifts. I accepted that, but it was hard on me. I was supporting both of us; now we'd have to live on a stingy portion of my previous salary. My daily tips, reduced to twenty or thirty dollars from the lunch shift, were barely enough to buy our daily rations of one shared submarine sandwich, two packs of smokes, and a case of beer.

Two weeks passed in this miserable state, yet since I was the best waitress on staff, management relented and gave me another chance at a forty-hour week. Rick was pleased with our reestablished income. In turn, his actions, so deliberate, impressed me. He rented us a house. It was a nice, older house in a better section of town, but I wondered how I'd get back and forth to work because the place wasn't on a bus route.

Well, what the heck! We were going to be happy, and I could permanently move out of my parents' house once again.

Besides, I was tired of Gary always being around. This time, we would be alone: me, Rick, and Rick's beautiful and smart dog, Sheba, a black-and-white (and always pregnant) border collie. The only thing I would have to do was to find a second job to pay for everything.

Rick hated being alone. While I was working, he regularly picked up new friends at strip clubs and brought them home like stray cats. My love for him was greater than my good sense, which meant that I had to put up with finding strangers in my living room. It kept me off center and forced me to work harder to make him love me, and only me.

Couldn't he just look forward to seeing me at shift's end? It caused a fight. Rick was walking the two-mile distance to work with me when the subject happened to arise.

"I'm sick of these guys hanging around. They're drinking our beer, they never help, and they never leave. Can't you tell them to get out?"

"They're my buddies."

"I'm not enough? You have to have them?"

"Oh, that's stupid."

"I'm stupid now? Go ahead. Tell me I'm stupid."

"That's not what I said."

"Okay, maybe I'm stupid for putting up with this shit."

"What are you putting up with? You're not even there all day."

"Because I'm at work!"

"What's that supposed to mean?"

I threw my hands in the air and stalked away. He chased me.

"If you love me, you wouldn't walk away. Don't you love me?"

Yes, I loved him, but I wanted him to say it first. I needed to hear him say it first. If I said it first, it meant he won, and this was about balance. Not to mention, he was the man. The man should say "I love you" first.

"Well, do you or don't you?"

"Do I or don't I what?"

"You know, love me."

I stopped walking and faced him.

"Yes."

"Yes what?"

"Yes! I love you!" My arms flailed angrily in the air. "Okay, you happy now? I said it!"

"See? That wasn't so hard, was it? C'mere, girl, and hug me. I love you, too."

And that was it. We were officially in love, even though I had to admit it first. As I look back, it came to represent one of those life-altering decisions that makes free will both exciting and terrifying at once. Rick and I were together for the long haul. I had lost the power of choice. From that moment, he became the master of my destiny. Shortly afterward, the abuse began.

24

Rick found us some furniture. Now we could set up camp in our two-bedroom house and live happily ever after. Rick was nothing if not resourceful. I didn't ask where he got them from, but he just showed up one day with some essentials, including a mattress and a kitchen table that was painted a deep shade of moldy green and randomly chipped from top to bottom.

Some of his scavenging included people. They were always homeless, jobless, and fun loving, Rick's band of merry drunks. In my absence, they entertained him and kept him company. Some of them brought girls. I didn't mind. Okay, so I'm lying. I told him it was fine with me. Even when I found sunbather Lisa topless in our overgrown yard, I surveyed the scene and managed to say, "Gee, looks like fun." The guys had created a water carnival for themselves on Lisa's waterbed. They couldn't fit it into the house, so they had tossed it on the back lawn, hosed it down, and made a combination trampoline and waterslide. It was a laugh-a-minute afternoon while bare-breasted Lisa lounged in a recycled lawn chair. I wanted to join them, but I was between jobs. Rick had caused another after-hours scene in the bar, which meant I was put back on lunch shifts only. I had to find a second job to compensate for the lost income. I was only home to get ready for the next shift.

I'd often return from the second job at two o'clock in the morning to find another party in full swing: laughter, drunken conversation, and loud music. Of course, I'd slide next to Rick, smile up into his wonderful face, and play the perfect girlfriend. After a few rounds of serving him (Rick expected me to wait on him, and, even if he were leaning on the refrigerator, I'd have to gently shift him to one side, reach in for a beer, open it, and hand it to him), I'd crash into bed, still wearing work clothes and try to sleep through the noise. Self-sacrifice was the least I could do for being so deliriously happy to be his ol' lady. As my protector and personal manager, he took care of me, including the money stuff. I never had to be concerned about paying the bills or buying food. All I had to do was hand over my paychecks and tip money and he "looked after" everything. I tried to remind myself that I should be grateful for his looking after me; it was something I needed, and it was compensation of sorts for the escalating punishment that dominated my days.

Consider the pizza episode. It taught me never to assume. I learned that rule on one of my lunch breaks between jobs when I asked Rick if I could order a pizza.

Yes, why yes, I could; I could order a medium and he dictated the toppings. No sooner had I ordered it when Rick's friend Eddy phoned and announced he was on his way over. With another mouth to feed, I called the pizza place again and changed the order to a large.

Stupid, stupid girl. Now why would I think that I should order enough food for the friends Rick loved so dearly? Rick and his friend Jack were already in the garage, well into their afternoon beer drinking. Eddy hadn't arrived yet. When the delivery van pulled up, I saw the guy hop out with the big orange warming bag and begin sliding out the pizza box. I ran out to pay from my lunch tips.

"What the fuck *is this*?" Rick was ahead of me, swaggering and gesturing with a bottle in hand. "I ordered a *medium*, you asshole! Take it back!" He rammed the pizza box into the guy's chest.

"No!" I sprinted across the driveway. "No, it's okay! See, I'm paying! I ordered!"

I got close enough to see Rick's jaw clench. Somehow he managed to park his beer bottle long enough to grab my shoulders and heave me into the chain-link fence. I hit the links with such force that I ricocheted back to his feet, which, for some obscure reason, intensified his rage.

Obviously, I couldn't do anything right. I should have hit the fence and crumpled on the gravel driveway. Instead, I found myself flying back to my assailant. Perhaps for my inability to be beaten properly, he boot-kicked me into the garage. Jack tried to intervene, and I'm sure the astonished pizza guy was speeding down the street by that time, but Rick wasn't finished. Just to emphasize his point, he slammed me to the gravel.

It doesn't take long to beat up a hundred-pound girl who is barely taller than the average twelve-year-old. Even though it felt like hours, the episode only lasted a few minutes. Who knows, I might have been beaten anyway because I hadn't ordered enough pizza, embarrassing Rick in front of his friends for my stinginess. Then again, he might have decided on a more peaceful tactic and given my portion to Eddy, leaving me to return to work hungry. It didn't matter; I was too battered to work anyway. That's the way it was with Rick. That's the way it was for me. Love meant control: exerting it and accepting it.

"Get outta my sight, bitch!" usually signaled permission for me to scramble to safer ground. When I was sober, these attacks confused me. I had that raw awareness of all battered women that I hadn't done any harm and what had happened to me was wrong. When I was drunk, I could easily be convinced that I deserved no better treatment since I had caused it and had asked to be beaten. The rules for normal in a cycle of abuse are defined by the abuser and are his privilege. He believes his might is right.

Once his emotional tirade was over, Rick strode back to the garage and flipped open another cold brew. I limped back to the house in a daze. To give him a little credit, Jack slipped out of the garage muttering about having to piss and came into the house to check on me. My arm was swelling from wrist to shoulder. I began to tremble. Despite my empty stomach, I was drowning in dizzy waves of nausea.

"Are you okay?"

Sheepishly, Jack held back at the doorway. He hadn't stopped the beating, nor was he standing up to Rick on my behalf. I told him I was fine and watched his hasty retreat.

My ribs ached. I couldn't move my arm; it was growing stiff.

This is not the time to be a crybaby. This is a survival thing. Stay cool.

If I could just make it around the corner, Rick had two friends living nearby who I was sure would help. As soon as Jack was back in the garage, I slipped out the front door and ran as quickly as I could to Roy and Tom's place. Occasional drinking buddies with Rick, they knew the kind of treatment I was getting. I hoped they'd take me to the hospital because they had a car.

As soon as they saw me standing on their doorstep holding my bloated arm, they knew what had happened. I told them my story. In return, I received a lengthy lecture about how I shouldn't put up with such abuse, how I should call the police, and how I should leave Rick. But they didn't understand. *I was really a rotten person and this was what I deserved.* Dad had told me no one would want me, and now Rick was proving it. I couldn't leave. It was my fault. I was to blame because of all the horrible things I did. And there was more. Leaving Rick would be admitting there was something wrong with me for choosing him and *nobody, especially an insecure, needy woman who doesn't feel she measures up to society's norms, wants to be wrong.*

After more consolation and beer, they took me to the hospital. Hours of waiting for tests and a diagnosis gave me my sympathy bid to regain Rick's attention. Doctors advised I'd have to be off work for two weeks for therapy.

That would show Mr. Macho! He had cut off his own income.

No, there were no broken bones, but they said that the bruising was extensive and unusually violent.

Good. I was a special case.

I got painkiller pills, the good kind. Narcotics. Roy and Tom took me back to their place. We drank a few more beers and waited until dark before I mustered the courage to go home. Rick was passed out in the center of the bed, snoring, and lying spread-eagle as usual. As the dutiful ol' lady, I quietly scrunched myself up on a corner of the mattress and tried to sleep.

25

I wanted an apology. In the late morning, Jack and Eddy were banging on the bedroom window for Rick to come out and play. I heard him grunt and stumble to the shower, but I sat positioned at the kitchen table, hurting and waiting. Next to the back door, where he couldn't miss them, I had placed two green garbage bags, stuffed with my belongings. Still pulling on his clothes, Rick stopped at the refrigerator for a beer breakfast and jerked a look back at me. He saw the plastic bags, but then, because I had chosen a short-sleeved T-shirt, he also had a good view of my swollen, bruised arm.

"What? Are you leaving?" His eyes were puffy and bloodshot, but he was able to calculate what the bags meant. At least he had sobered up enough to figure out that much.

"Yes, I am."

"You're really leaving me? How come?"

His stupid questions and phoney surprise opened floodgates of recrimination. I showed him my arm and pointed out my inability to work for two whole weeks. I spewed venom while he stood alternating his gaze between me, the plastic bags, and the ground. Yes, I do believe he got the message. And I, for a tiny moment in time, had the game advantage. His friends were just outside; his paycheck ol' lady was inside, but she was getting ready to walk out. I finished my tirade and fell silent. We both listened to the hum of the refrigerator.

Finally, he spoke. "What'll it take to get you to stay?"

An edge of worry. A note of hopefulness. *Ain't this romantic?*

"Try saying you're sorry."

"You already know I don't do that."

"My ride should be here in half an hour," I lied. "So, good-bye."

His mouth turned down like a sulky child's while he considered the packed bags. Too trapped to use his fists, he retreated. Maybe he expected that the slap of the screen door would set me into high panic and I'd come running. Whatever, I wasn't about to budge in my determination to win a point. I wanted the apology.

Within ten minutes, he was back under the pretense of retrieving another beer. Again, he paused at the door and stared at the bags. This time, he shuffled his feet a bit and rubbed his fingers across his mouth and beard.

"You're really going to make me say this, aren't you?" he asked.

"If you want me to stay, then yes."

It was an agonizing wait for his answer. I was trying to strategize how I'd cope if he stepped back out that door without a reply.

Then, abruptly, *"I'm sorry."* His face flushed with embarrassment and irritation. "There. All right? Are you satisfied?"

"I am. Thank you."

It would have been too humiliating for him to cross the floor to hug me. Instead, he beckoned me over to him. I got up and walked into his arms.

"I really do love you, you know," he admitted awkwardly.

"I know," I said, leaning on his chest. "I love you, too."

An anniversary of sorts. We had been together for two months. We kissed and made up.

The scene, complete with its packing and unpacking of green garbage bags, was very soon to become a too frequent ritual. Its climax was always "I'm sorry."

Once in a while, I still saw Ted's old gang members. I counted them among my friends, even though they detested Rick. Every chance they got, they cross-examined me about his business dealings. Truthfully, I didn't really know what the guy did, but he always seemed to have more money than I gave him. Grudgingly, I had to assume that he extracted it from his stripper girls, although I couldn't risk probing that possibility. I hated needles and shied away from shooting up drugs for myself, but, when I met Rick, he had a history of doing both cocaine and speed. His arms didn't bear any proof of addiction; I thought he had quit. Could he be selling the stuff? I didn't know. I did know that even when the others had coke at parties, I wasn't permitted near it and I obeyed, imagining I was being sheltered and protected. There was beer. What did I care? I had enough to take care of anyway by making sure my hair was blonde enough and that I was always dressed the way Rick directed. I really didn't care about his income, but my biker friends were always very interested. They were especially keen to learn anything about Lester, a fallen club member who had gone missing.

As a female, I wasn't permitted the whole story surrounding Lester, but he did spend some time holed up in our back bedroom. I was parked on the couch for a week because the bedroom was off-limits. I didn't ask any questions, but I pieced together a picture anyway. Shooting speed was against biker law. When Lester was caught shooting up, I heard that club members beat him up pretty good. Afterward, he went into hiding. I don't know where he was before he landed at our place, but one day when I came home between shifts, Rick was having a fit. Someone from the club had been in the house searching and had left a business card on the counter. (Yes, they had them.) Not surprisingly, I was thoroughly interrogated about the visit.

"What do you know?"

"Nothing."

"Who did you talk to?"

"*Nobody.*"

The next day, Lester was in our bedroom, completing his recuperation. I suppose that since our place had already been searched, Rick calculated it was time to sneak Lester out of the first hideout and keep him with us. I wasn't sure but guessed that the loyalty lay in the fact that Rick and Lester were partners in selling speed, coke, or whatever other profitable drug they could market. I appreciated being left in ignorance.

The pizza episode was followed by two weeks of uninterrupted harmony that ended abruptly when I was slammed once again into the gravel driveway. The morning after, I showered, cleaned my wounds, and set the garbage bags in the same place. This time, instead of waiting to confront him, I left for work. I didn't hear from Rick all day nor did I call him. At seven o'clock when I finished my shift, I sat down with some of the regulars and had something to eat. I needed to decide where to go because I had determined that this time...this time...I would probably leave. By eight o'clock, I was more relaxed. By nine, I was having a very good time. Shortly afterward, a lady came to our table and handed me a dozen red roses and pointed across the bar. At the same moment, my favorite song, Willie Nelson's "Always on My Mind," struck up with a dedication from the disk jockey.

"This song is for Sue."

I scanned the faces along the bar. Rick came forward and moved to the dance floor, waiting. It was a grand gesture considering he didn't dance. But how adept he was at playing my emotions! He knew exactly what to do. The situation was hopeless. Unable to stop myself, I glided onto the dance floor as though in a trance.

"I'm sorry, Sue."

"I know."

"I love you."

"I know. I love you, too."

One of my next lessons ended when I came out of a blackout on my hands and knees, groveling through broken Wedgwood plates, the ones my mother had given me for birthdays and Christmas. I was trying to gather up the bits with my bare hands, vaguely wondering what I had done to provoke the attack. Whatever it was had caused Rick's having to smash the entire collection. I was very defiant, very obnoxious, and always stubborn when I was drunk. Sometimes I was almighty about my position as the breadwinner, a situation that, by comparison, made him a loser and a wimp. He didn't like that. Would I never learn?

I asked for a broom.

"Here's your *broom!*" His foot flew to my ribs. Satisfied with the pain he had inflicted and the resulting cry from my throat, he added, "See if that teaches you!"

Oddly, I wondered what I was supposed to learn. I didn't ask for clarification. None was offered. I simply continued with the task of picking up blue and white shards that had skidded everywhere.

Rick's reaction to my multiple injuries would always hint at some measure of remorse.

"Why do you make me do this to you?" he'd ask with sad, concerned eyes.

I never had the answer. Heck, I wasn't sure I really understood the question. Once I recall coming out of my blackout just before I hit the bedroom wall. What could that have been about? You see, drunk means stupid and it wasn't just me: there were two of us. In my desire to be accepted, my distorted logic told me that *I had to please him*, even at the cost of my life. It seemed a natural conclusion.

The cellar of our house nearly became the final site where I would pay for my defiance. It was already an open crypt: weeping cinder block walls draped in cobwebs, the sharp stench of mold and mildew, rodents scratching in the shadows. It seemed a fitting end for what I feared was our final round. I came out of that particular blackout to find myself sitting on the filthy, damp floor with my wrists chained together in front of me. As I raised my head, I could just make out Rick's outline, seated on the stairs across the room. Across his lap, he held a motorcycle chain.

Was this it then? Was this how I would die? With a couple of quick lashes from that chain Rick held? Slow starvation? What did he have in mind?

I must have done something really terrible this time. He spoke. In the gloom, his voice seemed more menacing than usual.

"Well, I guess you won't do that again, will you?"

I shook my head from side to side.

What in hell had I done now?

Rick got up slowly, lightly slapping the chain on his palms. Mercifully, he headed up the steps. At the top, I heard the door slam. Hours passed. I watched a small brown spider string a web near my feet while my heart banged inside my chest. I hated spiders. When the door opened again, I stumbled to my feet afraid to look like I had been resting. Rick descended in slow, deliberate steps. Without speaking, he reached slowly into his pocket. I held my breath and waited. Unhurried, he drew out a key and clicked it into the padlock that held my wrists. The lock sprang open, the chain fell to my feet, and I stood there shaking.

A saner mind would have taken its owner straight outside to safety, anywhere. Clinging to the undercarriage of a speeding train would do. But, no. For the inmate in this invisible prison, there was a more compelling place. I went to our bed.

At work the next day, I told everyone that the scrapes and cuts to my face and wrists were from a bicycle accident.

"What a fool, huh? Flipped right over the handlebars!"

I also launched a new sideline to my career. I became a counselor to every waitress who had an abusive boyfriend, advising each one of them that they deserved better, that they should leave the bastard. Mind you, even as I was a poster girl for battered woman's syndrome, I couldn't apply the rules to myself, and I rationalized it this way:

1. I was getting what I deserved. My parents' motto is that you get what you deserve in this life. (Never mind that I had woefully misinterpreted the message.)

2. Normal people don't get abused. I was abnormal, lower than life because I was a bad person and no one would ever want me. My dad had said so.

26

One of Rick's demons was the dread of solitude. That's why the house was always crawling with people. They were there all day. They were there to greet me between shifts and they were there when I returned from work at two o'clock in the morning, sore and tired from hauling beer trays. If the place had been a person, it would have needed tranquilizers. It raged constantly with brawls and laughter.

Most of the guests were females who oozed seduction. With their breasts and hips always tilted in Rick's direction, they eyed me resentfully when he introduced me as Pebbles, his ol' lady. Sometimes it was Pebbly-pooh or Pooh. I accepted the handles because I was his. The names gave me the status of a brainless, four-legged pet, which was pretty accurate, but, in his way, my man was claiming me as number one. On the street, he was Gypsy. I never stopped to think about the significance of that; I was too busy fending off the girls that were willing to stand in line to take my place. Whether it was his mane of red-gold hair, his bad boy image that begged to be tamed, or his tight butt, he was definitely a babe magnet.

If the party looked too intense and the crowd around him grew too flirtatious, I'd strut into the circle and cheerfully announce, "Hi, I'm Gypsy's ol' lady, Pebbles."

Adjusting Rick's party profile became my favorite sport. Smugly settled under the curve of his arm, proud as a gold medalist, I applauded myself for my successive victories. Much to my pleasure, his audience hated me.

There were nights though when he didn't come home. Rather than admit he was sleeping around on me, I'd worry.

Is he hurt somewhere in an alley? Is he in jail? Oh God, please release me from this terrible fear and bring him home to me!

When he did arrive late the next morning, I'd ask careful questions to get to the truth. It became my quiet way of letting him know I disapproved. If I raised my voice and protested, I'd get beaten. It didn't make any difference; he continued cheating anyway. I just wanted enough control to be able to confirm his sexcapades and say, "Oh, yeah. I know." All he had to do was give names, which he did, proudly, hatefully, when I asked. What could I do with the information anyway? It was only a feeble game, but it was a way to feel I still had some power.

By allowing someone to control my life, I had given up my independence. I had traded my parents for a far more demanding keeper. Rick and I believed we validated each other's existence. Oh sure, anybody could take one quick look and say we were both such losers that we had to reinforce each other. I would have fiercely denied that assessment. My ideas of love had been formed by watching the old black-and-white Hollywood movies on late-night television. In my estimation, this was the same. It was kismet. Rick and I were the stars of our own ill-fated romance.

One day, I came home from work, and there was no party, although Rick was not alone. He had spread one of our bed sheets on the floor and was on his hands and knees with his new infatuation. Like all the women he toyed with, he was dedicated to his work. This time, he was not the master. His new love demanded attention all day and at odd hours throughout the night.

"Change my head gaskets!"

"Get these pistons timed!"

"Buy more parts. No, not those. I want expensive parts!"

And he complied. Since he could never do anything alone, I had to learn the skills involved in motorcycle repair by taking the thing apart and reassembling it to his satisfaction. Don't imagine I was allowed to sleep when I needed it. Don't imagine either that I could find a third job to afford this new love affair. That's when I realized that my idol was a drug dealer. He had to be. Even Rick's stripper girls couldn't have given him enough cash for this baby. It's not like he had a savings account; the guy didn't even have a social insurance number. I have already insisted that I am pretty smart, so I couldn't ignore the obvious. The money came through dealing. Let's check the clues:

1. Strangers showed up at odd hours.

2. I wasn't introduced to them and was told to stay out of sight.

3. They never stayed longer than ten minutes.

4. Parties meant a mirror passed around the table with a straw. On the mirror were powdery white lines. I wasn't allowed to participate.

"My ol' lady don't do the stuff," Rick would say and push it away from me.

Cocaine: addictive, dangerous, and profitable. Cocaine was plentiful in the house, yet it was taboo for me.

"You'll like it and get hooked," he'd tell me. *Of course he was selling it*!

Yet look where it got us. We had arrived in high society. We owned a Harley-Davidson. Truly, the Harley was one of his other women, but, unlike the others, this one caused major fights. Most of the time, I was run-down and tired from work while Rick, after a rough night with the bike, would be irritable and ready to fight. He'd start, I'd retaliate, and it wasn't long before I'd be wearing more ugly bruises to work. The transmission episode was one of the worst.

Dragged out of bed in the middle of the night to help, I argued, "No! I'm not getting up!"

"Get up, Sue, damn you! I can't do this job alone."

"Don't care. I'm tired. Leave me alone."

"Get up!"

"Get outta here! I gotta work tomorrow, or we'll have no money for the stupid bike!"

Oops. Mistake. Was this disrespect for Rick's inability to find or keep a job? Yes. In an instant, I was punched in the face and then forced, with his hand pinching my neck bones, to the kitchen where my nose bled all over the bike parts on the floor. As soon as he saw the blood, he went rabid.

"Look what you made me do!" he screamed. "Now you've done it, you stupid bitch!"

His feet slid this way and that over the tools. When he fell back into a chair, I saw that his eyes were crimson, warning me like brake lights. Before his fist collided with my flesh again, I left him smashing things in the kitchen while I charged back to our bedroom, grabbed some clothes, and dropped out the window to the ground. Under cover of darkness, I crawled along the bushes next to the house until I could get up and run. If Rick found me, I feared he wouldn't stop this time. His not being able to fix the bike was not my fault, but the dripping blood on his bike was mine, and that offence was worth another several blows.

I found a pay phone and stood in a daze wondering who to call at this forsaken hour.

My family? Why, for more lectures?

Who then? I called the police. I had barely hung up when a squad car appeared at the curb. A uniformed officer got out.

"Sue?"

"Lloyd! Thank God!" It was one of the cops I knew from the bar.

"Thought it might be you when we got the call."

"What am I going to do?"

"Get in."

He and his partner bought me some tea and drove around while I told them about my latest blow up with Rick.

"We can arrest him if you want us to, Sue."

They winced at my smeared face. Lloyd's partner handed me a tissue. Both of them knew my situation. They had done hundreds of domestic disputes like mine and were familiar with irrational, tangled emotions.

"He doesn't have a right to do this…not to you…not to anyone. You deserve better. You deserve to be safe."

Safe. He said it like it was an option. How, in all my guilt, did I deserve safety? This had all started because I had insulted Rick's manhood by refusing to help and by reminding him of his choice to be unemployed. I had provoked him.

"Well?"

Panic. "Please don't arrest him!"

"We've been watching him anyway."

Watching? For what? Uh oh, drugs. I was in deep trouble here. Fraternizing with the cops could get me killed. Returning to Rick could also get me very dead in a hurry. Which way? At that moment, something heavy happened inside me. It felt like an undertow, pulling me far out to sea. I wasn't sure how I had come to a decision, but I found myself thanking the officers and backing away as they drove off. Rubbing my jacket sleeve across my swollen nose to wipe away the caked blood, I set off in the early morning light to retrace my steps. I'd stay where I was.

Once again, I curled up in a corner of the bed where Rick lay passed out in a crucifixion pose. A couple hours later, I got up and prepared to go to work. That evening, probably because I looked bad enough to ward off customers, I was allowed to leave early.

When I arrived back home that night, I found only Rick and Jack. They were sitting at the kitchen table. Rick got up, lifted my chin to inspect the damage, and repeated his dreary question: "Why do you make me do this to you?"

No apology was given. None was expected. I knew what he was like when he was drunk. Why couldn't I just learn to do what he said?

The three of us settled in to play Trivial Pursuit, all pretense and goodwill despite voices inside me loudly protesting.

Said one: "Sue, your life is a mess. Practice what you preach to others and leave him!"

"No!" piped up another. "Don't think. Don't feel. Everything is fine now. We're together. He's being nice."

My mouth cupped around happy words.

"Let's have another beer." I smiled. "You too, Jack? Okay, fresh ones coming up."

That night, like a lost trio of dogs, the three of us crawled up on the mattress and slept together on the unmade bed.

27

The month of May was beginning. My black eyes and nose healed once again and, for a few weeks, life seemed reasonable. The Harley was on the road, and I had managed to keep two jobs; they were bar jobs, but they paid well. For the first time in a while, I felt positive and capable. Inside my delusional head, everything was rosy.

I called Sarah to invite her for a sisterly visit. We'd chat. The news would get back to my parents that Sue was settled: she has a nice house and an adoring boyfriend. No, there wasn't much furniture, and no television set…and, well, I didn't see anything in the fridge to eat, but she's happy. Just thought you'd be really glad to hear that she's not a screw-up anymore!

When the day arrived, Sarah turned into the driveway in her shiny, late-model car. The open garage door framed Rick, Jack, and me next to the motorcycle. We each had a beer in hand, celebrating the bike's move from the kitchen to its summer workshop in the garage. Through the windshield, I could see she was amazed. Sure, I thought she'd be impressed. A Harley is quite a trophy.

"Great, it's Sarah!" I ran to pull open her car door and breathed in on her. "Hey, c'mon over and meet Rick and our friend Jack!"

I expected enthusiasm. Instead, Sarah looked startled, like a tourist who had just taken a wrong turn into a ghetto's dead end. Before she walked the ten steps to meet the guys, she locked all of her car doors. With a bit of encouragement on my part and probably a small shove, she stepped up for introductions, being careful to keep the bike between her and the new faces. Once the introductions were complete, Jack shot her a leer, then drained his bottle and gave a satisfied burp. Remembering his manners, he wiped his mouth with the back of his hand and looked as if he might try to shake her hand. I was already excitedly pulling her away to show off the rest of the house.

"See," I said with sweeping gestures, "this is the kitchen. Well, it will be a little better when we finish getting the tools and stuff out to the garage, 'cause we had to keep everything inside for the winter." I was babbling, barely paying attention to the corners of her mouth beginning to twitch.

What was that look? Disapproval? It seemed like fear. "Hey, never mind the floor. I was going to wash it!"

My sister was crying, tears tumbling down her cheeks. Why? She was scared for me. I tried to reassure her that Rick would never do anything to hurt me, but she dashed back to the car as though being chased. I was stunned. For several minutes, I gaped at the empty driveway, wondering what had happened. If only I could have seen the truth. If only I could have acknowledged how much of my energy was spent in adjusting to life in a shack with my unemployed, drug-dealing boyfriend. Sarah felt I was living like riffraff, but I didn't view it that way. I saw her as a snob and that applied to my parents as well. Whether out of indignation or shame, it would be a few months before I would speak to any of them.

Summer arrived with its usual parties. In particular, there was the annual blue-grass weekend waiting for us at the beginning of June. Bluegrass wasn't my favorite music, but the excuse to camp and do the party-hardy thing was unquestioned. It was permission to get shit-faced with everyone else and to reconnect with old friends. Like the hours before a big lottery, the anticipation grew to a pitch. There would be fights, rapes, stabbings, the odd death, and the usual birth or two. The event was a time-honored tradition. I cherished it.

Rick had managed to borrow Gary's girlfriend's car. For some reason, we were only going for Saturday, but we loaded the trunk with beer and planned to have a full day. That's what we did, even though the beer didn't last long. Luckily, we had plenty of generous drunks willing to share. I recall square-dancing with some energetic old geezers in Western costumes at some point. We just socialized away the rest of the hours. When eight o'clock that evening rolled around, Rick announced it was time to leave. He was too drunk to drive, and I'd have to take the wheel. Drunk enough to be in a blackout myself, I was appointed to chauffeur us home.

The highway back to town had four lanes. I think I swooped across the lines dividing most of them before Rick took his turn trying to make the car behave and go straight. I was glad he did. Everybody's honking was getting to me. From time to time, oncoming traffic nearly blinded us with all those high beams flashing in our faces. (Some drivers can be so rude.) Miraculously we avoided being arrested, run over, or killed. Once home, we ordered a pizza. As we ate, we discussed our wonderful future together and then fell asleep in each other's arms.

Sunday morning was electric. I have always liked Sundays. After one blissful, lucky day that weekend, I was expecting another. Eddy and Jack were coming over to play Trivial Pursuit. We planned special treats to go along with game day: whiskey, rum, vodka, and mixes. We'd make pitchers of Tom Collins, whiskey sours, and Planters Punch. It was a family feast. Eager to get started, I got up early and found myself shockingly ill.

Hey! What's wrong with my stomach? Hangover? Nah. Bad pizza? Well, Rick's fine. Whoops! Back to the bathroom. Run!

"Rick, I think I'm pregnant!"

"Wha'? That's impossible."

(What was he thinking?)

"No, really!"

"How do you know, eh?"

"I'm sick. And I just feel like it."

"Ah, jus' try to forget it and enjoy the day."

Good advice. I shelved my queasy stomach and my instincts as I was told. A week or so later, the appearance of my period gave Rick leeway to say, "I told ya!" Of course, it was natural; he was right. I was an idiot. I was just having trouble forgetting some of my nagging inner voices.

A few weeks later, a Sunday afternoon bike show was held at the new club-house on the beach strip. Rick was totally fixated on the Harley now, polishing and primping the thing until he was edgy and short-tempered with alcohol and lack of sleep and food. He desperately wanted to make a grand entrance and then stand back while all the other guys admired his skills with a wrench. When I got home Saturday night, I had to admit I was impressed. Under the stark ceiling bulb in the garage, the bike gleamed. It was all shiny chrome and leather. Rick rolled it out to the driveway to start it up (ask the neighbors what time it was…two thirty? Three in the morning?) while I went inside looking for sleep.

After a couple clicks, false starts, and frantic cursing followed by a horrible silence, I knew the bike was not going to move. Two more tries. Nothing. Uh oh…this was not good.

Rick's first reaction to disappointment would be to seek out a scapegoat, most likely, me. Someone had to be accountable for this disaster, and he was coming straight for me. When he charged through the door, his fists were already raised. Too tired to resist, I stood as solidly as I could and braced for the blows. After the routine punches and kicks stopped, I cleaned myself up and went to bed.

Rick was gone by the time I woke, but just as soon as the sleep fog lifted from my head, I lunged for my wallet. Surprise. My cash was intact. Outside, the bike was still parked where he had left it. I showered, dressed, and called a cab. If he didn't return in time, I'd go to the bike show without him.

At the bike show, my face, bruised enough for a prize fighter, brought disgust even from the most hardened bikers. I was surrounded with voluntary lectures.

Happily, they were always accompanied by a beer. People came forward to offer me a place to stay, to warn me of Rick's disturbed character, to show concern for my obvious, numerous beatings. Guys were sent to the front to guard against Rick entering the show. I only had to ask, and I'm sure they would have sliced and diced him like a salad. Even though it was gratifying to see how much I was cared for, it was pathetic to have to build my self-esteem on pity. I let them take care of me anyway. The attention felt nice.

Later that day, Rick showed up on his Harley. I watched while a couple of club enforcers blocked him at the end of the street and turned him back. Wasn't I just in big trouble now! Who had caused him to miss the show because of her whining? This time, even while I felt twinges of remorse, I wasn't dumb enough to go home.

One of the kindest voices I heard that evening was Ted's. After what I had done to him and after all these months, he still cared. Knowing I had his full attention, I let him charge to the rescue.

"Where you gonna go now, Sue?"

"I don't know. Can't go back to Rick."

"No."

"And not my parents either."

"No."

"They've already kicked me out once. Well…" (a long sigh here and puppy-dog eyes) "I'm sure I'll find someplace."

"How will you get your stuff out of Rick's?"

"Oh, geez, I hadn't thought about that yet. I just know I can't go back."

"What about work?"

I widened my teary eyes at him. It was a ploy that never worked on Rick, but I prayed Ted would take the bait.

"Oh, Ted! What am I going to *do*?"

"Don't you worry. I'll round up some guys from the bar. We'll use my van and pick you and your stuff up tomorrow."

Oh, thank God! I held him in my hopeful gaze, hanging on to every word.

"Then you'll move back with me," he said firmly.

I was ecstatic with relief.

"Are…are you sure?" I asked sweetly, almost making myself sick with martyred appreciation. "I mean, I've been such a rotten person. How can you be so good to me?"

"Never mind," he said. "You just come back home. Everything will be fine."

Home. What was that?

I had never felt really settled anywhere. Every moment was insecurity. Every day felt like a loan. I accepted Ted's generous offer, if nothing else but to be calm, just for a while.

28

I spent the night at my friend Cassie's. In the morning, I took a cab home to get ready for work, not knowing what to expect. Rick wasn't around. That made me nervous. I expected him to pounce at me any minute from some shadowy corner. For all I knew, he might be hiding in the refrigerator and, if I opened it, he'd grab my wrist. Even during my lunch shift at work, I was convinced he knew what I was planning and would come flying into the bar, all wild-eyed and ready for a fight. I imagined him dragging me out of the bar and finishing me off in the parking lot. Of course, none of this happened. Except for my nervous fumbling with customers, the time passed without incident.

At one thirty, as soon as my tables were finished, I raced home to pack the usual garbage bag luggage. Ted had promised that his buddies would be at the house at two thirty. By two forty, I was pacing at the front door terrified Rick would arrive first. There would certainly be a scene.

Would I stay? Would Ted understand if I did? After all, I couldn't bear the thought of Rick being upset.

I should go with Ted.

I should stay with Rick.

Oh, I know! *I'll go with the one who arrives first.*

Being too overwhelmed by fear and choices, it was the only decision I could make. The problem was solved five minutes later when Ted's van arrived with three friends. They charged out, baseball bats in hand, ready to do battle and haul away the big goods.

"Where is he? Where's the stuff?"

"Not here," I said. "I don't know where he is, but my bags are ready."

"That's it?" The guys sounded disappointed. Their adrenaline was pumped for a fight. I think they were looking for a "wipe the floor" scene they could brag about for months to come. Not wanting to walk away empty-handed, they raided the fridge, taking every bottle of beer and stashing them in the van. We took off with my worries following the whole way. Rick hated being alone. I had abandoned him.

As soon as I thanked the guys and set my garbage bags down inside Ted's town house door, I knew I had made the wrong decision. Nothing had changed.

My parents might be overjoyed with my move, but I didn't have any intention of sharing the good news. They'd see me only as a common floozy, jumping from one warm body to the next. Could I sink any lower?

Ted still loved me. Anxious to prove what a fun, spontaneous guy he had become, the first thing he did to excite my soul was whisk me away for the weekend. We spent the entire quiet, peaceful, unbearably safe weekend on the sidelines at a popular campground, watching partygoers.

I had lied to my boss about being sick just to get that weekend off. When I got back to work, I told the manager something closer to the truth. I had really been scared of Rick's coming after me and causing some police action at the bar. He was appreciative for my candid explanation and told me I was a nice person, a good worker, and he hoped I could finally get my act together. He'd notify the bouncers and the rest of the staff to keep Rick out. I'd be quite safe that way. Since I didn't have Rick around to inflict damage anymore, he'd give me full-time employment. I could quit the other job.

My manger's welcome back to reality should have been confirmation that I was on the right track, but I could only think how much I had fooled him. I was *not* a nice person. I was horrible: a liar, a user, and a master manipulator who cared for nothing except her own pleasure. I was unworthy of such kind words and doubted I would ever be able to live up to my manager's mistaken view of me.

The normal life I wanted was in hand. I had a secure job, a stable man, a standard town house, and a predictable routine. I didn't miss being regularly beaten to a pulp, but, after having survived six months with Rick, I missed the drama. I missed the fun times. I missed my soul mate, and I was missing my period.

I was missing my period. *Again?* Same thing last month!

The doctor sent me for an ultrasound. For that test, you have to drink so much fluid you think your bladder's going to explode all over the examining room. I could drink that much beer, but who could swallow clear tea or water in such quantities, especially first thing in the morning? It was obscene! Ted came with me and sat in the examining room to show support while I squirmed impatiently in one of those backless hospital gowns and complained. (That was while we were waiting for the technician.) When she did arrive, she mentioned that my husband could stay. Ted was immediately front and center, placing me up on the table as gently as he could.

Gooey stuff slathered on my abdomen, monitor humming in the dim room, rubber scope working back and forth through the goo, and then the friendly voice: "There it is!"

Oh, I am going to die. She's found a growth of some kind.

The screen said nothing to me. It was only gray and white blobs.

"What is it?" I asked, panicked.

She smiled a saintly smile. "*It*? Too soon to accurately tell its sex now, dear!"

"Its...*what*?"

"Your baby. The sex of your baby!" she answered.

I knew it! And I had known for a while. I started counting backward.

April, May, June? What? Two months, three? But this couldn't be happening! I smoked a pack of cigarettes a day, drank myself into oblivion as often as I could...I had been beaten...how many times? I was going to be an alcoholic single mother with a baby I had damaged before birth. Fetal alcohol syndrome. Facial disfigurations, learning disabilities...oh my God! What had I done?

"Don't worry, Sue. We'll raise the child as mine," Ted said on the way home.

I burst into tears. "You would do that?"

"Yeah," he said, and a smile worked across his face that was so proud it haunted me. He reached over and took my hand.

We would marry. I'd have a husband and a baby. And I never wanted either. But, wait! Hadn't I *wanted* to be normal? Well, here it was. The worst part of the predicament was that I suddenly really needed Rick to be normal with me.

"Make the best of it" was always my father's philosophy. And I tried. Ted tried. He even arranged for us to take a weekend trip to New York with some of the other guys and their girlfriends. We packed up the saddlebags, slung them over the bike, and away we went. But things were different. I was an underweight pregnant woman, being rattled over miles of pavement. This baby didn't have any insulation. I was sure I was slamming it up and down like an olive in a cocktail shaker, and the bike's vibrations made me want to pee more often than I thought humanly possible. Because I still held the belief that you shouldn't upset others in public (behind closed doors is all right), I didn't ask for bathroom breaks when I should have. When we finally did stop, my bladder was so distended that at first I couldn't urinate. That scared me. This was not going to be a good camping experience.

The other members of the group already treated me with suspicion and distance; they knew what I had done to Ted, and they knew I was pregnant. They resented me, I knew, so I had to keep my mouth shut and try to quietly deal with my own bodily functions. By drinking less alcohol and not being the party animal, I'd survive the weekend without offending anyone's sensitivities.

Ted was excited because he knew how much I loved Willie Nelson. What he didn't know was how much hearing Willie made me think of Rick and our song, "Always on My Mind." I didn't want to disappoint Ted, but the concert was just another reminder of the old life. I had to keep trying to look forward. I was desperate to keep looking forward.

We had great seats for the concert, but I tried not to listen. I was doing pretty well until song number six, "Always on My Mind," when the tears started running down my face. I tried my best to hide them.

29

The day after we arrived home from our camping trip and concert, Ted returned to work and I was scheduled for a shift that evening. With an entire idle day for daydreaming, I called Rick. After several rings, I was about to hang up when a female voice answered.

"Hullo?"

"Who's this?" I was instantly annoyed.

"Misty."

"Misty?" Hmm, I was talking to my replacement.

"Well, this is Pebb...ah, Gypsy's ol' lady. What are you doing there?"

"I live here. What do you want?"

"I was looking for him. Are you his new girlfriend?"

"Un, uh," she said. "Me and Sandra just moved in to help pay the bills."

My tone mellowed, and I chatted her up. Seems she was only eighteen, and her friend was sixteen. Yikes, Rick was flirting with jail time. A few niceties got me a telephone number where I could find him and a very interesting comment from Misty.

"He'll be real glad to hear from you. He talks about you all the time."

That was something. I dialed the number she gave me.

"H'lo." Male voice.

"Is Gypsy there?"

"Who wantsta know?"

"Tell him it's Sue."

"Hey, Rick! Telephone!" Hand clamped over the receiver...muffled words I couldn't make out.

"Yeah, you want something?" It was Rick, his voice heavy and irritable with being awakened before noon.

"I need to talk to you."

"So? Talk!"

"No, no. I need to see you in person. It's really important."

Long, annoyed sigh. "When?"

"Today. This afternoon."

"Where? Hmm, guess so. Pick me up." He gave me a time and place.

Oh, lucky me!

I called my mother and explained that I needed to borrow her car to get to a doctor's appointment I had nearly forgotten about. I'm sure she had plans for the afternoon, but she clucked her tongue and agreed.

"Oh, Susan," she said. "You're a problem, you are."

The moment of the great reunion arrived. I buzzed Rick at the designated apartment and he came down. When the elevator doors opened, I stood in the lobby with my arms outstretched, expecting one of those romantic scenes from the movies, complete with soul-filling music piping from unseen speakers. It wasn't to be. Rick brushed straight by me with his hand out for the car keys. I held onto them, not so much out of duty to my mother, but because of my need for some sense of control. He shrugged and slid sullenly into the passenger seat. On his direction, we drove to a park that teetered on the edge of a cliff. I turned off the ignition and held my breath.

Was he going to push me off?

He hadn't spoken a word while I drove, but then…

"Why did ya do that, Pebbly-pooh?"

"Do what?"

"Leave like that. No warning, no note. Nothing."

"Ted convinced me," I lied. "Said you were bad news. But he was wrong and now I'm so, so sorry. Can you forgive me?"

His eyes shifted back and forth across my face. Without missing a beat, he said, "When were you talking to Ted about me?"

I sure didn't want to drag up the whole issue of the bike show again and my betrayal that day. I ambushed him instead with loud crying and blurted, "I'm pregnant!"

(There was no point in waiting for him to guess. At ninety-two pounds, I wasn't exactly looking plump.)

"Ted's kid?"

I shook my head violently.

"Mine?"

I nodded and hung my head. More sobs.

"Why didn't you *tell* me?"

Of course I had tried, but that wasn't the tactic here.

"I was scared," I whimpered, "that you'd get mad at me."

That worked. His face softened.

"I wouldn't get mad," he said gently and reached for me. "It's my baby, too."

"I'm stupid," I said submissively.

Naturally, that put the power squarely back into his territory. My imagination was hearing Willie Nelson again. "You are always on my mind…"

"Whadda we do?" he asked.

Ah, he said *we*. The next few steps were going to be a piece of cake.

"It's up to you." (Passive, stupid, and pregnant. How much more vulnerability could I offer?) I dabbed my eyes and waited for his wisdom.

"You'll have to move out of Ted's place."

"Mhmm." I snuggled closer. "Okay."

Poor Ted was getting dumped again.

"Then…"

"Uh-huh…?" I gazed hopefully up at him through damp eyelashes.

"You can move into your parents' place."

Bam! Switch off the music!

"What? Why can't I move in with you?"

I instantly knew the answer. He didn't want to expose his emotional weaknesses. Holding me at arm's length reflected his importance. I had wronged him. I had to earn my way back, but he explained it so that, poor silly thing that I was, I could understand.

"Misty and Sandra live there now. There's no room."

"Oh, right." I struggled to fight off sarcasm. "I'll just move back in with my parents."

When he took me to meet his roommates, I secretly wondered what had gone wrong in the lives of such young girls to take up living with the likes of Rick. One was a cleaning lady and the other worked as a counter girl in a fish 'n' chip take-out place.

When my parents asked why I had left Ted, I explained that it just didn't seem right. Unconvinced, they waited for the rest of it. I told them I was pregnant.

Silence. Sudden, intense studies of paint on the ceiling. Long, exasperated sighs.

Groaning, my dad said, "I told you so!"

Mom, her face tight with disappointment, her voice pitchy added, "What will you do? How will you raise a child?" The underlying tone to this comment was, "Since you can't even take care of yourself…"

Needless to say, I failed to mention that, in my hours away from their tidy, quiet environment, I was trashing my life again with Rick.

The part of me that was feeling motherly experimented with the good life. A customer I had known for a while asked me out. He was a good, decent, normal guy, a nonsmoker who talked about sports and his job selling insurance. I considered his offer and thought, sure! Gee, a real date with an invitation, an appointed time, a destination, good manners, the works! My conversation, limited to drugs, booze, bikers, and Harleys lasted through dinner before my date managed to remember "something important" and took me home.

The ruined date left me with the conviction that both Dad and Rick were right. Something was basically wrong with me; I made very bad decisions. That meant I was probably lucky to have an abuser like Rick for a partner. That my lack of self-esteem and poor coping skills were interfering with my ability to reason didn't cross my mind. I didn't know any better.

I started spending more time at Rick's place. Sandra had our former bedroom, the larger one at the back, Misty had taken the smaller bedroom, and, since Jack was still hanging out at the place, he took the couch. That left the dirty storage area for the expectant couple. I managed to lower my standards yet again in order to find the accommodations acceptable. I rationalized that it was worth it; I was with Rick. Our fun Sundays saw Trivial Pursuit replaced with cooking, but the drinking remained a staple. We made cabbage rolls and drank pitchers of Tom Collins and whiskey sours. We had hilarious, very messy food fights, stopping only long enough to mix more drinks. I was beginning to wonder what was in store for this baby. As it turned out, I wouldn't have to wonder about that too much longer.

Weeks blurred by. We were concluding an afternoon of drinking with friends. When I was once again past the stage of good sense, I began to nag Rick about our living together. With each comment, his jaw clenched tighter. His bottom lip curled forward until he bared his lower teeth, but I was determined to get my way. Finally, he snapped. Even as drunk and sloppy as he was, his blow to my face was stunningly painful. I fell back and tried to escape what I knew was coming, but it seemed I couldn't move fast enough. In an instant, he was smashing me through a window. I tumbled down a metal fire escape, down and down and over and over.

"When are you going to listen!" he screamed after me. It was probably my drunken state that kept me limp enough to avoid breaking any bones.

That night I ran. When I was sure my parents would be asleep and unable to see my injuries, I snuck home and collapsed on the family room couch. Avoiding Rick lasted less than forty-eight hours before I called him. Misty answered.

"Sue! Thank God, you've called! Rick's been so nasty! Just a complete asshole! He keeps staring out the front window and asking if you called. He asks about twenty times a day! And we can't get him to stop drinking. He's driving us crazy."

"Is he there?" My reply was purposefully flat and disinterested.

"No, he'll be back soon. Please, please, for our sake. Would you call him back?"

"I'll think about it," I said.

I'd let him sweat. He'd invite me back to live as soon as he grew desperate enough. As I see it now, my vision was so distorted that I thought I had won some critical battle. As a general, I would have probably instructed my troops to cover all territory by blowing themselves into bits with their own ammunition. I was that irrational.

Within days of the fire escape beating, I began to hemorrhage. The doctor said something about "placenta previa," meaning the placenta was separating from the uterine wall and the baby was losing its already precarious lifeline. My labor would have to be induced. Notwithstanding my drinking problem (perhaps it was because I had been thrown down a flight of metal steps or perhaps it was because I had endured a prior case of pelvic inflammatory disease), my uterus was becoming an increasingly hostile environment for a baby.

Normal women do not expose their babies to injury. Normal women do not flunk basic motherhood. Normal women wouldn't want me in their ranks. I was a useless failure at everything.

Just before noon, I took a bus to Rick's place. When I arrived, he was drinking with Jack and Eddy. Vaguely wondering if it were morning for him or still the night before, I went to the fridge to grab a beer. What harm would it do now? I was surely losing the baby anyway. I called Rick away from his friends. When we were out of view, I told him what was happening. Instinct wanted me to bury myself in his chest, to listen to him tell me he loved me.

A warning voice within held me at arm's length. "Don't think. Don't feel. It's better that way."

He half-turned away from me. "Is the kid going to be all right?"

"No," I answered. "No, it isn't."

The baby was stillborn. A few days later on November 5th, after a short, induced labor, a tiny baby boy slid lifeless into a sterile hospital world. I wondered whether my doctor had even detected a heartbeat when I visited his office. The baby may have been dead for some time. I will never know.

Rick refused to visit during my three-day hospital stay, yet he wanted me back. My parents were terrified of dropping me off to recuperate with him, but I persuaded them I'd be fine. There had been complications; I wasn't well at all.

Given the care I'd need, I expected Rick to keep me at a distance until I was healthy again. Surprisingly, he dashed out the door to greet us, cradled me in his arms, and carried me inside to the couch. He accepted the bag of groceries and medical supplies my parents brought, but sent them on their way. I can only imagine their emotions.

All of our friends were there to fuss over me. Rick sat at a distance and stared. I swallowed pain pills to forget, and lay curled on the couch, wounded and fragile. Voices and faces floated around me, but Rick's was not one of them. He was detached and edgy. Eventually they all converged into another room and left me to rest. Shortly afterward, Rick came back into the living room with an announcement. He and the friends were going out.

I can't describe my despair. Alone, barely able to crawl to the bathroom, I was terrified. When the door clicked shut behind them, the only thing I could think to do was put sad songs on the stereo, take more pills, drink from the case of beer they left, and let myself drift into something other than the cruelty of the real world. Early the next morning, Rick was standing over me.

"Get dressed!" he said.

"What?"

"Get dressed! We're taking you somewhere!"

Oh God. Now what?

I couldn't imagine which bar would welcome us before noon, but, with some help from one of the girls, I managed to pull on a pair of jeans and an oversized shirt. We all got into a van and drove.

"Where are we going?"

"It's a surprise."

"Where are we going?"

"It's a surprise!"

And it was. We stopped at the outer fence of a farm where two friendly dogs, one a Great Dane and the other a massive German shepherd, greeted us by running around and barking with excitement. Rick carried me over to pet them. I've always loved animals. These two were beautiful. Rick was pleased that I liked them.

"Why are we here?" I asked. "You're not going to steal them, are you?"

"Don't be silly! Just come with me."

He set me down and we walked together very slowly to the barn. It was a chilly November day. I remember wondering why I was in a freezing cold barn with Rick steering me to one of the stalls.

"Look here, Pooh!"

In a pile of soft straw were the cutest, roundest puppies I had ever seen. They were the babies of the two dogs at the fence, tiny bundles of love.

"What are we doing here?" I asked between gasps of excitement.

"Pick one," he said.

30

We called the puppy Wolf. He earned his name early on by biting deeply enough into a leather cowboy boot to leave behind a few milk teeth. Too bad the boot was still connected to the wearer, one of Rick's friends. Within weeks, Wolf grew to be a galloping pony. For some doggy reason, he thought of me as a chew toy. My love for animals is great, so, despite the fact that our new family member was a goofy attack dog, I adored him. When I sat, he climbed on my lap and tried perching on my head. In the mornings, he'd playfully clamp his mouth on one of my ankles or the hem of my housecoat.

Whenever Rick was home, Wolf was the model of good dog behavior. As soon as his master departed, Wolf became as loony as a cartoon character. He'd hide until Rick left. Then he'd streak across the linoleum at me, toenails skidding, backside crashing into chairs, and excitedly leap on my back. Rick didn't believe that I sometimes had to lock myself in the bathroom to avoid Wolf's version of tag. On one of those mornings, when I was having a tug-of-war with the dog yanking me by the housecoat and both of us yipping and thrashing around the room, I heard a louder sound just outside the window. It was Rick, doubled over with laughter. I discovered him after losing the housecoat to Wolf, which Rick considered even funnier.

Even though Wolf (my "Woofie") inflicted occasional cuts and scrapes on me, his companionship helped heal some of the emotional wounds for my lost child. Years later, when I got the news he had died of a heartworm infection, I was too devastated to grieve. I still can't.

The puppy pleasures distracted me from other more serious problems. It took a while to notice that Rick's addictions were intensifying. Our new cable television package enabled him to watch movies all through the night; he only slept when there was nothing on he cared about. Lack of sleep, cocaine, and alcohol became a lethal mix for him. When Christmas came, Jack, Sandra, and Misty planned to visit family. That left me alone to try to accomplish what regular people do at Christmas, except I was with Rick and I couldn't remember the last time I had seen him sober.

On Christmas Eve, I went shopping with my tip money, which I'd hidden in one of those nice, purple Crown Royal bags with the yellow drawstrings. Because I didn't have much to spend and the crowded stores sapped my energy, I came home early. Rick was busy tearing apart his bike, intending to rebuild it. Maybe the bike was a distraction from the season and the emphasis on warmth and family. It was easy to see he had been drinking since I left, yet typical of my own poor judgment, I decided I needed to play counselor.

"Rick?"

"Yeah what? See these head gaskets? Grab a wrench, would ya?"

I moved beside him to help and tried sounding as casual as possible.

"When was the last time you talked to your mother?"

"My mother! Why?"

"Oh, I don't know. Being Christmas and all, I figured she might be thinking about you and wondering where you are."

"What would she care, the bitch!" His eyes were narrow and bloodshot, but there wasn't any anger around his mouth to match the words. I thought I saw sadness. He only spoke again after he had finished his beer and was opening another. "Okay, maybe I understand why she wouldn't give me any money."

"I wouldn't either…I mean, give money to an eleven-year-old. That's the last time you saw her, wasn't it?"

"Yeah, so? She's probably married to her Indian boyfriend by now anyway."

"That doesn't mean she wouldn't like to hear from you. She is your mother."

Too many buttons were being pressed here. He resented the boyfriend; he missed his father; he was still holding a grudge against his mother for his father's suicide.

"Drop it!" he snarled. I did.

By late Christmas Eve, I crashed into bed exhausted, leaving Rick to his own devices; nevertheless, I wasn't going to spend the night enjoying sleep.

"Pooh!"

"Wha'?" I was groggy and wondering why the clock was telling me it was five thirty. Less of a surprise was the fact that Rick was shit-faced.

"Wake up, Pooh! Here, take the phone. Somebody wants to talk to you!"

"H'lo?" It was a woman.

Oh…my…God! He had called his mother. I remember nothing about our conversation except her assessment that I must be crazy. When we finished talking, Rick was scowling.

"*Happy now?*"

Well, no. Actually, I wasn't.

I still recall two images from that Christmas Day:

First, I remember my mother in her flowered housecoat and pink hair curlers at her front door. It was seven o'clock in the morning. Rick was still leaning on the doorbell when she appeared. He pushed a half-empty bottle of red wine at her and swayed dangerously close to her face.

"Merry Chrish-mash, Lynne. Gimme a big kiss, eh!" he shouted and then grabbed the poor woman, nearly crushing her with affection.

Second, I remember traipsing over to the home of my parents' best friends, "Aunt" Betty and "Uncle" Ted. Betty was wearing a plastic Santa brooch. Usually there was a string attached to those things that made Santa's nose light up. Rick, ever the puzzle-solver, didn't see a string. Instead, he repeatedly poked her pointy bra with an index finger.

"Is 'zis how you make the nose light up?" he grinned while I, shrinking into the nearest corner, prayed for the floor to open up and swallow me.

Christmas came and went. Rick's binge continued. Just before New Year's, I was at work adding up my tips for the night when a mountain of a man walked up to where I was sitting counting change.

"You Gypsy's ol' lady?"

Looming over me was a man as wide as a truck. His face, barely visible through the wild tangle of black hair and beard, startled me, although I was a little amused by his weird, extra-wide bell-bottom jeans, relics from the 1960s fashion scene.

"Why do you ask?" I was being cautious, but the guy didn't seem to appreciate the cross-examination.

He leaned emphatically near my face. "He needs to go to the hospital."

"Oh shit!" Another fight. "Where?"

"Outside. In the alley."

I dumped my tips into my purse and sprinted behind this big messenger, who gave his name as Lennie. Rick had picked a fight with a jumbo-sized biker and lost. Being stomped to the ground had done a number on his spine. He couldn't move an inch in any direction without pain. Lennie accompanied us to the hospital.

Rick was treated and sent home to rest his back. Within days, Lennie moved in with us. At least he relieved me from my duties of having to dress Rick, even to the point of putting on his socks and lacing his boots. He had regressed to some preschool age, and I was cooperating as the surrogate mommy. Lennie took over. I was glad to hand him the job. It didn't seem to matter to Rick whether it was me or this big gorilla that was dressing him anyway. Not long afterward, when Rick was again mobile enough to pick up his old habits, we had a talk.

"How long is Lennie going to be here?" I was growing impatient.

"Not long."

"How long is not long?"

"Soon. He's going to Florida."

"Florida?"

"Yeah." Without a pinch of emotion, he added, "And I'll be going with him."

"What about me?"

"Stay here, I guess."

Honest tears began to blur my eyes.

"What will I do without you?"

"Don't worry, Pooh. You'll find some nice guy."

Fat chance. I wasn't "nice guy" bait. Besides, I didn't want a nice guy.

"Is that what you want, Rick?"

"No…"

Good. A bit of hesitation. "Well then…?"

"Well, I want you to come, but I think you should stay. You need to be with your family. It's safer." My hero. He was caring for me.

"I want to be with you, wherever that is!" I was pleading now, alarmed and passionate.

"No! Stay here!"

"But who will be with you? Dress you? Who will take care of you? What happens if your back goes out again?"

I had a few good points there. He looked away and nodded.

"Okay," he said. "You can come."

"When do we leave?"

"Two weeks."

I was triumphant.

The one single time I should have listened to him, I had to take the lead and turn everything in my own direction. It probably counts for one of my most classically stupid decisions.

31

Never own more than will fit inside two green garbage bags.

That rule made packing easy. Along with my twist tie luggage, Lennie, Rick, me, two dogs, three Harley-Davidsons, two Stevie Nicks tapes, and a sizeable supply of acid and hash were on our way to Florida. I lied to take the easy way out with my parents. I said we were going on vacation for a week.

We sold what little jewelry I had for gas money and headed to the border in Lennie's van, which really belonged to his sister. I didn't ask why we were taking it to Florida because I was pretty sure I didn't want to know. How we ever got across the border still amazes me. As we approached the customs inspection booth on that snowy mid-January evening, I was already chain-smoking to ease my nerves. Lennie pulled up to the booth where a dreaded blue uniform stood waiting. Surely this was it! There was no way he was going to let bikers enter the United States, especially with two dogs, neither of which had papers. Never mind the motorcycles in the back of the van and, if they searched, the drugs.

"Citizenship?"

"Canadian," Lennie replied, seemingly for all of us.

Would he ask me the same question?

I wasn't a citizen. I had my English passport with me, but it had expired.

And what about Rick? Was he a landed immigrant like me or a citizen?

I suddenly realized I didn't know.

"Where you headed?" continued the uniform.

"Buffalo."

"What for?"

"Dinner with friends."

Dinner with friends? Where did that come from?

"Open the back of your van please, sir."

Uh oh. Here we go.

Lennie got out and walked around the back of the van with the customs guy. I was too scared to look, too scared to move. The dogs seemed to have a sense of the situation; this was not the time to play. They remained quiet and well behaved.

"What's all this stuff for?" I heard the customs guy ask.

"We're moving up north. That's why we're going to have dinner with our friends. To say good-bye," Lennie said, his voice not betraying the slightest edge of untruth.

Rick and I waited, holding our breath. There was some shuffling at the back.

The customs guy, either obviously satisfied with the story or in a hurry to get back to the warmth of his booth, simply said, "Okay."

Lennie swung back behind the wheel. We were just about to leave when the officer put his hand on the door frame where the window was still rolled down on the driver's side.

"Have a good dinner," he said.

"Thank you," Lennie answered. And we drove off.

"Rick! That's it? He didn't even ask for my citizenship or yours!" I couldn't believe we hadn't been detained, refused, or arrested. "We made it?"

"Yup. Looks like it!" he said as he laughed.

We were on our way to the Sunshine State and celebrated by stopping and getting some beer to drink. We also smoked a skinny hash joint. Magic and dumb luck were on our side.

The trip seemed brief. I remember the big sign flanked by palm trees that read: "Welcome to Florida." We were elated! Four hours later, we were driving across a bridge on our way into St. Helen's. Rick had lived there for a short time, so we were headed for a biker bar he knew. It was a dingy sandstone building, small and square, with double doors. Thirsty and tired from the road, we parked the van and headed inside to the bar's dark interior. Both dogs followed obediently along behind us, testing new scents.

It was midafternoon and there were few people around. The bar wasn't air-conditioned, but it was great after the Canadian temperatures we had left behind a few days earlier. The beer tasted good, yet I was feeling uncomfortable.

"Out of one's element," as my father would say.

Hours passed. At one point, I lost Wolf. I didn't know where he was. I started to panic. I got up, self-consciously aware of the regulars eyeing the pale, skinny chick. I started searching around for my beloved puppy when I heard a voice say, "Hey! Whose dog is this?"

I spun around to see a waitress pointing. Behind the bar, standing on his hind legs, was Wolf slurping from the open draught tap that he was controlling with his paw. Yep, that was my dog, alcoholic himself from a very early age.

"Wolf! Woofie!" He ignored me and continued to help himself.

Soon, everyone in the bar started to laugh at the antics of our giant puppy. When I looked over at Rick, he was beaming proudly.

That event became a quick introduction to the crowd at the bar. Now everyone knew us or, should I say, everyone knew Wolf. That still didn't help with where we were going to sleep. We didn't have any money. Rick and Lennie had brought the acid along to sell, but how they were making out with that I didn't know. Comfortably numb from the alcohol, I had lost my initial uneasiness. I took for granted things would work out. In a way, they did because we ended the day by crashing at the duplex of someone named Goldie, who had taken a shine to Lennie. Rick, ever the opportunist, convinced his buddy to playact a flirtation so we had somewhere to sleep. It must've taken some convincing on Rick's part and a fair bit of alcohol on Lennie's because when he came out of her bedroom the next morning, what trailed behind him was not a pretty sight. Judging by the deep, hard lines on her face, Goldie had obviously lived a rough life. Her cheeks were smeared black and green with last night's eye makeup. Her hair, bleached dry and yellow as straw, was standing upright as if she had already frightened herself. Regretfully, the bright morning light revealed (through her short, see-through nightie) belly and hips that drooped like sandbags; ditto her breasts. Lennie's face bore the dread of a condemned man. He looked to Rick for some sign of release, but Rick felt the free digs were just fine, especially with Lennie's "paying the rent."

Rick and I slept outside on the veranda. Our bed was a slab of foam on the floorboards with a sleeping bag to cover us. I remember waking up in the mornings so cold and damp I thought I was back in England. And still I imagined everything would be fine.

We spent our first couple of days in Florida exploring, putting the motorcycles together, and hanging out at Rick's old haunt. When Goldie started complaining about no one paying for anything, Lennie found a job a couple blocks away working construction. Rick also decided that employment was a good idea. That's when he began to check the classifieds in the newspaper. When he had a list of waitress and bartending jobs for me, we got on the bike and rode to a couple places where I could fill out applications. I wore my best jeans and T-shirt, but the black leather jacket and helmet-head hairdo probably spoke for me.

The first place was a nice restaurant, but on the back page of the application I ran into a snag. It was a liquor test: List the five top shelf brands; Name three call brands of bourbon…and on it went. I gave up and ran out to Rick in the parking lot. He saw the distress on my face. "What happened?"

I told him.

"Well then, we'll try someplace else," he said, filled with ambition for me.

The "someplace else" was a bar with chili dogs featured as a menu staple. Having summoned up all of my courage, I asked for the manager. Without any alcohol in my system that day, I was apprehensive and growing embarrassed to even ask. Amazingly, the guy hired me on the spot. I'd start that evening. It gave us time to find my required uniform at the local K-Mart, a T-shirt and a pair of short shorts. I hated shorts. They emphasized my chicken legs. I didn't even wear shorts in midsummer. But this was a job, and we needed the money.

When the time came, I was dressed and steadied with a few beers, carrying guilt and worries that no one could imagine. Somebody at home must be missing us. We had left basically without notice. The vacation lie I had told my parents would cause some pretty hairy conversations when I hadn't returned after seven days. Rick hadn't notified his landlord or his roommates.

And what about Lennie's van? It really belonged to his sister. *Didn't she need it?*

Back at the bar, I understood why the boss had hired me in a hurry. I arrived in time for a very crowded twenty-five-cent happy hour. As a waitress, I can testify that serving two-bit beers or shots does not bring much in the way of tips. I worked very hard for next to nothing. After two days, I quit. Even Rick agreed it wasn't worth the time. On the upside though, I did learn the difference between well brands, call brands, and top shelf brands.

We had no money. To top things off, Lennie was arrested (and released) because his sister had reported the van stolen. Our prospects seemed bleak until the night that Rick came back from the bar and told me I had a job that started the very next day. He had made a new friend whose girlfriend, Rosie, was going to get me in at the bar where she worked in Clear Bay. Rick promised I would make a lot of money. I was both nervous and excited at the same time. How could Rosie know I would qualify? I waited eagerly for the next day, hastening the time along with my Old Milwaukee brew. Imagine. There were jobs you didn't have to apply or interview for. This really was a strange land.

The following day, I was ready for my new challenge. I asked Rick what I should wear, but he assured me that Rosie would fix me up. At the appointed two o'clock in the afternoon, a blue El Camino pulled up with Rosie and the boyfriend, Stan. He was a tall, skinny guy who grinned at us through nearly bare gums. The few teeth he did own were brown with tobacco stains. My high spirits suddenly left me. I stood perfectly still while he approached me with his long, tattooed arms outstretched for a hug. To avoid any face-to-face familiarity, I turned my cheek away. Being pressed into his shoulder was enough personal information for the day. When he stepped back, his less-than-fresh scent clung to my skin.

Rosie lumbered out from the passenger side on her own, dropping a wide shadow on the pavement. She was as tall as her boyfriend, but she must have outweighed him by at least fifty pounds.

"This's Rosie," Rick announced.

Well it wasn't exactly like you could miss her! I was in no mood for the obvious. My mind was already trying to sort out what was probably ahead of me as I was being nudged into the backseat.

I rode silent and terrified. I didn't know these people. I didn't know where I was going, what I was going to be doing, or when I would return to Rick. What if these two were completely crazy, the kind you see in horror movies and they were going to take me somewhere and kill me? It was a definite possibility, but I hadn't consumed anywhere near enough beer to handle being murdered. I listened keenly while they argued, hoping to figure out who they were and where we were going. The only facts I could determine were these:

1. They lived together.
2. Rosie wasn't bringing home enough money.
3. Rosie was doing too many drugs.

Their arguing only established that Stan reminded me of Rick, which meant that I favored him over Rosie, whom I decided was an airhead.

When we stopped outside a stucco bar that featured the painted silhouette of a naked girl beside the doorway, I asked where we were. Could I have been more naïve?

"Oh, we're here," Rosie reassured me while she opened the car door.

Stan twisted in the driver's seat to speak to me. "I'll be back at closing time to take you home," he said. I must have looked horrified because he flashed a smile and added, "Go on now. You'll be fine. Rosie will show you the ropes."

Oh bloody hell!

No one needed to tell me what kind of place this was. I knew. It was a strip joint. What had I done this time? Here I was, stranded, hundreds of miles away from Canada, miles away even from Goldie's place. I didn't know anyone, I couldn't run, I had nowhere to go and no money to get there with anyway. I got out and watched Stan peel away, fighting the urge to run after him.

"C'mon!" said Rosie. She tugged at my wrist and led me inside.

The place hadn't opened yet. The bartender met us at the entrance.

"Who's this?" she asked, rudely.

"Sue," replied Rosie. "She's going to start work here today."

"Hmph. Another one? Just make sure she follows the rules," said the woman.

As soon as my eyes adjusted to the dark interior, I saw my fate. I couldn't believe it, but there it was in black and red décor: a circular, raised stage with a mirrored back wall and bar seating around the outside. On either side of the stage were booths on two different levels. On the right-hand side of the stage was a jukebox. Rosie led me around behind the stage to a large dressing room with chairs and a wall mirror that ran the length of counter beneath it. I uttered not one word. I was already well aware of what would be expected of me.

"Nervous?" asked Rosie.

I nodded stupidly.

Nervous? Yes, you could say that.

My stomach was so tight that it hurt. Is this how society punishes bad girls? It lets them fall into pits like these to take off their clothes for men so disgusting they can't get women on their own?

"Don't worry!" Rosie's voice was so booming and cheerful it made me jump. "You'll be great," she said. I wanted to drown myself, but the sink wasn't large enough.

The other girls began arriving in twos and threes. After Rosie introduced me, they organized themselves into a kind of factory assembly line to undress me and put me in some sort of outfit that I don't remember. They also took turns putting makeup on me, something I was not adept at doing myself. (When you're always chasing drugs and alcohol, there isn't much time to learn about feminine things.) One of the girls even curled my hair. I was combed, sprayed, powdered, and painted. By then, I needed a drink, but the joke was on me. This was Clear Bay, a nude strip club in Clear Bay, where no alcohol was allowed, only soft drinks. Somehow that didn't sound right.

"I can't have a drink?" I asked, refusing to believe the bad news.

"Well, yeah, you could," explained one of my new coworkers, "but 'cause it's ten dollars to get into the club and the soft drinks cost four dollars each, the patrons smuggle in their own booze from the liquor store across the street."

Liquor store? "Oh, then what about me? I drink beer."

I sensed some hesitation while they exchanged looks. After some hurried whispers, someone was sent for a six-pack. They cautioned me though that I'd have to sip my beer from a plastic cup and pretend it was a soda. I agreed, but my mind was stuck on the errand in progress.

A *six-pack*? That wouldn't last me long.

32

The bar was open from four o'clock in the afternoon until two o'clock in the morning. If you left early, you had to buy your way out. The cost was whatever the bartender at the time said it was. Each girl had to dance three songs on stage. The girls were also responsible for getting the quarters for the jukebox to play their own music. They usually danced one song with their clothes on, one song while taking them off, and one song nude.

Nude? As in *naked*? Oh geez!

If I couldn't wear shorts in public, how was I ever going to dance in my bare naked skin? When you weren't on stage, you performed private dances for patrons in the booths at ten dollars a pop. They were, of course, performed nude. Unfortunately, this is how the girls made their money. I just didn't see how any of this was going to happen. I just couldn't imagine myself doing it. After the instructions, I drank my six-pack and dismissed myself to go to the bathroom, which was on the other side of the bar. The lounge was so dark (I guessed, to protect the integrity of the patrons), I could hardly see. Someone was swaying on stage. Too embarrassed to look, I stumbled forward to the restroom. It wasn't as though I had never been in a strip bar before. I had, but I had gone with Rick and I concentrated on playing pool or drinking so that I wouldn't have to watch some poor girl with her clothes off.

I was scared. Even the bathroom scared me. There were no doors on the toilet stalls, and my bladder was way too shy to take care of business in front of someone else. Luckily, I was alone long enough to use the facilities and exit. I decided to ask Rosie about the door thing, but her answer wasn't exactly, "Well, we must report that immediately!"

Instead, she said more things that scared me.

"Some of the girls, if they have drug problems, they clog up the toilet with their needles, so now they can't shoot up behind closed doors."

Great. Anything else I should know, Rosie?

"The other thing you gotta know," she continued, "is really important. If you're doing tricks, you have to get out of the building, but you better not come back that night."

"Why is that?"

Tricks? Now she was talking about *turning tricks?*

"The bartender, you know, the lady we talked to at the door?"

"Yeah."

"She don't want you coming back in because it looks too suspicious, and Joey don't want us to get busted again."

"Oh."

"Besides, if you do it, you better make it good. Remember, you gotta pay a hundred bucks just to get out early. And…make real sure you don't take some-one else's john." The look on my face must have been pretty blank because Rosie had to repeat that last bit for me. "You don't want to go hittin' on some other girl's john!" I didn't have a clue what she was talking about, but felt I should pre-tend I did. After all, I did want her to like me, although in hindsight, I'm not sure why.

"Uh, okay. Who's Joey?"

"The boss. He owns this place and another one up the causeway. Last time he got busted for living off the proceeds, they took his boat, his cars, everything. He's not real anxious for that to happen again."

Well, alrighty then! Wasn't this just the grand initiation. Drugs, prostitution, stripping, and a big stack of rules to go along with it!

"Is that it, then?" (Please tell me that's all?)

"One other thing…"

This wasn't happening. It was a bad movie. Had to be. It couldn't be real. With any luck, somebody would fire me for incompetence, and I'd be gone.

"And that thing is…"

"Some of the girls are bi, and you have to know which ones."

"Bi?"

"Yeah. You know, they go both ways. If they come on to you, just tell them to fuck off."

Lovely. Strung-out lesbian prostitutes to contend with, too. I needed beer. Rosie suggested we get started by going out on the floor to find someone (a cus-tomer) to buy me some.

Embarrassed, I followed her as she held her head high and strutted along on four-inch plastic heels. The cheeks of her ample backside bloomed on either side of the thong (which, in the world of dancers, is called a T-strap) and bumped along rhythmically.

My brain struggled with the fight-or-flight thing. Stay and get beer and money. Leave and end up alone on some dark street wondering how to get back to where this game started. And where was that? My head was low, my shoulders slumped. I had to lift my chin to notice the customers that Rosie pointed out. We explained to the bartender that I was new to the trade, which allowed me to sit out for the first while and watch. Rosie added her name on the rotation list for her turn to dance. Then, with me tagging along, she slid up next to a dark-haired young man with the standard line, "Hey, want some company?"

"Sure!" he grinned up at us. He must have thought, "Ooh, double fun. One very big and one very small."

I wondered if I looked as frightened as I felt. Rosie started to chitchat with the guy, and, very shortly, the conversation turned to my being nervous and needing beer.

"Here," he said, all wisdom and concern. He shoved a small, round black container at me. "Go do this. It'll make you feel better."

Happily I complied and took the container to the bathroom. He had also given me a short straw, so I assumed what I had in hand was cocaine. I had never done it before, but I had watched people snort often enough to know how. After shaping a matchbook cover as a small scoop, I lifted some of the fine, white powder and carefully placed it on the flat, chrome lid of the toilet roll box in one of the stalls. Then using the closed matchbook as a scraper, I formed the powder into a line. With the straw up into one nostril, I held the other one closed and quickly inhaled.

Not sure whether I was feeling any better at all, I made my way back to the table, only to find Rosie dancing naked at the table, swaying her hips and rolling her breasts in the guy's face. When she turned and introduced her jiggling butt to him, I was mortified. Even my "don't think, don't feel" defense didn't help. I needed a drink...fast.

After an eternity, the song stopped. Rosie climbed back into her halter and T-strap as nonchalantly as if she had just stepped out of the tub in the privacy of her own bathroom. The patron, feeling either relieved or elated, asked if I'd like a drink.

Yes, oh my God, did I ever!

I got some ice in my plastic cup. While he poured the Jack Daniels under the table, I asked what I had snorted.

"Crank. Why? You feelin' better?"

"Yeah." I lied.

I wasn't feeling better. I was feeling weird. Crank? That was crystal meth, or PCP. In the 1970s, we called it angel dust. It was, as now, dangerous stuff and the reason I had stopped smoking pot. Friends at parties had taken to secretly sprinkling angel dust on the pot before they rolled it into a joint and were ending up in the hospital. Two of them died. Now, sitting half-naked in a strip joint, I was expecting the same fate. It would be a bad way to go. I downed the sour mash, hoping to live through the night.

That's all I remember about my first night on the job.

The next day, Rick was pissed off at how trashed I was when I came home: "No money and totally fucked up," as he put it.

Well, no kidding! I didn't want to dance. I couldn't dance. Okay, I wouldn't dance.

Rick insisted I return to the bar. This was my new job. It was what everyone else's ol' lady did for a living.

Oh yeah? Well, fine then. I'll go, but I wouldn't dance. I wouldn't make any money. I'd show him!

That afternoon, Stan and Rosie showed up again, but, even knowing what I was in for, I felt I had no choice. After packing a makeup kit, I braced myself for the night. I had swiped ten dollars from Rick's wallet, enough to get myself a few six-packs. With a can of beer already in hand, I pranced out to the El Camino with Rick at my shoulder, giving me a lecture about not drinking too much and making money…blah, blah, blah.

Stan was standing outside the car listening to us.

"Hey, man! Don't be too hard on her," he said to a very surprised Rick. "It was her first night!"

That was all very nice, but, once I was in the car, he too began to preach about my having to do better and how Rick would be really pissed off if I didn't. What were my choices? Could I get beat up every night and not die?

In time, I learned the game. I was too shy to go on stage. Instead, I spent most of my time watching the other girls and getting sodas for the guys. As a waitress at least I was making money without taking off my clothes. The girls were so confident and their movements so fluid. I was scared to death, and it probably showed. Rosie tried helping, but I didn't like Rosie. She left the bar to turn tricks on a regular basis, and I wasn't going to take that route. I started hanging out with a girl named Dallas. She seemed nice. At least she talked like she was nice. She was really pretty with long, auburn hair and milky white skin. All the other girls hated her. That seemed a good sign because I hated them. They said she portrayed herself as a goody-two-shoes when in fact she lived with a big, ugly Cuban guy who was her pimp. When she wasn't at the bar, she was out turning tricks for him.

I never knew what to believe. Everyone seemed to have some kind of story. Some of the girls were prostitutes and just used dancing as a cover. A couple of the girls were junkies and only stripped to make enough money to support their habit. And since some of them were gay, I couldn't figure out for the life of me why they stripped for men. I didn't care what they said about Dallas. As far as I could see, she never left the bar with anyone, which meant she didn't turn tricks (at work anyway). She was modest and demure on stage, without the bump and grind pelvic thrusts and wide-legged invitations used by some of the other girls. She was straight, she had a boyfriend, and I never saw her do anything disgusting when she was doing table dances, which is more than I can say for the other girls. There were two girls in particular who were rumored to be having sex with the guys they were supposed to be dancing for. They preferred to do table dances in one of the dark corner booths. Both of them always had their back to the guy. It did look at times like they were bouncing on the guy's lap (all the more reason, I suppose, to call it a lap dance).

That's why I liked Dallas. She didn't do that, nor did she chase me around the bar, trying to kiss and fondle me, like Sass and Coco did. Dallas didn't do drugs and very rarely drank. I didn't understand that part because I couldn't imagine how anyone could perform this way without drinking. It seemed unlikely that anyone could actually enjoy taking her clothes off for money, but Dallas admitted she did, so I hung out with Dallas. Maybe I'd absorb some of her confidence.

I hated the job. I hated having to ask guys if they wanted a dance, so I didn't do it. It felt like begging. "Please, let me take off my clothes for you. Then you can tell me if I'm worth anything by giving me money."

I hated myself for even being there. I hated the filthy, perverted patrons. Most of all, I hated Rick for making me go there. Every night was the same routine. I went to work with a six-pack, drank it in the dressing room, and then set out to find someone in the bar with booze. I'd sit and drink with him and try to convince him to feel sorry for me and give me money. If I could manage to make a hundred dollars, I'd coast until quitting time. Most nights, I went home with far less than my goal. No one wanted to give me money unless I was willing to dance for them, which was not going to happen. I was already scantily clad, what more did they want?

Of course, I couldn't tell Rick that I was begging instead of dancing. Some pretty homely girls were working at that bar. They seemed to make a lot of money without a lot of dancing. What was wrong with me?

Was I too skinny, too shy? Did my disgust show?

Every once in a rare while, some guy would come in and just pay me to talk. That I could do, provided I had more than enough to drink.

Drinking was the only way I could get through the day. I would wake up, start drinking, go to work, keep drinking, come home at four o'clock in the morning, and pass out. The next morning, I'd have such a hangover I'd have to start drinking again to feel better. I hardly saw Rick, which was fine. He sent me to a job that made me feel cheap and dirty. I didn't want him or any man to touch me. All of them were loathsome. I was loathsome.

It would be a long time before I could tolerate sex again. What Rick did in the interim was his problem. While I spent my afternoons and evenings at the strip club, he spent his afternoons wheeling and dealing. It wasn't long before we moved out of Goldie's place and in with some guy whose wife had just left him. That didn't last long either. We moved again after two weeks. Lennie, for his own reasons, remained with Goldie.

By hooking up with Stan, Rick found a new crowd and a new place for us to live in St. Helen's. To hear him tell it, it was great. We'd be sharing a house with two young guys who were looking for someone to share the rent. Best of all, we could take Wolf with us. Until that point, we had to trust one of the bartenders to look after both Wolf and Sheba, but when we went to pick them up, we were told that Sheba had run away. Rick was crushed. At least we still had my Woofie.

Our landlord friend was very happy to get rid of us. He even offered to deliver us, along with our two trash bags worth of possessions, to the new address. We went ahead on the bike. When he arrived, he simply deposited our stuff and left. As for the wonderful house, it was an unpainted brown shack on a sandlot. I had never seen anything so shabby. The drapes in the front window were bedsheets. The front steps sagged, and garbage substituted for a lawn.

Welcome to my ever-shrinking world.

33

We soon connected with a family whose matriarch was a gaunt-faced woman named Gertie. She lived in the small, run-down house next to ours along with a divorced son, an unmarried daughter (whose young son lived down the street with his father), and her current boyfriend. Also roosting with Gertie were the two grandchildren of an absentee daughter, one of whom was pregnant. *Have I lost you yet?* Let's summarize it this way: counting Gertie and a lame, aging biker who rented a room with them, there were seven (eventually eight, with the addition of the newborn) people in that house. The expectant father was a teenager. He and his buddy, another grandchild, were to become our roommates. I grudgingly accepted them.

Gertie was divorced from her husband, but occasionally (just to complete the picture), he'd tear down our road in a rusted pickup truck loaded with trash to pay a drunk and disorderly family visit.

At our shack, which I secretly christened the cockroach clubhouse, Rick and I established our bedroom by nailing a tired-looking blanket across the doorway of what was once a small, enclosed back porch. Rick, wise in the ways of street life, salvaged a grubby sleeping bag from somewhere as our bed. To dilute my disgust and anxiety, I kept a bottle close at hand. If I couldn't be passed out when the cockroaches tried sleeping with me, I'd at least have a weapon to bash them with.

We were barely adjusted to our new setting when our young roommates, along with their rent of thirty dollars a week, moved out. That meant that somehow I had to work harder or longer to make up the difference, yet I was the happy fool, convinced it was a small price to pay for being Rick's ol' lady. Since he was busy and cheerfully rubbing leather shoulders with the local motorcycle club, his good mood meant fewer beatings for me. He had finally found somewhere he was accepted and he was settling in very well. His new world included survival practices, which his cohorts readily shared and which he was grateful to learn. First, his ol' lady would support him in one of two occupations, working in a strip club or hooking. Second, for his personal protection, he was given a gun.

To offer a view of how well those two privileges blended for him, imagine my arrival home from the strip club at four thirty in the morning to find Rick and his new "main man" Billy Lee, Gertie's son, having a great time shooting cockroaches off our living room walls. The game is even more fun it seems if you're totally hammered and sitting in the dark. It also helps to be in a neighborhood where the sound of gunshots in the wee hours means harmless entertainment.

One day while I was alone, I received a personal visit from four of Rick's heavy-duty biker friends. The largest of them was called Hog, the pig kind or the motorcycle kind, I didn't know, and I didn't care. He strode in ahead of the others.

"We wanna talk to you about Gypsy," he said. "Whadda you think about him spendin' so much time with us?"

"Oh…" I was caught off guard, but kept talking anyway. "He's so glad. He really likes you guys. It makes it fine with me," I answered dutifully, keeping my grin stretched as wide as I could manage.

Wow. They were interested in my responses! Yes, that was me, soaking up attention from guys who possessed all the charm of cavemen. My dear mother wouldn't have known where to faint in their presence. Everywhere was too dirty.

The hint of a smile on a grimy pock-marked face. A grunt of appreciation. "We want you to get him to join up with us. Every time we ask, he jus' says he's thinkin' about it."

"Yeah, I can do that," I heard myself boast. "Just leave it to me."

Nods all around, the social niceties were concluded. They withdrew, pleased as gators backing into the swamp with a fresh carcass.

Rick heard an altered version of the visit.

"What'd you tell them?" he snarled, eyes narrowed.

"I told them it was up to you. I've got nothing to do with it."

He was pleased not so much by my attitude, but because an invitation had been offered.

"I'll go see them tomorrow."

I thought I had arranged quite a deal. We were in St. Helen's. The biker club was in another city, so while Rick was hanging out with them, I was the lady of cockroach manor. I didn't have to worry about being beaten up for looking at him the wrong way. On my warped scale of contentment, things were good, so good in fact that with the bar closed on Sundays, we'd spend the day at the beach on Clear Bay. Wolf learned to doggy paddle in the waves and we partied with another group of bikers, some Vietnam vets. When we did get time alone, we pretended to be tourists. While I played in the water, I could wave to vacationer Rick with his gun tucked into the waistband of his Levi's.

Look at him up there, propped in the sand with a cooler of cheap beer! Check out the dark sunglasses, black T-shirt, black leather vest, studded belt, heavy wallet chain, and motorcycle boots. Ah, yes. The total tourist. Just to blend in more perfectly, sometimes he'd sunbathe by removing his boots and socks. What a postcard for the folks back home! When I joined him on the sand to dry off, my swimwear was a pair of cut-off shorts and a T-shirt, but that's only because I was too self-conscious to wear a swimsuit. Somehow it was all right for weirdo creeps at the bar to ogle me while I served them sodas half-naked, but normal people would see shame imprinted on my skin. I had to keep that concealed.

I knew we weren't regular people, but Rick's sense of importance grew as he spent more time with the club. Because he was relatively stable and I wasn't getting too drunk too often, we had found a kind of balance to sustain us. For my good behavior and because he was feeling so manly, he bought an automobile for his ol' lady: a pale yellow, thirteen-year-old Cadillac. It was a barge of a car to park and maneuver, but when I drove it I felt like Miss Florida Sunshine.

"Do you know this girl?"

The photo my boss held before my "twelve beers later" vision meant nothing to me.

"Uh-uh. Why?"

"The cops were just here, dropped this off asking questions. She was found all cut up in a dumpster down the road."

"Cut up?"

"Stripper. Her body parts were in a garbage bag."

In an instant, the issue had some personal sisterhood attached. I realized that this profession drew psychotics who were capable of murder. Whoever killed this girl could have been in our bar, too. Everyone was jittery, especially when another girl's body was found two weeks later. Coincidence? A serial killer? When my turn came, I was behind the wheel of my yellow Caddie.

The headlights had held steadily in my rearview mirror, no matter which turns I took. At four o'clock in the morning, drunk, alone, and steering unsteadily along a dark, deserted highway and then exiting to narrower roads, I knew I was in danger. Stopping at any of the all-night convenience stores to call Rick would probably prove useless. He was likely passed out drunk. Calling the police could invite more trouble. An intoxicated waitress from a strip club complaining about a phantom stalker? Hardly an emergency. I had to make it home.

Please, big sunshine car, don't fail me!

I careened around corners, always with those headlights glaring at me from my mirror. When my driveway loomed up ahead, I yanked the steering wheel hard without slowing down, nearly driving up on the unlit stoop where Rick and his latest live-in best buddy were sitting. Wolf bolted from the porch and began barking crazily at the car behind me that had by now come to a near stop in front of the house.

"Somebody's following me!" I yelled, arms flapping at my sides.

I flew straight to the front door with Wolf chasing me in playful welcome. Behind us, Rick and his pal, both drunk, were in a wild foot chase, shooting at the fleeing car. Part of me was afraid they'd kill him; the other part was afraid they wouldn't. There was no doubt in my mind that this was the deranged murderer who had chosen me as his next dumpster victim. Now that he knew where I lived and how much time he'd have to intercept my drive home, he could try again.

The next night, I was a tangle of nerves. Every patron seemed worthy of suspicion. I couldn't help but dread my drive home that night. Yet, as I have found over and over in my life, if it weren't for blind luck, coincidence, or some loophole in the great scheme of things, I would have been dead many times over. Of all the regulars I unwittingly chose to trust with my scary tale, the nephew of a mob boss was the right one. When he left the bar, I resumed scanning every face, looking for my would-be assailant. Little did I realize that my Mafia friend was out finding me some peace of mind. An hour later, he returned with it: a six-pack of beer and a beautiful, pearl-handled derringer already loaded with two bullets. Perhaps he had slipped it from his wife's lingerie drawer or borrowed it from his mom. I never knew.

His voice was lowered and his dark eyes shone with confidence when he gave me the gun.

"This'll keep you safe," he said.

Yikes! *No kidding.* "It's a loaded pistol!" Rick would never let me even touch one.

"If you're gonna carry a gun, you better know how to use it," Rick would shake his head sadly. "That's why I can't give you a gun, Pebbly-Pooh. You'd have to shoot to kill, and you wouldn't be able to do that."

Shoot to kill.

Well, this Pebbly-Pooh airhead might have done that very thing, had the need arisen. Every night on the way home, the pretty little weapon sat reassuringly on the passenger seat next to me. I never told Rick about it, nor did I mention my casual connection to the guy who gave it to me. I kept the gun. It took its place at the bottom of my handbag, right alongside my lipstick and tampons. Rick never did find out about it, nor did the killer strike again.

34

"Why can't you be like the other ol' ladies!?" If what Rick meant by that was that I refused to prostitute myself, he was right. "They work. They make serious coin and come home sober. But no, not you. You go to work to get drunk! You come home stupid, with nothin'. Why do I keep you anyway? Why?"

The lecture was getting old. Every day, a new version. Was I supposed to offer answers to this crap?

"You're just a worthless piece of shit!"

Like I didn't already know.

And there it was, the noose I allowed around my psyche for years to come. I would hear it so often I could never forget. Rick volunteered the label, I believed it myself, and my own father had already predicted my worthlessness. I had to recognize myself and behave accordingly.

You'd think I would be able to ignore his verbal abuse with "sticks and stones will break my bones, but names will never hurt me." I had been physically hurt by his fists and survived, yet emotionally I couldn't heal the wounds those words inflicted on me.

Owen liked me though. He was quickly becoming my favorite customer. When I reported for work, he'd be waiting for me with a six-pack of beer and a bottle of Jack Daniels. We'd talk, and he'd ramble on about his two kids and how hard it was for a man to raise a family alone. His wife had run off. Even though I saw that Owen was searching in the wrong places for her replacement, I began fantasizing about accepting the position. While he spoke, I built daydreams of my playing stepmommy in a singlewide trailer under Florida palms. He'd go off to work, working at whatever he did, while I stayed home with the kiddies and made pink, frosted cupcakes. The picture played out so nicely in my head, had it not been for my knowledge that I was a "worthless piece of shit," I would have gone home with him. That phrase, Rick's invisible choke chain, was too snug around my neck for me to say yes to Owen's numerous offers.

I can't blame Rick entirely. There had to be something wrong with me to hate myself so much. Still, it was nice to listen to the drone of Owen's mild, coaxing voice. So wrapped in what he was saying that the appearance of two men standing in front of the table startled me. One of them was pointing at me.

"She's the one."

"You're under arrest," snapped the other.

Undercover cops in jeans and denim jackets.

Terrified and confused, I was escorted by the elbow, straight out to the parking lot where police cars had converged everywhere. Behind me, a steady parade of dancers was being ushered out of the building, some still in scanty costumes, to be lined up and handcuffed. They weren't going quietly either. The raid was a noisy affair, complete with flashing lights and sirens. At some point, I was flung against a wall next to Terana, a tall, black prostitute who had been behind bars often enough to consider it normal. We stood in stark contrast against the spotlighted flamingo-pink walls of the club, she as unmoved as I was upset.

"Don't worry, honey," she crooned, seeing my fright. "You be okay. This yer firs' time?"

I nodded, every muscle in my body quivering.

"Sugar, you looks like you be needin' help worse 'n I do." With one handcuffed hand, she reached inside the waistband of her T-strap and drew out a small, light blue capsule. "Take this. It'll relax ya."

I took it before I even asked, and then looked up at her.

"Downer," she said, anticipating my question.

Apparently, what I had just experienced was routine. The local police force kept the strip joints stirred up by coming in, paying for a few dances, and then arresting everyone. The girls would be taken to jail, released in the morning, and, a few months later, they'd appear in court and pay a fine. No big deal. It happened all the time.

I wondered why I was riding in the back of squad car while the others were being taken away together in a paddy wagon. I hadn't even been dancing. I'd been drinking beer in my street clothes.

Had I had been singled out? Was it because of Rick? The jerk! What had he done now?

I sat in silent disbelief. What would my parents say? Oh Lord...my parents! They must never know about this. Maybe I'd be deported and sent back to Canada. Oh, how in hell was I going to get through this night?

At the precinct in Clear Bay, after a brief wait, I was directed to a chair at the desk of a young detective.

"Do you want coffee?" he asked.

I shook my head from side to side and tried to look casually disinterested.

Why was everyone being so nice to me?

I had been already offered a whole variety of donuts, sandwiches, cookies, and bananas while I was sitting on a bench in the hall.

"Half my lunch?" he asked, yanking a brown bag from his desk drawer. "Peanut butter."

"No thanks."

He sighed, picked up a pen, and tapped it over a form laid out on the desk pad. For a second or two, he scanned my bleached hair, my make-up, my frail arms, and assorted fading bruises, and I felt his pity. Such a waif, he must have thought. This is somebody's daughter.

"How old are you?

"Twenty-three."

"Hmm." Hasty writing. "Know why you're here?"

"No." I was very curious though.

"You've been charged with lewd and lascivious behavior." He looked me straight in the eye. "It carries three months in jail and a fine."

I felt myself stiffen. All those dark awful things that happened to women in prison movies scared me nearly senseless. "What? I haven't *done* anything! I was just sitting there...talking!"

He shrugged his shoulders. "How long have you been dancing?"

"I don't dance. I waitress."

He looked at me quizzically. "Why do you work there?"

"It's a job." Why was he taking a jab at my conscience?

"Would you like something to eat or drink?"

"I'm fine." I wondered where we were going with this and where the other girls were all this time.

"You have a boyfriend."

"Uh, yeah..." Rick! I knew it. That's what this was all about, wasn't it!

"We've been watching him for some time." They had his name. I couldn't deny my connection. "How does he treat you?"

"Fine."

"Does he ever hit you?" A brief glance at my arms again.

"Never."

"Because, if he did, you know you don't have to be treated like that. Stuff like that happens to pretty girls. They don't stay pretty very long." He was playing on my nonexistent self-esteem. I didn't budge. "How long have you been together?"

"Two years."

He leaned back in his chair and crossed his arms, willing to wait for the truth. "Two years. And he's never hit you?"

"No."

"You're lucky then. So, what can you tell me about him? What he does for a living...that sort of thing."

"Nothing. He's not working right now."

"What does he do with his time?"

"I'm at work all day (not true). I don't know." The exit sign at the far end of the room was calling my name. The sedative was beginning to calm me, and I just wanted to lie down somewhere and dream nice dreams.

He tried again. "Listen, are you sure he treats you well? We can protect you, you know. You won't have to go to jail. You don't have to be scared."

I mustered a carefree laugh. "I'm fine!" I insisted. There, that should get him off my case.

Ha, protect me all right...probably ship me back to England.

Enough games. He got to the point. "We want him on suspicion of murder."

I was living with a murderer? Goosebumps ran down my arms. How could I respond to *that*?

"I don't think I can help you. I don't know anything," I said firmly and looked away.

My interrogator sat silently for a moment and then stood up.

"Think about it," he said, and walked away.

For several minutes, I was left alone, feeling watched. Would I gasp for air with the news I'd been given? Would I throw myself at their mercy and end this punishing, ever-riskier relationship? With the sedative dulling my senses, it became increasingly easy not to care. I chose to sit quietly in the chair, stare at my handcuffs, and wait.

The officer returned. "What would you like? An orange? Coffee? A sandwich?"

"No. Uh-uh. No thanks." I'd die first. "What's going to happen to me?"

"You'll probably be out soon, so there's no sense taking you back to a cell."

"Out?"

"Ask the bail bondsman in reception."

Rick had put up bail for me. It was after four o'clock in the morning when the bondsman put me into his car and drove me home. All the way back, my mind raged. Leave the bastard! Go back home! Then again...wait and see if he's awake. Act depressed and traumatized. He'll treat you good for a couple days because of his guilt.

Wolf and Rick greeted me in the driveway where they had been sharing a six-pack.

"I've been so worried, Pooh! Me and Wolf been waiting for hours!" Rick was visibly shaken, maybe even more so than I was.

My anger was immediately replaced with self-recrimination: how guilty I now felt for having thought such nasty things. I could have at least called someone to get a message to him. Oh, how much pain I had caused him! Why was I always so selfish? What a truly bad, bad person I was.

I hugged Rick and kissed Woofie. All of us sat down for a beer.

35

According to Rick, who had checked with the wisdom of his biker buddies, I had just experienced the county's tax system.

"They get money off the dancers. They arrest you, you pay a fine, and that's how they score their cash."

Naturally, the law was the enemy. That the cops could clean up some crime, rescue a few underage runaways, or use the raids to keep an eye on the dancers' boyfriends and assorted pimps was beyond us. Rick and I were both indignant. He was disturbed enough about my arrest to keep me home the next day. Let them arrest dancers, but I didn't dance. I was determined not to pay the fine, so much so that I decided to defend myself in court.

It was in Rick's best interest that I not get cross-examined again; it was also in his best interest that I find an alternate job. That sent me job-searching the strip joints in St. Helen's.

The first club I tried was considered classy. The girls were not expected to cavort around nude. They were given G-strings and pasties, a tease, I assumed, for soft-core perverts. Despite its more upscale reputation, they hired girls as young as seventeen, a policy I found distasteful. Unfortunately, they were only hiring dancers, not waitresses. Could I do it? I didn't know. Physically, I felt jeopardized because the pasties were applied with a glue I was certain grew roots into flesh. The first night, I came home in tears, unable to peel the things off. I worried about whether the chemicals in the glue would cause blood poisoning, cancer, or worse. My high-toned values over the junior dancers and my overactive imagination about the glue drove me to seek another bar and yet another.

After a determined search, I found a boat-shaped bar that needed waitresses. This time, my costume was a white, lacy sundress, a pink G-string, and a pair of shiny plastic slide heels. The first night started out well. Encouraged by a couple beers, I started flirting with the patrons while serving them drinks. During a lull, I settled at the bar, lit a cigarette, and took a nice long pull on my beer. I think my head was still tilted back when the police arrived. Another raid. Only this time I didn't get arrested, but the bar did get closed down.

I went back to work in Clear Bay. The money was better at the Clear Bay bar anyway, as were the drugs. Besides, I was set on fighting the fines. The trip to downtown Clear Bay afforded me an excuse to use the library to research my case.

Every working day, I'd direct my yellow Caddie to the library before checking in at the bar. I discovered that the statute being used in my case dated back to the late 1800s in Florida, Georgia, and Louisiana. Among other things, the "lewd and lascivious" law made it illegal for a man and woman to present themselves as a couple without benefit of marriage. Wasn't that just another charge looming over me, my living with Rick? Emotions always override common sense, so I immediately saw another excuse for the authorities to ship me to England. I'd need alcohol to settle my nerves.

Rick required references to get into his exclusive club. Joining the bike club wasn't a matter of receiving a fancy, printed invitation in the mail. There were checkpoints and hurdles, one of them already secured by having a supporting ol' lady working at a strip club. Passing each test gave the would-be member privilege and achievement. Making it to their ranks was a source of deep, macho pride. The problem was that the club members Rick had left behind in Canada wouldn't vouch for him. They hated him.

Enter "always eager to be accepted" Sue and her poorly thought out schemes. When one of the club members showed up at the bar to invite me to their clubhouse, I immediately saw an off-season valentine moment to prove my love to Rick, and I'd do it with my own references. After all, I knew the president of the Canadian chapters. Everyone there liked me. Because I didn't have my car that day, a trip to the clubhouse would also net me a ride home. Double luck! So off I went to play out my game. For security and appearances, I took along a dancer friend.

Like every other biker clubhouse I'd been in, this one was a small, run-down house surrounded by a ten-foot-high chain-link fence. Its interior focal point was a bar. Already feeling no pain when I arrived, my first order of business was to help myself to a beer. Hog, the shaggy, overweight giant, was tending bar and picked up conversation with me. His beefy arms, so tattooed they appeared to be wrapped in gift paper, kept sliding another round in my direction, keeping me talking, impressing, and persuading. I saw myself as the most important person in the room.

"You want recommendations for Rick? Well, start right here!" I boasted, rummaging around in my purse. "Take this number. Call this clubhouse in Canada. *Just ask about me.*"

After a few more beers and my nonstop babbling, Hog gave in and called. As he spoke, he kept looking back at me with growing interest in his eyes.

Ah, yes. The prospect's cool girlfriend and her great biker affiliations.

He was becoming quite impressed with the celebrity before him, teetering on a bar stool. They were *definitely* discussing my reputation.

My memory of that evening starts to dim at that point. The image blurs to sitting on Hog's knee...going upstairs to the bathroom, beer in hand...my way downstairs blocked by Hog pressing me to a bedroom. Resistance. Struggle. Blackout. Everything is lost until the morning and grinding pain.

The sharp Florida sun was burning into my cheek. I felt myself moving, being kicked and dragged, first by the leg and then by the hair, to the house. Rick was a madman. His rage was more intense than I had ever experienced. Sometime during the night, I had been pitched from a moving vehicle; every cell of my body could recall that much. I was already raw from being thrown onto the road, but Rick was inflicting even more injuries on me.

"Stupid, worthless bitch! You embarrassed me...made me look like a wimp asshole! What the fucking hell were you thinking!"

I knew enough to crawl to our room to find some shelter inside the sleeping bag. I knew enough not to try to defend myself. I knew I had to lie still and keep quiet, especially about my fears about what had happened with Hog. As for my damages, I was afraid to look. Rick would soon stalk out, leaving me to hide from daylight with the cockroaches.

Later in the day, I scrounged around for some loose change and managed to scrape together the price of a six-pack. Too sore and swollen to work, I trudged to the store for my medicine. When I finally passed out weary from misery that night, Rick still had not returned, but he had negotiated a trade. The next day, when I heard loud, stubborn gears shifting in the driveway, I ran out to see Rick backing up a monstrous pickup truck that possessed a death rattle. Attached to it was a camper, the sort they call a fifth wheel. That seemed appropriate. The truck looked like any extra help would be welcomed to keep it upright.

"What's going on?" I called, expecting to hear he had found his new treasure in a ditch and had saved someone the trouble of transporting the whole mess to the junkyard.

"None of your business!" Teeth clenched in annoyance, he backed the camper up to the house and jumped down to unhook it.

I waited and watched, wondering what all the fumes, dust, and activity meant for me.

Rick pushed a wad of bills at me and grunted, "Get me something to drink!"

Once again, I made my way to the store and returned with beer. I sat at a safe distance while he drank, vaguely beginning to fear that my beloved Caddie had been swapped. After about five or six beers, he finally faced me. Blind to my bashed forehead and open cuts from the previous morning's events, he was seeking approval.

"What do you think?" He was cheerful now, gesturing at the truck and its camper and patting the rusty fender.

Afraid of saying the wrong thing, I kept my face turned to the driveway while Rick climbed inside the camper and leaned back to beckon me. "Hey, Pooh! C'mon in! Have a look!" He was all smiles, filled with pride and accomplishment.

The tour started at the door in the back on the passenger side. We passed a sink the size of a shoebox and a stove where something had boiled over and sealed itself to the surface. We paused to marvel at Rick's favorite feature, a toilet/shower combination where you could sit on the toilet and shower at the same time. I wondered where the water would come from or where it would go afterward. The table, presumably where I'd serve drinks and food, folded down into a bed. Another bed, with whatever crawling in it, awaited us on a shelf two steps above the floor. I was less than impressed, but acted astonished and pleased at every step. After edging our way back to the door through the narrow galley kitchen, we stepped outside to greater news. The package came with one more surprise: a boat. I couldn't imagine it was still floating, but I suspected we'd be working on making it seaworthy. And what had he used for money? Was it my car?

"Yeah, I got *everything* for one old, piss yellow Cadillac." The hard stare in his eyes warned me not to protest. Instead, I was supposed to be thrilled. The truck was transportation for me to get back and forth to work. It even had a name. Gothic, black lettering across the front bumper would announce to everyone who could read and see me coming: "Swamp Slut."

"But…it…" I had to be careful with my choice of words. "It's a standard transmission. I can't drive that." I hadn't even tried since the disastrous driving lessons with Derek in England.

"You can ride a bike, can't you?" Rick said, still admiring the new toy. "This is just as easy. Three speeds and a granny gear."

Gears? A bicycle? Was he talking about a speed bike? I had never owned one.

"It's the same thing," he continued. "Billy Lee will show you later."

"Okay." My heart sunk. I missed my car. I did not want to drive this thing.

Primed with forty-five minutes worth of instruction from Billy Lee, I drove to work the next day, lurching and stuttering all the way down the highway. The ABC liquor store came very close to finding me parked in their front display window, but I managed to pick up my beer for work and churn my way down the road without incident. Swamp Slut and I were trying to understand each other.

If he could have peeled away the layers of violent mistrust, anger, and chemical addiction and replaced them with any measure of emotional stability, Rick would have been a very successful salesman. His sense of bartering and persuasion was uncanny. The boat turned out to be a twenty-five-foot Chris Craft cabin cruiser. It was old, but Rick had negotiated the deal without cash. Along with Woofie, Rick and I enjoyed that boat for many Sundays, drinking away the day and fighting all evening. Predictably, when the marina started demanding back payments for docking privileges, the boat went to market. It was replaced by three motorcycles—Harleys: one for spare parts; one for Rick's "brother" Billy Lee; and one for Rick. The one he kept for himself needed a new engine. It was pretty banged up.

"Devil bike," he laughed. "It's got 666 in the serial number, Satan's telephone number. Bad luck machine, though. Its owner had an accident, so nobody wants it now." He stroked his hand appreciatively along the damaged fender. "She's a nice bike…good, smooth ride."

As another discard from the real world, I couldn't help but relate. Rick obviously wasn't superstitious. The bike's owner, a Vietnam vet we'd met on the beach, was killed in a nasty accident on a bridge. I remembered reading about it. He died, but the bike survived.

I drank with Rick to toast his devil bike. Privately, I was considering the bad karma that came with it.

"But hold on a minute here! What was happening to my feelings?

An unexpected, bright emptiness had just replaced my usual dark fears that came with new challenges. I wasn't sure how I felt about Rick's getting into an accident. Would it be a good thing or bad?

The thought surprised me.

36

One night, Lennie, Rick's manservant who had driven us from Canada to Florida in his sister's van, was sitting out front drinking with Rick when I arrived home from work. I hadn't seen him in months, nor had Rick mentioned him. He knew the guy was not my favorite person, but it didn't matter anyway. Lennie was no longer with Goldie. Naturally, Rick had already invited him to move in with us. We could never be alone. Always, there was someone living with us, and, this time, I was furious. In the morning, when Rick was close enough to sober, I intended to persuade him to toss the baggage.

"Rick…"

"Don't call me that. My name is Gypsy." His threatening tone quickly weakened my opening.

"Okay then, *Gypsy*." I was careful to smile approvingly. "How come Lennie's here?"

"He's got no place to live."

"Oh, but you know we just got rid of people staying with us. I was kind of looking forward to being alone, just you and me spending time together."

He turned the tables on me. Now he was being the persuasive charmer. With a sad, weary face, he framed his answer to make me feel like a rotten kid who rejects the new addition to the family.

"But he's our brother, Pooh. He's got nowhere else to go!"

And wasn't I just the evil woman to want to turn away this large, obviously helpless, stray man. Since I had to work seventy hours a week to support us, and since Rick had to have a keeper and a playmate or two while I was out, and since all of his babysitters were live-in, unemployed heavy drinkers, I began to feel a rage creeping up around me. No one cared I had to work at a job I hated in order to live a life I hated. No one cared I drank to dull the ugliness of it all. I was so tired of the burden.

I tried to defend myself in court and failed. Evidently, all the effort I put into studying the lewd and lascivious law was useless. The judge found me guilty, handed down the standard $250 fine, and put me on probation for six months. Rick wasn't immune to the long arm of the law either. He spent two months in jail for aggravated assault, without a revival of murder charges. What was with that?

My days without him were peaceful. Dutifully, I visited him every week and was waiting for him in the parking lot with a bottle of Jack Daniels when he was released. We went home, back to our hovel, and picked up where we left off. That period of relative peace lasted until Raven's entrance.

Raven had been flirting with Rick for weeks. The passionate groaning coming from the direction of our bedroom window as I walked toward the house wasn't any surprise. When I peeked in, I couldn't identify anyone or see very well through the gritty panes. In my post-work drunken state, I just guessed who it was. Consumed with rage and crying tears of disappointment, I threw myself back inside the truck and headed to the bar to find a sympathetic ear.

"Hey, babe, you know you can crash at my place." Ethan was a crippled member of the club. Whether his injuries were sustained on a motorcycle or at the hands of another biker, I didn't know. He was a good listener, though. He ordered us another round while I considered my options. Here was one of Rick's "bro's" who was offering sanctuary. It wasn't that he was nursing a grudge against Rick, it's just that among members of the organization, women were considered casual possessions. As such, they were interchangeable. Maybe he was prepping me to move in with him next, but, for whatever reason, he left me alone that night. In the morning, I took a cab home. Rick was still in bed, but heard me come in.

"Is that you, you ungrateful bitch?"

Ungrateful bitch? Who was the one screwing around in my bed in the house I pay for? "Yeah," I said, throwing open the curtain covering the entrance to the bedroom, half-expecting to see Raven still curled up beside him. I was ready for a fight. There was no way he was winning this one. "Who else would it be?"

"Where were you?"

"Why do you care?"

"What are you talking about?"

"I was here last night, Rick. I came home early to surprise you." That wasn't exactly true, but guilt worked well on him. "Guess what I found when I got here?"

He pulled his standard scowl that told me he was quickly building a case against my accusations. "What the fuck are you talking about?" Of course, anger was his usual standby.

"You and your girlfriend, Raven. Right here in our bed! That's what I'm talking about."

His face contorted somewhere between surprise and guilt.

"Rick," I said with exaggerated patience, "I was standing at the window. It looks right over the bed, or did you ever notice?"

"You're nuts! You don't know what you're talking about. You must've been hallucinating!" Desperate now, he challenged, "If you were here, then where'd ya go?"

"I didn't want to disturb you and your girlfriend, so I left. By the way, your friend Ethan is pretty nice!"

"Ethan?"

"Yep."

"Where'd ya see him?"

"At the bar," I said, pointing up the street.

"And...?"

"And nothing. He bought me a beer and let me spend the night at his place. I don't know how much of a friend he is, though. He tried to get me to leave you and move in with him!" As a final shot, I added sarcastically, "Should I have?"

Rick's mouth went slack. He was considering my question, and not at all reacting the way I needed him to. "Yeah, that's Ethan. Did he hurt you?"

"No! I told you. He wanted me to move in with him!"

"And...?"

"I guess that's up to you." I was sidetracked, but steered right back to the point. "What are you doing with Raven?"

"Nothing! I told you. You're crazy!"

"Oh, so you're telling me I was hearing things? She wasn't here?"

"You were probably drunk as usual." Normally that ploy would have worked. I would have shut up, but not this time.

"You're wrong! I only had three beers." A lie to be sure; whenever anyone asked how much I'd had to drink, three beers was my standard answer.

"Bullshit!"

"You're telling me she wasn't even here?"

"She was here, but nothing happened."

It was my turn to scoff. "Yeah right! What went wrong, Rick? She got bored before breakfast?" I was being a smart-ass, but I was mad.

Silence. End of discussion.

Later that day, we broke up. Rick felt that our being apart for a while was a good idea. I didn't argue, especially when he said I could have the truck. I knew what that meant. If we were really breaking up, he wouldn't have allowed me anything. We weren't breaking up; we were just having a break, and I was looking forward to it. After all, my unhappiness was all Rick's fault, just like it was my parents' fault when I lived at home.

I went to work that night. The next day, I packed my few clothes into the Swamp Slut and drove to the main strip where I worked in Clear Bay, looking for a motel room.

37

By chance, I found a small, clean motel ten minutes away from work for a hundred dollars a week. The lady who managed it insisted on several strict guidelines, including no men, drugs, or alcohol and definitely no noise after nine o'clock in the evening. I liked the regulations. In a neighborhood crawling with hookers and drug addicts, rules made me feel safe. On my first night in a real bed with clean sheets and crisp pillowcases, sleep arrived immediately.

I was a single woman with an income. Just having enough money for rent and gas to run the truck were my only concerns. I had no long-term plans. I didn't even know how to make them, yet people at work commented that I looked better the very next day. I even felt different. Freedom is healthy.

If I'd seen the light long enough, this story would end abruptly, right here. I would have understood that no woman needs to be slammed with fists, bruised with boots, or emotionally assaulted with anger, foul insults, or put-downs. Above all, I would have realized that working to support an abusive partner is never a privilege or a source of pride. Another few hours might have even brought enough clarity into my spirit to hold my own needs above Rick's. It was not to be.

Forty-eight hours after my departure, a call came to the bar for me. Rick was asking me to meet him at the restaurant down the street the next day. He even left a time. A woman with a true sense of self would have taken her pay, climbed on a bus, and headed out of town, never even giving a backward glance. I was emotionally feeble, however, and unfamiliar with planning for my own daily existence. One of the girls at the bar, seeing my distress, offered to let me stay with her that night. We could talk and be girlfriends. I needed that. Given that she was one of the nicer girls at the bar, meaning she wasn't a drug addict with needle punctures all over her arms or a predatory lesbian, I accepted. I wish that she had told me she lived in a nudist colony; I would have declined her offer. I know it seems a double standard, but I had to put up with nudity as my job. Nudity in a domestic setting was taboo for me. My modesty surprised my hostess. Even so, she was nice enough to provide a nightie for me to sleep in, which I gladly accepted. She said good night and went to her room, leaving me alone in the dark with my six-pack and her nightie.

I also wished she had mentioned something about her roommate. Late the next morning, while I sat on the floor in her living room waiting for my friend to awaken, a naked man came into the adjacent kitchen to pour himself a glass of orange juice. Not wishing to appear standoffish (and I wish he had), he walked over to shake my hand, all the while cheerfully introducing himself. From my position, the view was gross. I replied to his kneecaps, hoping I was merely having a nightmare.

When my friend appeared, I was very eager to get going, but she insisted on a tour of the compound.

Weren't we supposed to talk? *I thought we were going to talk!*

I really didn't feel prepared to chat with the tall guy standing near the barbeque wearing only a hat, nor did I want to view the swimmers in the pools or watch players jiggle across the tennis courts. I tried easing myself into conversation by asking why everyone carried towels.

"It's a rule," she said, smiling. "Sitting in public areas and all."

"Oh." Good point.

The second hurdle of the day was the command performance with Rick. The nudist camp had made me feel awkward and displaced. It was good to see a familiar face, even Rick's, and even if I was hooked on his approval.

"Pebbly-Pooh! I wanted to make sure you were all right!"

How sweet!

I knew he loved me despite himself, but he also cared. I was touched. I guess "touched" is the right word. In the very next breath, he asked me for money, one hundred dollars, to be exact. I guess that made sense since we had been apart for three days and he needed cash. His monetary needs were as great as my emotional poverty. I began to try to convince him that my drinking was under control, my new image and all. That was nice, but he still needed folding money. I promised I'd get it.

Lucky for me, there was a convention in town that night, which made it easy to score a few large tips. Girls were dancing everywhere to cheers, hooting, and all the four-legged animal noises one would expect in mating season. I made not only the hundred bucks for Rick, but enough for me to pay rent and buy my own food and drinks. Rick would have to acknowledge my worth this time and admit he'd made mistakes. He needed me. To help him see our destiny, I decided to gather up my things and move nearby to a motel in St. Helen's. That way, we could start to get back together. It would be his idea, of course.

Rick was happy with the news.

"It's good. You're closer. Wolf misses his mother."

I took that as an invitation to visit and suggested the coming weekend. Yes. That was acceptable.

On Saturday, I packed my things and proudly collected my deposit from the motel in Clear Bay. I had been a good tenant. It was a big deal for me to be rewarded for behaving like a normal person.

The new motel room, with its queen-sized bed, was quite nice. I popped a beer to celebrate my triumph over love and set off up the street to my family. Woofie was delirious to see me, but Rick was nowhere around. I hung out with my dog for a while, drank my way through a six-pack, and left. There wasn't any time to feel dejected. I had only been at work an hour when Rick called. Apparently, it was urgent.

"You gotta come home!"

"*What's wrong?*"

"Nothin'. Just come home. I'll tell you when you get here."

Home. The word sounded sweeter than I had imagined. Whatever was waiting for me there, I had to be part of it. I wanted to belong. After begging off work, I threw the rest of my evening's six-pack in the car and drove madly down the highway. It was early evening when I pulled into the driveway to find Rick and Billy Lee sitting outside drinking.

"What's wrong?" I called, barely out of the car.

Rick ambled over to greet me, arms open for a hug, albeit one hand was still clutching a beer can.

"Nothing. Like I told you, I just wanted to see you."

I was flabbergasted, caught between rage and love.

"Glade City," he said. "I just wanted you to hear the good news. I've joined up. They're sending me north to Glade City."

The bike club had accepted him. Not exactly the young executive with an important transfer and promotion, nevertheless, he was eager to share his acceptance with me, knowing I'd approve and rejoice. Rick would be a "probate" (on approval). After all, they didn't just accept *anyone.*

"Lennie, too. They need him, too."

Once again, Rick couldn't do anything on his own. By now, I was curious.

"Where do I come in on this?" I'm sure my sarcasm wasn't missed. What was I? His cheerleader?

"You need to stay here," he explained. "Hold down the fort for a few weeks." I could feel myself sinking. "Then," he added, "I'll come get you. We'll go back up with the camper."

Hmm, maybe this was a good plan.

For the time being, I'd stay behind on my own without supervision. At least I had a vehicle. I could shop, rest, eat, and sleep when I pleased.

"Okay!"

Over the next six weeks, Billy Lee lurked around me protectively, but my time alone was worth it. Every several days, Rick would place a call next door to Gertie requesting money from me. I'd send it via Western Union. In turn, I'd get compliments.

"The guys up here think you are one really cool ol' lady in how you take care of me!"

Wonderful. Somebody appreciated me.

What a shame. I saw friends, but soul-destroyers awaited me. Unseen, they were already lining up on the roadside of my life to help me complete my self-destruction. And I'd find most of them in Glade City.

38

Six weeks later, as promised, Rick was back in our driveway, dismounting from his bike. After my brief freedom, I was lonely and glad to see him. Had there been any other girls in his life during all that time?

"Only one," he assured me. "A stripper at the local club. See? You worry too much." Their relationship was impersonal, "strictly casual." Besides, it was in my best interest not to care. Translated, that meant shut up. It was my reputation at center stage, anyway. The guys in Glade City had praised me as a righteous ol' lady who sent money. I was already a star. Even so, I was still terrified of meeting these people. Uncertainty and self-doubt had returned as soon as Rick opened the door.

With our few belongings packed into the camper, including the new sheets and pillowcases I had splurged on (much to Rick's disapproval) and the pots and pans he decided to steal from our rented home (much to *my* disapproval), we set out. My worries sat right up front with me. We had stolen goods with us, and I obsessed about being caught and put in jail before we even reached our destination. Rick said my worries were stupid. Perhaps he was right. Have another drink. Don't think, don't feel. Just drink.

We were on our way in Swamp Slut, dragging the trailer and the bike behind. I had a stack of questions to last all the way down the highway.

"So, what are they like, these people in Glade City? Where will we live? Is there anyone there I can be friends with?"

The trip would take about four and a half hours. Rick simply patted my knee and reminded me that things would be fine. He was always right, wasn't he? Besides, I was the "righteous ol' lady." Everyone would love me on sight. There were other ol' ladies there. We'd all be friends.

"But, where will we stay?"

"At the clubhouse. In the camper."

"Is the clubhouse like the one here?"

"No, way nicer."

"Nicer?"

"Yeah, it's a real house. Mack lives there with his ol' lady, Vicki. He's the vice-president and my 'father.' He's responsible for me."

"And…the house. What's it like?"

"It's off the main road, surrounded by bush. It's got farm fields behind and a big, open space where we can park the camper. We can even run an electric line from the bar so we can have power."

"A bar?" My ears perked up.

Well, maybe this wouldn't be so bad after all.

"Yeah, it's attached to the house, but bitches aren't allowed to get their own brews. Only brothers can do that."

Bitches and brothers? He had picked up a new vocabulary. The significance of the titles made me nervous. "What if I wanted a beer?"

"One of us would get it for you."

So, I was a child. The "brothers" would be my guardians. As my mind filtered these thoughts, I wondered what else I was in for.

"Where do I shower and go to the bathroom?"

"In the house."

And how I hated imposing on people! My upbringing had taught me not to inconvenience anyone.

What if I really had to go and someone else was already using the bathroom? Where would I wait? If I did, would somebody get mad at me?

I really needed a drink, right away.

"It's hot!" I complained, hoping Rick would pick up on the cue.

"Yep, sure is."

"Just let me know when you're thirsty," I offered. "You can pull over, and I'll go to the back and get you something to drink."

The game was on. I was craving a beer, but I had to make him feel he needed it, not me. It's the great skill of salespeople and alcoholics. Let the other guy initiate action. It proves they're the weak ones. I had set the idea. Time and a few more miles would do the work for me.

"I'm fine," he assured me, gruffly.

Damn. I'd have to wait. Was he making me wait? Probably.

Miles passed. I tried again. "How ya doin'? This is a long ride."

"Oh, I could use something to eat. Gettin' hungry!"

Good. That meant we had to stop.

"I could use the bathroom, too."(Translation: I could use a beer, you idiot. A friggin' beer! How long until I could have a cold one in my hand to calm me down?)

After what felt a very long time, we found a restaurant and I was able to quench my thirst before setting off again. Rick pulled the cooler from the back. I was relaxed enough to resume my interrogation. With a few drinks to guide me, I could deal with the facts.

"Tell me about Mack. He's your sponsor, right?"

"Yeah, Bone wanted to be, but he can't because he's the chapter president and the regional president, too."

"Oh. What does that mean?"

"It means he's a pretty important guy."

I tried to sound impressed that such an influential person liked Rick. Regardless of how I felt about it, I knew it was a prestige thing with him.

"Tell me about Bone."

"Well, Mack and his ol' lady live at the clubhouse, but Bone and his ol' lady, Dixie, have their own place. Bone's a good guy, and you'll like Dixie. Mack's teenage son is living with them at the clubhouse right now. Dodge."

"His name's Dodge?"

"Yeah. Hey, did I tell you my new name? It's Flash. Don't ever call me Gypsy again."

Like I ever called him anything except Rick.

"*Flash?*"

"Bone calls me Flash, 'cause he says I'm one flashy motherfucker!" His face was alive with the flattery of it all.

Where did I fit in? Who were these larger-than-life people I had to cope with?

"Who else is in this club?" I wondered aloud.

"Wart, for one. He's Lennie's sponsor, but he lives out back in a yellow school bus."

"Oh. And does Wart have an ol' lady?"

"Nah, but he's looking."

"How about Lennie?"

"No." Rick shifted in his seat a bit to give me a sideways look of amusement. Was I that worried about girlfriends?

"How do they live?" I wanted to know. "Don't they need money?" I knew that the club members didn't work for a living. They lived off their women.

"We support them."

My greatest fear: *We.* That meant my money would be going to support Rick's new friends. What else was new!

"How does that work? Do we just *give* them money?" I asked, bracing for the answer.

"No, no, no. Every week at our club meeting, brothers only, we pay our club dues and the money is used to buy food, pay for the clubhouse, support the brothers…"

"How much?"

A confident smile spread across Rick's face. "That's not for you to know!"

I reached behind the seat for another beer. This was looking worse and worse. "Okay, who else is in the club?"

"Diesel, the ex-Navy guy. Him and his ol' lady got two kids or something, but I think they're going to live with her mother."

"That's probably a good idea." (Children in a motorcycle gang?) "Anybody else?"

"Nope. That's it. That's all of us."

"I can see why they needed you in Glade City."

Another beer would keep me from jumping straight out on the road. As the miles sped past, I was beginning to panic. The only thing holding me together was the thought that Rick and I were back together.

"Where will I work?"

"At the bar. With the other ol' ladies."

"Where?" Oh, please, not at the clubhouse!

"Up the street. Vicki will show ya when we get there."

I was supposed to feel sheltered and tried to be comforted with that while I took a few more pulls on my beer and watched for a while as the flat scenery along the highway rolled by. Rick must have been feeling the monotony as well because he broke the silence with another surprise.

"Look," he said, picking up a rag between us on the bench seat to reveal an old gun. "We're gonna show you how to use this."

"You did already, remember? You showed me how to shoot in St. Helen's."

"Nah, this is different. Bone gave it to me. Shoots black powder instead of bullets. Makes it legal to carry because it's an antique. It's got to be cleaned all the time, though. I'll show you how."

"Anything else I should know?"

"Uh, yeah. I've got guard duty tomorrow night. It was supposed to be tonight, but they switched me because you were coming up."

How thoughtful. "Gee, you have to stay up all night by yourself?"

Rick reached over and playfully squeezed my knee. "Not all by myself. You'll be staying up with me, Pooh. While I watch, you can clean the house."

Anger burned in my chest like acid. I didn't have to say anything. Maybe he sensed my reaction by my rapid breathing or the rising flames along my neck.

"Don't worry," he said. "You'll get used to it."

39

Somewhere on the outskirts of Glade City, Rick pulled off the road and traveled down a long driveway crudely cut through the bush. The going was slow; our belongings clunked and shifted over every pothole and, while he concentrated on steering, my impatience grew. I just wanted to get there and get the preliminaries over so that I knew where I stood in this situation. Self-doubt was taking over.

At the end of the driveway stood a plain, wooden cabin surrounded by sand. Rick headed to the far back corner and attempted a U-turn, presumably to position the camper, but the wheels spun into the sand. We were stuck. Embarrassed by his helplessness in front of the brothers, he panicked.

"Fuck! Get out. Get *out!*"

Never taking his eyes off the windshield, he reached sideways and shoved my shoulder.

"But, I don't know anybody…"

"*Shaddup!*" he screamed. "Just get the fuck *out!*"

By now, everyone was outside watching the sand whip off the back wheels, wondering why the girl and the dog had jumped from the truck and darted away to stand by a fence.

Two guys trotted toward the camper. One had long, matted blond hair and a reddish beard and moustache. The other had a brown ponytail and a Fu Manchu moustache. Both were yelling directions to Rick in that macho "we're in this together" way that guys do, hardly the insulting shouts a woman driver would have to endure for her misjudgments. When the crisis was finally over and the trailer was in place, it was time to meet "the folks." I was summoned from my retreat by the fence.

Wolf bolted ahead of us to the stable that had been converted to a bar. I followed behind Rick, who was already in stride with Mack, the Fu Manchu guy, and Bone, the one with the tangled blond hair. Inside the stable, Wolf already had his front paws up on the bar and was slurping up a vodka and orange juice. All the guys were laughing and slapping Rick on the back, complimenting him on how well the dog fit in. The wheels-in-the-sand episode was immediately over. No jokes, no ribbing about it, just a glad welcome. Then it was time to turn attention to my presence.

Rick, er, Flash, introduced me around the bar while I stood quietly sipping a can of beer and trying my best to fade into the background. Surrounding me was a forest of heavy, bearded men, each wearing a black leather vest with a patch on the back signifying their membership. While I gratefully started to inhale my third get-acquainted beer, a pickup truck pulled into the yard. A tiny brunette with waist-length, wavy hair jumped out. This was Vicki. She had come home early from work to welcome me, but no sooner had she arrived, then both of us were sent back in the truck to the store.

I never got to shop much, so the thought of a big grocery store with shiny lights and organized shelves, real people, and the scents of fresh produce appealed to me. At the same time, I felt very awkward leaving with Vicki. For me, it meant a forced get-acquainted moment with a stranger. Fortunately, she opened the conversation.

"How long ya been here?"

"Oh, Rick and I got here about an hour ago."

"Rick?" she replied, amused. "You mean Flash?"

"Uh, yeah. Flash."

"He's really cute," she volunteered. "We think he's the cutest one!" Her eyes were sparkling when she said it. Was this a test? I held my cool and changed the subject.

"You're Mack's ol' lady, right?" There, that would remind her of her own territory.

"Yeah."

Small pause while I searched for something else to say. "So, I guess I'll be going to work with you."

She accepted the new topic and ran with it. I needed to know what was in store for me and I listened gratefully. "We work just up the street. I'll show you when we get there. It's not bad. You have to take your turn on stage, but you make all your cash in the table dances."

Here we go again. How was I going to manage this time?

"Okay, good. Ten bucks a dance, right?" I replied knowingly.

She gave me a quick glance before she set me straight.

"Ten? No, no, three dollars a dance. Two for five. But before you even start, you gotta go downtown and pay eighty bucks for a license. Then you get your picture taken."

Eighty dollars for a license? Three dollars a dance? Oh my God! I had avoided having to be a dancer for all those months in Clear Bay. Now it looked like this would be my payback. I had to catch my breath before I spoke again.

"Do you mean I have to dance naked for a measly three dollars?"

"Ah no, not naked. You wear panty hose and a T-strap."

"Panty hose?" I wasn't sure whether to feel relieved or weirded out.

"Yeah, you roll them down in front and back and pin them. I'll show you."

I thought I'd wait to see how uncomfortable that felt. What really concerned me was cash.

"So, in a night, how much do you make?"

"About a hundred bucks. Sometimes more if you got regulars."

My mind was whirring with calculations. Okay. A hundred dollars meant forty table dances. "How many turns on stage?"

"Three."

Three. Just like Clear Bay. I hated this already. How was I going to avoid dancing this time?

We finished with the business discussions and went into personal histories, probably searching for common ground. Vicki had been around for a while. When her ex was killed (in the line of duty?), she was moved to Glade City and given to Mack.

Given? Like an orphaned *cat?*

I felt sorry for her. The pity helped ease my misgivings about our friendship, but it did nothing to relieve my fear of what I had gotten myself into. That night, with all the whooping and hollering of drunken bikers in the background, I tossed and turned trying to sleep, wishing I had enough alcohol at hand to help me pass out.

40

Moments of conscience told me that I had caused my own problems. What troubled me more was that I didn't have any solutions. When a loud wake-up rap on the side of the camper startled me the next morning, I wanted to dive under the blanket and stay there. It was Sunday, and the boys wanted to go for a run. That meant they would load their ol' ladies on bikes and take off for unknown destinations. I didn't want to join them. I wanted my old life, the one in Clear Bay in the small security of Gertie's compound. I woke up Rick and told him we had to get ready. He bounded out of bed, and we headed to the house for showering. Given that I had to wash and dress him, we went together, even though the bathroom in that house gave me the creeps. Somebody's ol' lady had committed suicide in there, which caused a new rule about bathroom locks. There were none.

I didn't get the privilege of curling up for the day with my dog and a case of beer. These people, as Rick explained, were now my family: Bone, Mack, Wart, Diesel, among others, and their respective ol' ladies. I hardly had time to imagine what my parents would say. After a liquid breakfast at the bar, we had to ride.

On the road, oddly enough, I felt safe in the center of the pack, protected by the powerful roar of engines around me. The stares of people on the street and in cars made me feel like part of a royal motorcade. Separate. Elite. After what felt like a very long time, we drove to the end of a gravel drive and stopped at a run-down bar. More like a shack than a bar, it was furnished with plain chairs, tables, a jukebox, and a pool table. It was good to set foot on firm ground and let the vibrations in my middle die down while I sipped a can of beer and stretched the cramps from my legs. After the long ride, I needed the drink to quiet the insecurity of being the new kid on the block. Feeling nostalgic and wanting something familiar for comfort, I asked Rick for a quarter to play our song and pointed to the jukebox. He doled it out with the attitude of indulging a tiresome child, but I didn't care. Willie Nelson was waiting for me. He would sing "Always on My Mind," and I would bite back tears and try not to think or feel. After a while, Vicki and I talked a bit, but mostly I kept quiet, trying not to attract attention. Dread of saying the wrong thing was always present. Silence was best.

The being invisible routine was going pretty well. After about my third beer, I realized no one was looking in my direction anyway. I could breathe normally, that is, until Rick mentioned that his bike didn't seem to sound right. Maybe it was the transmission. I thought we were just making conversation when he suggested I have a look at it.

"*Now*? I don't think that's a good idea."

"You put it in, Pebbly-Pooh. You should check it out."

I knew better than to argue. I hadn't put the tranny in. He had. He was trying to impress his friends with the usefulness of his ol' lady who fixes bikes. He'd show them by example, even allowing me another beer to take outside. Well, since I didn't really want to be inside with them, I went willingly to the bike. It would be good to be alone and quiet.

I set (oh, so carefully) my beer on the gravel, removed the tool pouch from the handlebars, and slid under the bike with a wrench to look at the transmission. I truly wasn't sure what needed to be done, but I had been helping him build and rebuild engines for years; something would come to me. I didn't want to screw up, though. It could cost us our lives.

Without warning, Bone grabbed my ankles and was dragging me across the gravel parking lot, cursing and spilling my beer. He let go of my feet and sat so heavily on my chest that I could barely breathe.

"Cunt!" That word I so hated, so loud in my face. "Fucking cunt! What the hell do you think you're doing, huh? No one touches a brother's *bike*!"

More screaming. This time, it was Rick, running to the scene.

"No, Bone. *No!* I told her to do it…I told her!" Rick was pleading, gulping for air, trying to stand between us. "She's a crack bike mechanic. She was the one who installed the transmission!"

Bone stood up, crazy with anger, and glared down at me.

"Don't ever touch a bike again!" he shrieked.

He must have been certain that he had caught an ol' lady in the act of sabotage. Did he think I was suicidal? Rick and I would have hit the pavement together had I been playing that game. There was more yelling, this time at Rick. While Rick stood back and took the blast, I fumbled for my beer can. A small crowd was watching from the doorway of the bar, but no one stepped forward. Bone kept shouting for what seemed forever. I hated the outburst, hated the unfairness of the whole incident. When he left, we were alone beside the bike.

"Why did he do that?" I cried, and apologized for whatever I had caused.

"He has to. He's chapter president. He was protecting my life," Rick said simply.

"From *me*?"

"Yeah, he doesn't understand. He'll get to know you and love you, just like I do. You'll see."

I doubted it. Now I understood my worth in this kind of family. Wolf ranked higher than I ever would. I was also becoming aware of what my defiance would mean for Rick.

Our next stop was a bike shop in Glade City where the extra two beers I drank after the Bone episode hit my bladder. Embarrassed because I had to go to the bathroom, I waited as long as I could before asking where it was. The group had all piled into the shop to view the merchandise, but I held onto Rick's hand and balanced a beer in the other.

"I have to pee," I whispered when I could no longer stand it. "Where's the bathroom?"

"I dunno," he said. Before I could stop him, he was hollering across the shop to the owner. "Hey, Jim! My ol' lady's gotta *squat*! Where is it?"

"Outside. Don't have one in here."

Rick turned to me. "There you go."

I was mortified. The last thing I wanted to do was draw more attention to myself. I ran outside to find some privacy in the tall grass. Gladly I would have stayed in the yard, alone with my anger over Bone's attack. What I couldn't understand was how he could get so many grown men to cower in his presence. I saw only a filthy, matted-haired old warrior who fought with everyone around him. He had grown children somewhere and a four-year-old with Dixie, his new "wife," who was younger than me. Rumor had it that Bone never showered. Standing close to him confirmed that. I didn't like him, and I certainly didn't like the ultra-macho way Rick behaved with me when he was around Bone.

Boots, jeans, and a black leather jacket can be very warm under the hot Florida sun. When my beer was finished and I couldn't stand the heat anymore, I ventured back inside. When I reached the door, laughter rolled out at me.

"Hey, cunt!" Bone was behind the counter. He was calling to me with that word again.

"Get over here, cunt. It's your turn."

For what? I wondered.

I scanned the room, trying to figure it out. And there, on the other side of the room, were Vicki and another ol' lady, Paula, backs to the wall and topless. Dixie was walking over to join them. Her upper body was also bare, but when she turned to face me, I was horrified. Hanging from her nipples were vise-grips.

Bone was swearing again at me, expecting me to be next in line for his sick idea of pleasure.

"Get the fuck over here. Now, you fucking cunt!" He was snapping another pair of vise-grips at me.

"No," I said as steadily as I could and stalked outside.

As soon as I stepped over the doorstep, I shuddered with what I had just seen. How those grips must hurt! Who was crazy enough to allow that to happen? This couldn't be real.

Rick hurried out behind me, followed by Mack. They both started in at me for my stupidity, my stubbornness. Apparently, no one—absolutely no one—ever refused Bone! I kept my eyes downcast, rubbing semicircles into the sand with the toe of my boot. Inside, I was feeling triumphant for crossing that line. Not even Rick or Mack had the guts to do what I had just done: I had rebelled against a rebel. When Rick finally saw I wasn't budging to submit to the vise-grips, he pushed me onto the bike and we sped off down the road. I didn't care what anybody thought. I had done the right thing.

Back at the clubhouse, Rick continued reaming me out. He screamed, he paced, and he ranted while I remained locked in silence.

"All the other ol' ladies were doin' it! What the hell is wrong with you?"

That speech again. I couldn't answer his delicate questions. I was afraid of what the vise-grips would do to my breasts. If I told him that, he'd want to test out the theory. My nipples would fall off. Maybe because the other girls had borne children they weren't so sensitive. I didn't know.

Rick did his best to frighten me. Would Bone kill me? Who cared? Maybe I was better off dead anyway. My family would be spared any more grief on my account. I suspected Rick's greatest concern was that I had shamed him. Whatever, I wasn't changing my position.

"Maybe you'd better get out of sight for the rest of the day," Rick said nervously.

Personally, I was thrilled at the prospect of being left alone.

"Can I take some beer with me?"

"Yeah, yeah. I guess."

Yippee! I win! I win! I could mind my own time without having to play anymore stupid games.

When the motorcycles finally roared in, I was outside with Rick and Wolf drinking beer. I quickly scooped a couple more cans and flew into the camper where I could watch the proceedings through a narrow rear window. One by one, the brothers stopped and dismounted. Rick walked over to greet them. Almost immediately, Bone resumed yelling and waving his arms. I couldn't hear what he was saying, but it caused Rick to race toward the camper.

"Run," said a voice in my head, but that would show weakness. Later in my life, I would learn that this was the only voice I should have listened to. To desert this mess and stay away from it forever was the only wisdom I would ever need. At that moment however, I pushed it away. I wasn't going to run. I'd stay and fight.

Rick burst through the camper door. "Bone wants to see you! Now!"

I rolled my eyes and followed.

"Just do what he wants!" Rick whispered and then ducked away.

Alone, I walked up to Bone and stared him firmly in the eye.

"You wanted to see me?" I asked defiantly, all the while tightening every knot in my stomach for enough support to remain standing. Outside, I was cool and calm; inside, my heart was pounding so hard I was sure he could see it through my shirt.

He bared his bad teeth and leaned into my face with his stinking breath.

"Yeah, I wanna see *you!*"

My instinct was to back up, but I resisted and held my ground. Bone began his tirade by poking me in the chest with a long, yellow fingernail.

"You think you're better than the rest of us, you worthless, low-life cunt? How old are you anyway, bitch?"

"Twenty-three."

"Well, you're too *old!* Ya hear that! You're *never* gonna make it here!"

And so it went. Really? Well guess what, you sleazy old bastard! I'll survive in spite of you. Just watch me! My thoughts were so forceful, I was almost sure he could hear me. I had to make it. If a bottom-feeding animal such as this rejected me, then I really was nothing. At the time, it seemed crucial to prove Bone wrong. That my strength was directing itself down the wrong path didn't occur to me. The very fact that I didn't crumple into some weeping mess made me proud. He hollered himself hoarse and stomped off, but his failure to break my will encouraged me to strut triumphantly to the bar past the other ol' ladies, one of whom was Bone's woman, Dixie. She was busy clucking her tongue at me when I turned and shot her a look, too.

I had faced the Beast and lived to tell the tale. From that day forward, I was no longer afraid. The battle of wills between Bone and me would rage for a long while, but ultimately he became my ally. Somehow this man and I developed a bond of mutual respect. He would become my protector, my mediator, and, later, at a club meeting, he would venture an unprecedented move which would shock the members. He would bestow on me a high club honor.

My alcohol and drug addiction would get much worse. I lived in that compound, shut out from the real world, for several years. The addictions caused me to lose my sense of time, yet they were also my coping mechanism, a way of smothering the voice in my head that begged me to run. Although I can remember many things that happened in Glade City, I can't recall whether they are in the right sequence. For that reason, the events that follow may seem disjointed, yet they speak for me from moments when I had no worth or mind.

41

My first night on the new job arrived after three hours worth of sleep. The night before, I was required to remain awake all night cleaning the clubhouse while Rick was on guard duty. Since I had no idea how or what to clean, Rick helped. By seven o'clock in the morning, I was allowed to sleep, but not before I undressed Rick and put him to bed. Later that morning, I had to go downtown to buy my license for work.

Vicki, Paula, and I went to work with a quick (and what would become routine) stop for panty hose. The bar was impressive; they sold beer, wine, and hard liquor. That meant I could have beer and shooters. My favorites! After the preliminary introductions and verification of my license with the manager, we were shown to the dressing room to get ready. Dixie was there ahead of us. She laughed mockingly when she saw me.

"How ya doin' today?" she sneered. What was that supposed to mean? How was I doing after my face-off with Bone? I decided I did not like Dixie.

As it was my first night and I wanted to look nice, I brought along my curling iron and began putting on makeup. Out of the corner of my eye, I watched Vicki load on more cosmetics than I knew existed, although she did pause to help me with the panty hose. I had been given instructions to buy sandalfoot sheers in the shade labeled "nude." Vicki showed me how to roll them down low in the front and back and pin them to hold them in place. Then she handed me a black T-strap, a sort of thong to wear over the panty hose. The gear felt so weird it was like working with a constant wedgie. My butt cheeks were already protesting with the stuffing between them. I pulled on my borrowed top, slid into four-inch heels and was ready to go…without Vicki. Apparently, she had several more coats of makeup to apply. Personally, I needed a drink. Paula was already on the small, mirrored stage doing a dance for some guy. I was left to figure out how to get myself a beer without any money.

There were three or four naval bases in town. I surveyed the room for a friendly sailor who looked generous. I settled on a young guy at the bar.

"Hi," I said in my best perky tone. Now what?

"Hey there. I haven't seen you before. Are you new?" Whew. He spoke. Now to get him to buy me a drink. I'd need at least six before I could attempt this dancing thing.

"Yeah, I'm new. This is my first night." I took a quick glance at his beer. "I'm kind of nervous."

"Oh. I'm sure you'll be fine. Where'd you work before?"

"Clear Bay." I followed his beer to his mouth and back down again.

"Clear Bay," he said and nodded. "Aren't they nude down there?"

"Yes."

"I guess this will be different for you then, right?"

I took another long look at his beer. "Yeah, I'll say. I've never danced before. I was a waitress there, so this is going to be really different." Big, forced smile. "Hopefully, I'll be okay." I was going for sympathy.

Pause in conversation. I remained at his side.

"Can I get you a drink?" he offered. Finally!

"Umm…" I hesitated, trying not to appear too eager. "Well…okay…I'll have a…umm…beer."

"Sure thing."

He ordered me one, and we introduced ourselves. That was my first hurdle of the evening. I crowded him long enough to manage a third round. Holding it in my happy hands, I excused myself and wandered around. Vicki was still in the dressing room. Guessing she had been crushed in there under all the weight of the face paint, I went back to check on her. She was busy straightening her hair.

"What's up with Dixie?" I asked, not giving away any real feelings on the subject.

"Whadda ya mean?" she frowned, leaning her head to one side.

I had to be very careful here.

"She doesn't seem very friendly, that's all."

Vicki smoothed her hair in front and back of her shoulders, neatly lining up every strand. "She's not allowed to have friends. He doesn't want her to."

I immediately understood the "he" was Bone. The ol' ladies weren't allowed to mention names in public, just in case someone could be traced through us.

"Oh," I said. "I'll remember to stay away."

"One more thing…" Vicki, her hair completed, got up and was ready to go on the floor. "Be careful," she warned. "She's like his tape recorder. She reports everything."

That was something to keep in mind. I appreciated her telling me. I was already feeling a little more comfortable by being able to drink openly and stay at least partially clothed, even though the three-dollar per dance deal still worried me. I'd have to solicit my pathetic dancing to a lot of men in an evening, and I dreaded it. Men were loathsome to me. I needed acceptance and wanted love from them, but I hated all of them. The idea of asking them for money was unjust. It put them in a position of power over me.

I wondered how anyone could do this job without being drunk. My sense of dignity wasn't ready to allow me to wriggle or jiggle in front of anyone. Instead, as the night dragged on, I searched for more pockets and more kind faces to buy me drinks. A lot of enlisted guys were in the bar, and I wasn't disappointed. By the end of the evening, I had managed to scrounge up fifteen dollars. Vicki had made nearly eight times as much.

Rick was going to be really mad.

42

When we pulled into the compound, everything was quiet. Everyone was at the house. I took my time to drop off my stuff at the camper before I joined the others and had to face Rick. Wolf was in the doorway watching for me. How I loved my good ol' doggy. He never got mad at me.

"Hello, baby!" I crooned. I patted him on his big, loveable head and kissed the top of his wet nose. The next thing I knew, I was flying backward. I hadn't even seen the fists that hit me until I was sprawled on my back in the sand and saw they belonged to Rick. Before I could react, I was snatched up and slammed into a tree.

"*What the fuck*! You say hello to a *dog* before you speak to me? What the fuck is *that!*" he bellowed.

Each sentence was punctuated by driving my face into the bark.

There was only one thought in my mind at the time: At least he wasn't mad about the fifteen dollars. Not yet, anyway. When he finally let go of the back of my neck, I slumped to the ground and lay there. That was my version of playing dead. I had learned long before that, if I seemed to be seriously hurt, even unconscious, the beating would stop. Just for good measure, he kicked me in the side. Even though I wanted to coil up against the pain, I remained still. The quiet was nice.

Maybe, just maybe, I could play on his sympathy later when I gave him the bad news about not making any money.

The front door slammed. Someone else had come out. Mack called to Rick, "What did you do? What the fuck did you *do!*"

There. Now, would someone come and help me? I stirred, hoping there were witnesses to stop Rick's brutality. My fingers traced the swelling starting to rise on one side of my face. I sat up against the dark tree trunk, bleeding from a gash in my forehead.

"Hey!" Rick was at the door, shouting into the yard. "Hey! Get in here!"

He was jerking his thumb for me to come inside. Slowly, I hauled myself toward the light. As usual, he pinched my chin and yanked it upward to inspect the results of his work. I neither spoke nor looked at him.

"Get cleaned up!" he said with disgust.

In the bathroom, I picked bark from my cheek, pressed the blood from my forehead with a towel, and, through the eye that wasn't swelling, I could see the bruises beginning to form along my jawline. I took as long as I could before returning to the living room under the glare of bare lightbulbs and staring faces. When I finally came out, Rick once again took my chin in hand, this time more carefully, and made that "why did you make me do this" expression on his face. It was his version of concern.

"I'm going to sleep," I mumbled. "May I please have a beer to take with me?" Women weren't allowed behind the bar; I couldn't get one myself. I didn't need any more trouble that night. It was wise to ask permission.

"Yeah. I guess. Lennie…?"

"Yep," said Lennie. He was on guard duty. It was his job to get me a beer.

"G'night," I said to no one in particular and started to the door.

"Hey!"

Now what? I walked back to Rick to kiss him on the cheek. This time, I looked him dead in the eye. I wanted him to know I was hurt and angry. An average human would have realized that much and felt some sort of shame. Not Rick. He didn't reveal a flyspeck of guilt. Never did.

The girls were supposed to address everyone. Ignoring a brother was another punishable crime. Not to cause another scene, I bade everyone in turn a good night and left. I'm sure Vicki wanted to come after me, but she wasn't allowed. Club rules. Keeping the women's emotions isolated prevented them from bonding. How could we protest if each of us stood alone?

I trailed behind Lennie out to the bar, hating my life and clueless how to change it. When we were a safe distance away from the house, he said, "You never learn, do you?"

"Learn what? Not to pet my dog?" I mistrusted Lennie. In my estimation, he was weak and stupid.

"You know what I mean."

"Well, then, I guess I don't," I shot back.

I knew that I wasn't supposed to irritate Flash, yet I never knew what would set him off. Lennie, in his dull way, was trying to help me, even as he shook his head in disbelief when I asked for two beers. He slipped me the second one and told me to hide it. Nurse Lennie. He must have realized I needed an extra tranquilizer.

The next morning, I awoke to a steady throbbing along my cheek and jaw. Although I hadn't heard him come in, Rick was beside me sound asleep. When he woke, would he be sorry, or would he even remember what he'd done to me?

We had been in this place less than a week. It wasn't hard to imagine that I could probably die here and be replaced quickly. I rolled over to look outside the camper window. Wart was making his way over to knock at our door. I got up to greet him.

"Get Flash out here," he said. "Bone wants to talk to him."

I nodded and walked back to Rick, who was by now awake.

"Who was that?" he mumbled.

"Wart. Bone wants you," I said without any tone to my voice.

While he sat up, I turned to gather his clothes so I could dress him. He was like my child. There were times I even had to help him pee or he'd miss completely. After I finished lacing up his motorcycle boots, I returned to lie across the bed. The window there afforded me a good view of his encounter with Bone, who stood impatiently waiting. The window was cracked open just enough to eavesdrop.

"What the fuck happened with you and your ol' lady last night?" Bone had his hands on his hips. Rick's back was to me. I couldn't hear his response, but I heard Bone loud and clear.

"You can't be doing that man! What if the cops see her? You wanna end up in jail?"

Wow. Was I being defended? Great. Somebody was finally telling Rick he was wrong, and he had to take it.

But then, Bone made his point.

"You can't hit her in the face, man! It shows!"

Oh. It wasn't that Rick beat me that anyone should feel concern, it was that he left clear *evidence* for anyone to see. Soon afterward, I was summoned to Bone for a face inspection, which took only a few seconds before he assigned Vicki to damage control. She would show me how to hide the injuries with makeup. Until then, I was set to work sweeping the camper.

The girls at the bar felt sorry for me, as did the customers. Getting beaten up was at least worth something while the cuts were fresh. People were nice to me. They gave me money and beer.

I wanted to get away.

"Clear Bay," I told Rick. "If I can work back there, I can make some serious money, not like here."

I think Rick suspected my real motive for going to Clear Bay. My life as an ol' lady was an ongoing nightmare. I was told what to do, when, where, and how long to do it. That included sleep and my every waking hour. I was told when to eat and how much to eat. Even my hair was under supervision. Bone demanded I curl it for work so I would "look better."

Rick agreed to my suggestion. For a month, I'd spend half the week in Clear Bay and half the week in Glade City. Life was almost tolerable until I returned early one night, happy and with some good money in my purse. Lennie was in the yard, waving his arms at me to stop.

"The ol' ladies are at Bone's. You have to go there!"

"Why?"

"Just go!"

"Where's Flash?"

"With us. Now go!"

When I pulled up at Bone's, Dixie was in the yard. She was standing with a shotgun pointed directly at my truck and held it there for several heartbeats before putting it down and motioning me to come inside. Vicki was sitting with her arm around Paula, but no one was volunteering any information.

"What's going on?"

Paula was staring at the floor looking grim. Dixie gestured at me, jerking her head toward the kitchen. I headed with her to the back of the house.

"There was a fight in the bar," she said, leaning back to catch whether Paula and Dixie were listening. "Diesel (Paula's man) got stabbed."

"Our bar? The one we work in?"

"Yeah."

"That's why Paula's upset?"

"Yeah."

"Is he bad?"

"Don't know. Mack and Bone are stitching him up now."

I was visualizing Diesel being laid out on the pool table with Bone and Mack playing surgeon with a sewing needle and fishing line when Bone drove up. All of us knew who it was because we could see him through the front window. That meant that Dixie had known it was me when I drove in. She merely wanted to have some fun at my expense. I really didn't like the woman.

Diesel was going to be okay, or so Bone told Paula when he pulled her to one side. The rest of us got the news secondhand.

Because of the stabbing incident, the girls weren't allowed back at that bar. Instead, we could pass the time cleaning and packing up to move to a new location. The whole club was moving to an abandoned, condemned farmhouse. There would be power because Bone had managed to get a generator somewhere, but there wouldn't be any running water. The toilet was a group bucket. Without running water, we had to find our own means to bathe. The guys immediately set up a bar with beer, soda, and bottled water. They were already settled, but my mind reeled. I never thought I could stoop to living in a camper, yet this…this was ten times more disheartening. This was nearly homeless. To make matters worse, within hours of arriving, Rick became dangerously ill. His skin was yellow, and he couldn't stand up. He said his muscles were mush. I went directly to Bone.

"We need to take Rick to a hospital." It was all I could think to say.

He must have read the panic in my voice or seen it in my eyes.

"Take him," he said.

43

The choice without insurance was a state hospital. Even then they could turn us away, but they didn't. We waited hours with Rick flopping over in a wheelchair before they called his name. He was in their hands now, which gave me some time to go to the bar for a beer or two. At least, that was my plan, but Rick wouldn't let me out of his sight. He insisted I remain right by his side, my hand locked in his while he went through blood tests and a camera being inserted down his throat while he gagged and heaved. Twelve hours later, we had a diagnosis. Rick's liver was failing. He needed bed rest and no alcohol. His drinking could be fatal.

Then what? Without Rick between me and the rest of the brothers, I'd be passed around like a jug of whiskey.

No, I wouldn't have that. I'd need to do something. But what?

I dressed Rick and took him home. The way I saw it, there was only one thing I could do. Talk to Bone. The guys would have to protect Rick from the booze. But then, what were the odds of being hurt for my troubles? I was ratting on Flash. He had expressly told me not to tell the others what the doctor had said.

"Get me a Jack Daniels!" Rick insisted as soon as he rolled into bed.

So soon? I was standing between Rick's life and death, yet he saw me as the enemy.

"No! You heard the doctor!"

"Pffct! They don't know what they're talking about. They're all quacks! Get me a drink!"

"No!"

"Bitch! A Jack and Coke, *now!*"

"Please, Rick, no! I love you. I need you. How can I stand by and watch you kill yourself?"

"Okay," he said after a few moments of considering what I'd said. "I guess Jack's kinda heavy. How about a nice glass of red wine?"

Because I was familiar with that gnawing feeling of desperation when I needed a drink, I felt sorry for him.

"Okay," I said at last. "I'll get it."

And while I was out doing that, I'd talk to Bone. I found him at the new makeshift bar.

"It's about time you got back," he barked. "How's Flash?"

"Okay, I guess. Can I talk to you?" I kept my eyes averted and my voice low. This was not the time for defiance.

"Whaddya want?"

"Uh, I need to talk in private," I said, pointing to the door.

"Fucking cunt! What now?" Bone stormed out and glared at me, taking his usual stance of leaning back on one leg and keeping his hands firmly planted on his hips.

"I need your help."

"What for!" His scowl deepened. "What's wrong with Flash?" he demanded.

"Well…he sent me to get him a drink…and, um…it's his liver. He has to stop drinking and get some rest or he'll get worse. It could even kill him. I don't know what to do."

Bone sighed with annoyance and stared into the distance.

"Whaddya expect me to do?" he snarled.

I shrugged, hoping he'd offer something.

"What did the doctor say?"

Once again, I detailed the situation: the liver, the alcohol, the need to abstain. He nodded and then appeared surprised.

"And he sent you here to talk to me?"

I was into it now. I might as well finish the mission.

"No, no, he didn't. It's just that…he wants me to bring him a bottle of red wine. I don't want to piss him off, but I don't know what to do!"

He paced back and forth as grandly as a general planning some important strategic attack, glancing alternately at the ground and at me. I had acknowledged his authority.

"Take him the bottle," he decided. "I'll talk to him tomorrow." Whether he did or not is anyone's guess. I had to work the next day at a new bar the guys had found for us.

The manager at the new bar expected an audition. Dixie was already there by the time Vicki and I arrived. From what I saw initially, it seemed a larger, nicer place. Like the other bar, dances were still three dollars or two for five, but what did that matter? My performance as a dancer was nonexistent. I considered myself neither sexy nor seductive. The thought of gyrating and swaying in front of strange men, pretending to be something I wasn't, was revolting. The manager smiled broadly while I struggled through an embarrassing attempt on stage.

He pronounced my act "very smooth. Like a ballerina."

Given that I didn't have any hips to bump, grind, or otherwise thrust in some-one's line of vision, ballerina would have to do, although I'm not sure I believed him. About an hour later, the manager approached me to ask me if I'd ever been a waitress. Why yes! As luck would have it, I had!

The next day, Rick instructed me to leave earlier for work so I could join a gymnasium.

What? Work out? I was only ninety-two pounds.

"Why?" I wondered aloud.

"So you can *shower.*" He peeled out thirty dollars for the monthly member-ship fee and added, "You don't want to go to work stinking, do you?"

Oh. Since he had put it so pleasantly, and since it would mean more time away from that hovel and any stupid chores he and the brothers could dream up, I agreed. For the entire month before we moved to a new clubhouse, the gym was a blessing. Vicki and I joined a new aerobics class and even tried the workout equipment. Rick let me continue my membership for a while after we moved. He said it made a difference and poked my stomach. What that meant, I didn't know.

We moved into another new clubhouse on a Sunday to coincide with the girls' day off. Much of the labor, especially the cleaning, was the responsibility of the "bitches." My special chore was to scrub the bathroom with a toothbrush: floor, bath tiles, sink, and toilet. It was a real bathroom, even though it lacked a lock on the door. No lock meant no privacy in the shower, even from the tiny green tree frogs who'd find their way inside to sit on the windowsill and watch. Once we were all settled, Bone produced the rules:

1. No women (*He used the c word—it still revolts me*) allowed behind the bar.

2. No women using or answering the phone. (*It was a pay phone.*)

3. No women in the kitchen unless told to be there.

4. No women in any of the bedrooms unless invited by a brother. (*No thanks. I'd sooner stay in my camper anyway.*)

5. Nobody walks outside at night without a flashlight. Especially after rain.

The walking around at night thing was about snakes, specifically the poison-ous water moccasins that swim in fresh water. I had already seen their kind twist-ing their way through swimming holes in St. Helen's. The wisdom of Bone's rule came home to me one night when I stepped into our camper and met one nearly eye to eye as I bent to push aside Rick's boots. It was coiled under our table, its white mouth opened wide in my direction. I jumped back outside, screaming my way to the clubhouse. As true knights in shining armor, every one of the guys trooped out to the rescue. I expected they'd take out the heavy artillery and shoot up the camper, but all they did was lift the snake out on the end of a broom. Good thing I got enough booze that night to pass out. I would have never slept without help.

44

My trips back to Clear Bay began to taper off as I settled into the new bar. Slowly, I began to understand how Dixie and Vicki made so much money without touching any alcohol. It was Vicki who shared the secret with me. Both were into cocaine.

What? I didn't think the ol' ladies were supposed to be into drugs.

"How do you get away with it?" I asked.

Vicki shrugged. "We just stop doing it an hour before we go home...and, besides, we don't do that much. Just a line or two."

"Who do you get it from?"

"Dixie."

"Dixie! Does *he* know?"

"God, no! He'd kill her!"

This was just ideal. Dixie, the proud and haughty one who had shown only contempt for me ever since I arrived, had a bad secret. I waited until she was alone at the bar before I struck back at her the only way I could.

"Hey! Got a line?" I asked, smugly.

Her face went ashen. "Who told *you*?"

"What does it matter?" I said. "I just wanted to do a line."

"Yeah?" Round-eyed with fear, she knew she was at my mercy.

Five minutes later, I followed her, as instructed, to the restroom. I peered under a stall to find her familiar brown heels and pink leg warmers. Fashionably speaking, it was the 1980s.

"That you?" she called.

"Yeah."

She opened the metal door and handed me a rolled-up dollar bill. On the toilet roll inside the stall was a line of cocaine. I only had to snort it with the bill and exit.

"I'll pay you after I make the money."

"Whatever," she answered and left the room.

Within minutes, the white powder was in my system, my heart racing with its energy. I felt glorious! Mighty! Invincible!

As I coasted onto the floor, I offered Dixie a smile. Now, I had a reason to make money. Alcohol was good, but my new habit would require more money and attention. Rick had always warned me that I'd like the stuff too much. He was right. I liked it way too much. It was an instant passion.

I was soon splitting baggies of cocaine with my pal Dixie. We were secret conspirators, but I became much more hooked than she was and much more quickly. She didn't drink and could stop snorting before we went home. I drank heavily, anything in a bottle or glass I could wrap my hands around. It fortified me to keep my mind on the real issue of doing coke right up to the last minute before leaving the bar. The manager who checked in for second shift was best friends with a major dealer in Columbian cocaine. Often I got the stuff for free, it was so plentiful. The trick was to disguise my condition when I arrived home by collecting my beer and heading straight to bed.

On our Sunday runs when we hit the highways on the bikes, I could hide my drinking in the bathroom of whatever sleazy bar we happened to find. The club runs were longer. One member would stay behind to guard the clubhouse while everyone else would go "on vacation," visiting other clubs in various cities. It sounded like fun until Vicki told me that the ol' ladies would be expected to dance naked on the bar and afterward were traded like sports cards. I decided not to be included.

"Uh, Rick…" I began. "I've been thinking about the club run to Orlando."

"Yeah. What about it?"

"It sounds like a lot of fun, but…"

Rick looked up from his reclining position in a lawn chair, puzzled. "But what?"

"It's just that…umm…I've been starting to get some regulars at the bar. There's a ship docking this weekend. That means money coming in, and I thought, well, I'd just like to stay here and make some good cash." It was such a lie I was surprised he didn't catch on. "And you know, Bone doesn't like me anyway. I don't want to cause you anymore trouble if I do something stupid." He screwed up his face while he considered what I was saying. Before he could answer, I quickly added, "And someone needs to look after Woofie."

"How will you get to work and back?"

"Oh, I think Vicki's staying here, too."

"Okay then. If Vicki's staying, then so can you."

"Good," I said, carefully disguising my triumph. "I'll make lots of money, you'll see."

Rick smiled. He was satisfied, but I was feeling conflicted. I won, but how was I going to get my hands on the "lots of money" I had just promised?

I found another way to earn love points. Vicki had overheard Mack saying that Rick was up for getting his "patch"—full club membership, which meant a graduation of sorts and something of a celebration. At the end of our five liberated days, Vicki and I went shopping. I bought Rick a congratulations card and a lighter. I waited while it was inscribed with his club name followed by the date. We rewarded ourselves by going out to brunch at a real restaurant. Later in the afternoon, when we heard the rumbling of the bikes returning home, I ran into the camper to wait. Rick hadn't yet revealed his honor, so he was thrilled when he stepped inside to see my party decorations with streamers and a handmade sign announcing his new position.

"How did you know?" he asked, laughing and hugging me.

Always needing to feel important, I answered, "Oh, come on. I know everything!" I handed him his gift, wrapped in gold foil. He opened it, stared, and then started to laugh again.

"Do you like it?"

"Ya done good, Pebbly-pooh! Oh, hang on…I wanna show this to the guys," he said, motioning to the sign and balloons.

Seconds later, the brothers were crowding the doorway to inspect the shiny, new lighter. After all the approval noises died down, they retreated to the bar, but one person remained behind. Bone had waited long enough to give that look of disgust he reserved only for me. We were staring each other straight in the eye, yet, did I see a small nod of approval? I think so. Was I winning some small battle in my war with him? I imagined he had finally seen some redeeming quality in me.

When Bone left, it was obvious even to Rick that I was one righteous ol' lady. In fact, he was still beaming at his new lighter even as he ordered me to unpack his things and wash his bike.

During all the years we were together, I managed to avoid absolutely every club run. I considered it an accomplishment, seeing myself as a master manipulator. Yet I wondered who I was deceiving. When I could have fled the situation in their absence, I was clipping my own wings each time I hopelessly sat and waited for their return. My invisible prison kept me locked in Glade City.

45

Mom and Dad had booked a Florida vacation in Clear Bay, assuming I still lived in the area. They wanted to visit with me over Christmas. I had managed to keep in touch with them by phone. I left out the parts of my life they didn't need to hear, but I never imagined they would consider coming down to visit me. I had to break the news to Rick that I'd be spending the holidays with my parents.

His immediate reaction was predictable. "What about me?"

"You'll be okay. I'll ask Vicki to look after you."

"I don't want Vicki. I want you!"

"I have to go, Rick. It's my parents."

"What about money? You already don't make enough. How am I gonna do without green for a whole week?"

"Uh, I'll work really hard to make extra before I go. How's that?"

"You'll come back with money, right?"

"Uh…"

"Well?"

"I dunno. I guess."

"Just ask for a few hundred bucks. For the cause."

(Oh sure. My straitlaced parents would be delighted to donate money to support the likes of Rick and his friends.)

"Seven hundred bucks. That would be good. Bring that."

Rick saw opportunity in his self-sacrifice. He repeated the figure, just to make sure I understood.

Without any intention of even trying, I promised to return with the dough. Rick said I could have the truck, and I was all excited. When I rolled into the airport arrival area to collect my parents and their baggage, they would be so impressed. I do have to wonder what I was thinking driving our twenty-year-old truck, Swamp Slut, with a six-pack firmly set between my legs. Who was I kidding?

When the day arrived and I rolled into Clear Bay to stay at Billy Lee's house for the night, I was very nervous. By now, you understand the routine. Anxiety meant calming myself with booze. When I reached the old neighborhood, I was so trashed that I couldn't remember how I got there. The next morning, when I awoke to get ready to pick up my parents, I knew I had arrived at Billy Lee's place because he was in my bed, along with his nineteen-year-old nephew on the other side of me. At least I was still fully dressed. Hung over, with three or four beers for breakfast and consumed with guilt for not being able to remember what the hell happened the night before, I set out for the airport. Always the thoughtful daughter, I had asked Billy Lee to disguise Swamp Slut's name. More tasteful by far, sitting in its place was a Confederate flag roped across the bumper. I repeat: Who did I think I was kidding?

As I was weaving my way over the bridge into Clear Bay, I kept an eye out for dolphins. Rick had believed that seeing one was good luck. The bay was a good spot to catch them leaping over the waves, but not that day.

So much for luck.

"Oh, Sue," Mom said when she saw the truck, "you're not expecting us to ride in that, are you?"

Why hadn't I let them rent a car? They had wanted to rent a car, but no…I had to insist on picking them up.

They got in anyway. I babbled mindlessly about dolphins, fishing, herons, and anything I could think of to distract them from what I really didn't want them to see. You can ask me again where my mind was.

In response to my mother's thirst, I took them to a bar in my old stomping grounds where everyone knew me. It was nothing more than a shack that only served beer or soft drinks (and assorted infectious bacteria if you wanted your drink in a glass). Mom, a tea drinker, had ginger ale from a can and Dad had a beer straight from the bottle, although he preferred a draft in a glass. We left after he had managed to drink half a beer and I had smashed back three cans of Busch. So far, things were not going well.

The reason I didn't throw myself at my parents' mercy was a matter of pride. I wanted them to be as oblivious as I was and see that my life was ideal. I wanted them to be proud of me. There was also the matter of bringing home cash so Rick would be compensated for my absence, but I quickly took care of that by slipping out to work for three nights. The teenaged liar in me dealt with my parents. I was going to spend some time with old friends. Luck afforded me a bar patron who gave me $200 just to go drinking and dancing with him. Once I had the money in hand and put in a couple of hours dancing with him, I slipped out to a cab and left. He had expected sex, but his complaints to the bar would go unnoticed.

What could they do anyway?

I didn't care. At the end of the three nights, I had $500 to take home to Rick.

Apart from the fact that I had to suffer through endless tourist attractions with a limit of two beers the whole day, I enjoyed being my parents' child for a week. They gave me a beautiful sweater for Christmas and bought me a decent pair of shoes at K-Mart for walking around with them. I should have left with them. It was a good chance to escape. Stupid me. It was another missed opportunity, but the cost of it would have been too great. It would have made them right. I would have had to admit failure, and I wasn't ready.

When I returned to the clubhouse after my trip, a pig roast was in full swing. Wart had a new ol' lady. Her name was Gail. Rick was happy to see me, happy to collect his token gifts, and happy to line his wallet with the money I scored. The place was bouncing with good cheer and visiting club members from another state, which meant I could drink myself into a haze without being noticed. Even in that condition though, I couldn't help but wonder about Gail. She looked out of place. No leather clothing, skin too pampered, and eyes filled with fear. Vicki told me that Gail's husband was a Navy man, currently on duty out of the country. She had two kids and a nice house near the base, but she was just bored being a housewife.

"So, she's *here*?" I asked, amazed.

"Here" was physical and emotional abuse. "Here" was a life uneasily carved out for someone like me who felt she didn't fit into the real world. But for someone who had already achieved a decent standing as a wife and mother? I knew the difference between the normal, moral, middle-class world and this outside existence. She was a fool, and I told her so. It didn't matter. Before long, Gail's husband found out what she was doing and divorced her. She lost custody of her children, her dignity, and her sobriety. Once she moved in with Wart, she started stripping and doing cocaine. When Wart grew tired of her, I heard she supported herself by doing tricks. She started shooting up and working in the seediest of the local bars. The last I saw of her, she was living in a shack, her arms and legs tracked with needle marks.

Paula, Diesel's ex, was now living with a club probate named Speedy, a name he earned by being too eager to draw his gun when he heard a noise on guard duty one night. He shot himself in the groin. After spending weeks in the hospital fighting infection, with Paula dutifully at his side, the club decided he was now "good for nothing." He and Paula moved about a mile away. After that, we only saw Paula at work.

Diesel, on the other hand, managed to find a new ol' lady from the outside world. Her name was Inez. She was a tall, slender, Spanish American princess of a girl with long hair that cascaded down her back like a dark waterfall. I don't know what attracted her to Diesel. He was a grubby blob of a man. If she had been attracted to the bad boy image of the biker patch, she certainly didn't understand the power these men had to ruin lives. When she moved on from Diesel's bed, she took up with some drug dealer from the bar. None of it made sense to me. She was well dressed, wore good jewelry, and was planning to return to school full-time. The new guy offered her a nice place to live, yet her slavish devotion to his every whim was just as demeaning as being an ol' lady.

Inez's and Gail's sad stories didn't have any personal impact on my life. I thought I had adjusted very well to my new family. There were patterns of behavior I became familiar with enough to make them ordinary and tolerable. For example:

Brother: (to me) "Hey, bitch! Show us your tits!"

Me: (to anyone asking) "No!"

Brother: (to me) "Then have this!"

Smack! Upside the head. That scene being concluded, I would go to work with a black eye or swollen lip. I'd play the poor, injured girl and accept sympathy money, drugs, and booze. When the club went for a run, I would find some excuse to remain behind as sort of a mental health break.

One day, Bone announced all of us were going camping.

"All of us," he emphasized, drilling his gaze in my direction. "And that means you, too!"

He closed the space between us enough to poke a finger in my chest. Perhaps he was losing ground with me and felt he needed to be aggressive. There had been a restful time of six weeks when Rick was doing time in jail. Bone played the big brother, making sure none of the other guys bothered me. He even favored me, giving me an old sewing machine. While Rick was gone, I made a long sundress for myself. Everyone laughed at it, but I felt good about creating something worthwhile to call my own.

I remember the dress. I wore it on that camping trip. It tried to drown me.

46

All of my usual tricks to get out of the weekend camping trip were unsuccessful. I hated the job, but I dreaded the coming weekend even more, so I convinced Rick to let me work the Friday night and join them afterward. Spending a weekend with the brothers would mean that my alcohol consumption would be monitored and limited. The first challenge was transportation. Rick expected me to borrow a car from one of my regulars at the bar to get to the campsite at Lilac Pond, actually a small lake.

That Friday evening filled me with dread. Both my manager and Vicki kept telling me to slow down with the drugs. The more I drank, the more I needed coke to make me feel sober. By the end of the night, I could barely stand, but, somehow, I convinced my young regular, a Navy guy, to give me his car for the weekend. How sober was he? Giving his new car to a waitress at a strip club, so trashed she could barely stand, wasn't his finest decision.

When the bar closed, Vicki climbed into the passenger seat and watched me swerve and wander along the road until she insisted on taking over the wheel. We tried that for a while, but since she kept getting lost, there was an argument and I was back in the driver's seat, snarling and nasty. The trip to Lilac Pond was taking too long. More beer…I was coming down off my high and needed more beer soon. The road was darker than my mood. With my reaction time slowed and my temper flaring, I missed the first turn. We plunged down a steep embankment.

"What the hell are we going to do now!"

As soon as we landed at the bottom, Vicki burst out crying and swearing, calling me more names than I think Rick had ever invented.

"Maybe someone will come by."

Nobody was hurt. What was her problem?

"Come *by*? Sue, it's three o'clock in the fucking *morning*!"

She had a point. "Then, let's just walk and see if we can find the campsite."

There, that was good. We'd be doing something. Besides, if I admitted I was drunk, that might mean I had a problem.

We climbed up to the shoulder of the road and stood arguing until headlights appeared. Wart and Lennie! They had been sent to find us.

Well! See, we were close to our destination.

Wart took one look at me and said, "Ooo-wee! Man, are you ever trashed! Bone and Flash are gonna be really pissed!"

"I'm fine," I shot back. Vicki groaned in disagreement. There was going to be a scene.

At the campsite (I never would have found it—too many turns), a lone figure stood waiting by the fire. It was Bone.

"Get over here, you…" And he used that word I so hated.

"What?" I tried not to sway, but the ground kept shifting and throwing me off balance. Bone glared at me.

"I think you better go sleep it off! Flash is in the tent asleep, so be quiet. If you wake him up, all hell's gonna break loose."

"Can I have a beer first?"

He shook his head in disbelief. "You never quit, do you?"

"It was a long trip. I need it to sleep."

"Then make it quick!"

Even Bone didn't want to discipline me. He let me have the beer. I drank it on the spot. Before I retreated to the tent, I crashed my way into the underbrush to pee, but it wasn't easy. I had thrown my big, homemade sundress over my shorts and T-shirt. Trying to get everything arranged to squat and not wet myself became a major operation. The cocaine had worn off. I was simply drunk, devoid of any motor skills or judgment of space and time. The first thing I did when I entered the tent was stumble over Rick.

"What the…?"

"Oops. Sorry, honey. Jus' go back to sleep."

"You're just getting here *now*?"

"Go to sleep…tell you all 'bout it inna morning."

"You're *drunk*. You're goddamn drunk!" He sat bolt upright with a flashlight trained on my face. "What did you do?"

"Nothing!"

Just because I had had three beers or so (more like thirty), why did Rick assume I had done something wrong?

"Worthless lowlife! Answer me, you stupid, stupid slut!"

"Don't get mad…"

"Yeah, whaddya want me to do? Be happy? My ol' lady's shit-faced again, making a fool of herself! Why do you do this? Why?" His voice was strengthening now, accelerating into rage.

"Run!" That familiar voice deep within me told me to get myself out of there and fast. Rick grabbed me by the foot. I kicked my way free. In the pitch black of the night, with bare arms, legs, and feet, I dived into the underbrush. Anything waiting for me that could sting, bite, or claw me to death was better than waiting for another beating. I just kept running and falling until there wasn't a breath left in me. Blood and sweat trickled down my arms, and roots and fallen twigs shredded my feet. From the dark behind me, I could hear Rick calling and there were other voices. He must have alerted the whole camp. In my drunken state, unable to run anymore, I squatted on the damp ground, trying to ignore the mosquitoes that seemed to be biting me everywhere. Lights flashed and disappeared through the trees. Rick's pleas, "Pebbles, where are you? C'mon, you've got to come out of the forest. You could get hurt," were reaching me. I had a choice. Die here or die at his hands. Here, there were no guarantees. I knew what to expect with Rick.

"Where are you?"

"Here," I called, defeated.

"Just stay where you are. Keep talking. We'll follow your voice!" Rick, filled with wisdom and concern, the ultimate forest ranger. He arrived with the probate, who acted as the point man with the flashlight. Within minutes, we were back at the tent. In the early pale dawn, Rick inspected my cuts and swelling mosquito bumps. Then it started.

"You could have gotten hurt!" *Smack! Slap!* "I can't believe you sometimes!" *Punch.* I fell to the ground, realizing I had to get away, but there was only one place left: the lake. Before Rick could drag me up again and start into me, I made a running lunge into the lake.

Damn the sundress! It was dragging me down, slowing my progress. I waded toward the rising sun and a finger of land. If I could just reach it, there was a chance at a highway and hitchhiking somewhere, but the resistance of trying to run through water was beginning to exhaust me. Behind me, Rick was bellowing from the shoreline. The entire camp was now awake and watching the drama unfold.

"Get back here! If I have to come in and get you..."

Oh, right! Rick had just given me an idea. He couldn't swim.

"You can't get me! You can't swim!" I yelled back. Dropping to my knees, I began to stroke with my arms to make it look like the water was deep. I rationalized that, if he thought it was deep, he wouldn't try to come after me.

Halfway to my goal, I turned to see Rick and the probate launching an aluminum boat. I heard the motor start up.

"Stupid bitch! You're gonna drown!" The stream of abuse rose over the sound of the engine, driving me to crawl faster along the bottom. That bit of land was looking promising. It seemed so close!

"Grab the oar, and we'll pull you in!" Too soon, it was over. Rick was holding out the oar. I knew I had to concede. I stood up and threw my hands straight over my head in surrender. A roar of laughter went up from the shore. Every brother was laughing so hard that some of them were rolling in the sand.

"I'll walk back," I said, pushing aside the oar. Perhaps I had taken things too far this time. The scene had been far too entertaining at Rick's expense. I had made a fool of him in front of his friends.

To my great surprise, there were no more lumps that day or that weekend. Bone, standing on shore with his hands on his hips, was shaking his head. I stood before him like a captured prisoner, dripping, head hanging in misery.

"You are such a fucking asshole," he said. "We got the car outta the ditch."

"Where is it?"

"Parked up there with the rest of them." He nodded toward the road.

"The keys are in it?"

"Yeah. Why?"

"I want to go home. I've caused enough trouble, don't you think?"

"Hmph! Damned right. Maybe you better get some sleep first."

This wasn't concern; it was more of an order. I'm sure they didn't want to scoop me out of another ravine.

"I don't want sleep. I want to go home."

My stubbornness was becoming legend. It even tired Bone.

"At least go get Dixie and get her to help you clean up a little. You're bleeding."

"Then can I go home?"

"Just go find Dixie!"

I wanted to see my injured face. Dixie didn't have a mirror, so I headed to the car to look into the rearview mirror. It was as I had expected: black eye, fat lip, scraped cheeks, forehead and chin dotted with insect bites. Dixie arrived with paper towels she had soaked in lake water for me to clean the sand crusted into my knees and shins.

"You never learn, do you?" she sighed, handing me the paper towels through the window.

"Probably not." I had nothing more to offer her.

Bone approached, and she left quickly.

"Tsk, tsk, tsk." I hated that slow sound. Bone was good at drawing it out in dramatic tones. "What are we gonna do with you, Num?"

"Num?"

"Yeah. Short for Numskull. Get used to it. You earned it." Something of a smile of admiration creased his leathery face. "I gotta hand it to you," he continued. "You got balls. Flash's really pissed off."

"I know. Why do you think I want to leave? He's going to…"

"No, he's not. Flash ain't gonna hit you," he said, anticipating what I was going to say.

I eyed him incredulously. "You don't know that."

"Yeah, I know that. Because I won't let him."

Was I hearing this correctly? Where had Bone been during all the other beatings?

"He loves you, Num. And you love him. Hey, why doncha both just kiss and make up so we can get on with the weekend."

"I don't want to make up. I've had enough. I'm leaving."

"At least talk to him before you go."

"No! Look at my face!"

"And whose fault is that?"

I had asked to get maltreated. He wanted me to believe that I had begged to be slapped around. This was all about me and all my faults.

"Go talk to him," he implored.

"No!"

"Think about it," he said, snatching the keys from my hand.

Dixie came back.

What did she want? Was she playing matchmaker along with her darling man?

"Want a beer?" Dixie was holding out a can of Budweiser. They knew me so well. This time, Bone retreated. Dixie waited until he was out of earshot before she asked, "Bone's not going to let you leave, huh?"

"Doesn't seem that way."

"Stands to reason. If the cops see you like that, they'll arrest Flash for domestic violence, and Bone's not going to let that happen."

So, that was how it was. Bone wasn't going soft. For a few minutes, I almost believed he cared. At least there was consistency in my life. The world was still as cruel as I knew it to be. Nothing had changed.

There wasn't enough strength left in me to deal with my life anymore. I sipped my beer as best I could through swollen lips and realized that all I really wanted to do was to drink myself into oblivion because beer erased all my grief. Vicki had told me to quit drinking. I had refused, damaged a borrowed car, and made an absolute fool of the man I was supposed to love. Maybe Rick would have done me a favor by beating me to a pulp. With any luck, he would have killed me. Then it would be over and done with.

While I thought over my few options, Rick approached the car and leaned into the open window.

What now? More punches or a round of criticism?

"Uh, Bone says you're leaving."

I bobbed my head once without looking at him.

"Why? Why would you want to leave me?"

Was he that clueless?

"I'm doing you a favor. I'm nothing but trouble, you said so yourself. Obviously, you'd be better off without me."

"No, I wouldn't! Who would look after me? What would happen if my back went out again? You're the only one who can help me." Such a soft voice. Such dire need.

"You've got your brothers for that."

"No, I need you. I don't think you should leave."

"Why? So you can keep beating me?"

"No, so we can have fun together like we used to." Did he think that would make me melt into his arms? Desperate now, he tried another ploy. "I love you, Num."

"Num! You too?"

"Yeah…well…you got to admit, you sure do some numskull things. That pretending to swim act was a classic. You really had me going." He was smiling tenderly. Both of us had to laugh. He was seeing my behavior in a more accepting way. His attitude bolstered my courage.

"I don't want to get hit anymore," I said, staring straight ahead at the muddy windshield, trying not to think about how I'd explain the damage to the car.

"I don't want to hit you, Num. I just want you to come out of the car and come back to camp."

"Can I have another beer and think about it?" What choice did I have anyway? Bone had the keys. It was just nice to put Rick off for a while.

"You'll think about staying?"

"Yeah, I'll think about it."

"I'll get Dixie to bring you a Bud."

When Dixie came over with my beer, she was all ears for the latest news.

"You staying?"

I took the offering. "Maybe. What do you care?"

"No reason. I kinda like having you around, that's all."

Was that a compliment? Dixie had just said something nice to me. Had Bone put her up to this or was she softening? Maybe I was good entertainment as the camp clown. Either way, I was curious enough to stay and find out.

I took my time to finish the beer and then walked slowly back to the campsite to where Bone sat cross-legged by the fire. He nodded as I passed. In return, I gave him a hesitant smile to convey my uncertainty, and then walked over to where Rick was standing, waiting. He opened his arms. As usual, he inspected my face. This time, he skipped the mock guilt trip.

"I'm tired," I said. "Do you think I can have a nap?" I didn't feel up to facing the others yet.

"Yeah. But just for a couple hours."

"Thank you," I said submissively and kissed his cheek. I had just opened the old, iron door and locked myself in again. To compensate, I deceived him. "Can I have a soda?"

"Yeah, there's some in our cooler. Just leave me some. I'll come by and check on you later."

"Okay," I answered wearily, then promptly disappeared around the side of the tent to the cooler and helped myself to a couple of bedtime beers.

By Sunday, I could have received a gold star on my forehead for good behavior. To keep my record safe and to keep the day quiet, I woke up and opted for a swim with Marlene, Lennie's ol' lady. We got on our rafts to paddle around and relax, soaking up some of that good Florida sun. It was lovely and quiet, just drifting and nursing one of my ever-present hangovers, when all of a sudden, the shoreline erupted with shouts.

"What's that?" Marlene turned her attention to the noise.

"Sounds like it's coming from our camp." Sure enough, I picked up my head to see a chorus line of bodies leaping and waving their arms at us.

"Looks like they want us to come in," I guessed.

Marlene, much older and wiser in club ways than I was, understood our only choice. "We'd better go then."

We began kicking and stroking to shore. Even as we did, the noise and activity there got more frantic. Every hand was pointing to our left.

Did they want us to go there? Fine then. I twisted in that direction to start the maneuver, but that's when we saw the cause of the excitement: alligators, five of them, two large and three smaller ones. As we watched in terror, they dived. With hearts pounding, we burst into frenzied paddling. As soon we got close enough to the beach, hands from everywhere reached forward and yanked us to safety. The rescue was so forceful that I had bruises on my arms for two weeks.

It was Mother's Day. A couple of the ol' ladies were heading up the road to the store, and I joined them. A call back to Canada was in order at the payphone beside the store. Scrounging up enough money for a "Happy Mother's Day" greeting was a present in itself. Mom would be happy to hear my voice, and, to please her, I would endure another lecture.

"Oh, Susan. Are you all right?"

"Uh, yes, I'm fine."

"Well, you just be careful, swimming and all. I just heard about a little boy in Florida who was bitten by a shark. You don't swim near sharks, do you?"

(No, I lived with them and swam with alligators.)

"Oh, never. Don't worry. Nothing's going to happen to me, Mom," I said, all confidence, as usual. "Happy Mother's Day!"

"Thank you, Susan. I am so glad you called."

"Me, too."

Following that camping weekend, Bone issued an order. Within days, an aboveground pool was set up next to the clubhouse. Rick had to learn to swim. Not that the process solved any of my problems, but it satisfied Bone. It would save any future embarrassment.

Bone began inviting Rick and me along on various outings with him and Dixie, even camping and fishing on his boat. I suspected that Bone was beginning to accept me, so whether I liked it or not, I went along. I had hardened myself to getting used to the lifestyle of a biker's ol' lady, which included being a waitress in a strip club. As much as I hated it, the other choices were worse. Sex had become meaningless to me; it was a commodity to be bought, sold, or bartered for. Men, in my estimation, had to be tolerated. I hated them. Women were compassionate creatures and, in that, I had an emotional connection. That's why I began to be less critical with the girls at the bar who traded sexual favors with each other. I even sympathized with the new girl, Cindy, who didn't turn tricks and didn't want a female lover. She was a skinny little thing. Because she was so lonely, I stepped up to help out. I offered Rick.

To my happy surprise, she accepted. It was like having a maid. While she was doing "the housework," I could relax. We arranged for her to visit the coming Sunday while the club was partying at Gator Pond, a bar they set up next to a pond—yes, with a gator in it. Rick was all anticipation, thinking he was going to have two chicks with him in bed. He pawed at Cindy's breasts and butt the entire afternoon.

By five o'clock, the whole group was getting pretty hammered. Wearing black leather in the hot sun always contributed to unstable behavior anyway, but one of the new ol' ladies, Tippi, was an exhibitionist nymphomaniac. Nudity everywhere and anywhere was her standard practice. She was beginning to get on my nerves. She liked to sunbathe naked right under our window for Rick's pleasure. The brothers were expecting all the ol' ladies to follow her example. On that particular party day, I decided it was time to leave when Tippi lost her clothes and reclined on the bar shouting lewd invitations. She even disgusted Rick.

"Time to go to Cindy's," I sniffed in high moral tone, and he agreed.

The three of us headed in the Swamp Slut to Cindy's to pursue our version of civilized sex in Cindy's trailer, except Rick thought the event would include me on the mattress. He had been drinking very heavily that day. (I suppose his ailing liver was too weak to protest.) Unfortunately for me, he insisted I join them in the bedroom. Our compromise saw me sitting beside the bed holding his hand and drinking beer while he had his way with Cindy. It suited me fine. Later, when I had left Rick and was homeless for a while, Cindy was good enough to let me share her gorgeous boyfriend who was a regular at the bar. Any of the girls would have fought for the chance, but Cindy felt she owed me the favor of some company. My values had become so seriously misshapen that I saw the gesture as gracious and accepted without hesitation.

One morning, I noticed my breasts were swollen, but after some fearful prodding and poking, I realized there were no lumps. At work, Vicki noticed the change in my figure, as did Dixie.

Dixie was the first to guess. "Are ya pregnant?"

My period was very late, but, with all the drugs and alcohol and less than nutritious meals I was consuming, it seemed natural for my body to act up somehow. Pregnant? No, it couldn't be. Rick and I had sex so seldom. Please, don't let this happen! It wasn't happening…was it?

Nature has its way with a young body and I soon miscarried. Life, mean and uncaring, went back to routine.

We had just returned from a Sunday run and barbeque when Bone said he had an announcement. He had a new leather vest and was removing the club colors from his old one.

"I'm thinking I'm going to give my old vest to somebody here." Like children at Christmas, all faces became hopeful. I turned to Rick with a knowing look.

Flash, the favorite son, it couldn't be anyone else. Rick thought so, too. His breathing quickened and he leaned forward, blinking.

"Who should I give it to?" Bone wondered aloud, teasing the crowd. He held the vest above his head. "It should be someone who deserves it." He surveyed the group while Dixie stood regally as a princess beside him. She made me sick.

"I think I'll give it to…" He paused for another moment before pronouncing the lucky and deserving recipient. "…to Num!"

Jaws dropped. Dead silence. Confused expressions everywhere. Bone paraded over to present me with the trophy. Was this a cruel joke? I waited for him to snatch it away with, "Ha! Just kidding!" followed by gales of laughter. Instead, he shook his head with an unmistakable yes and shouted, "Put it on, Num!"

To heighten the drama, he stepped back. With uncertain hands, I put on the battered leather vest, even though it was too big for me and drooped around the armholes.

"Go hug him or something!" It was Rick, babbling excitedly.

I walked forth on trembling legs and hugged the man I loathed.

"Thank you," I whispered into his ear, as though we shared a secret. I imagine the prize vest was Bone's way of acknowledging my achievement for the challenge he had presented at our first clash.

"You'll never make it," he had predicted. But I guess I had.

Rick was immensely proud. I was shaken. Why had Bone given me this "honor"?

When I asked, he merely said, "Why not?"

I thought I had risen to biker royalty. My existence was golden. But then, my parents came to visit.

47

We were in the middle of a tropical depression. A storm was on the horizon. It was still hurricane season, but my parents had decided that late October was a fine time to visit the Gulf Coast. To make matters worse, they were coming with my Aunt Betty and Uncle Ted, their longtime friends. The complications for me were enormous. I had to break the news to Rick that I'd be off work for a week, which meant working extra hard ahead of time to cover his living expenses until I returned. Luck brought in a navy ship, and I poured my energy into a new waitress routine that included performing. My clothes stayed on. If the guys offered enough money, I'd get onstage and dance to a piece of music.

The best part about being a waitress was that I could stash away money. I'd give Rick the bills and keep the coins. At the end of the week, I'd cash them in at the bar, often having as much as a hundred dollars to take home and hide. It gave me spending money for when my parents arrived. I wouldn't have to be dependent, which meant I could avoid the usual, "Oh, Susan, what are we going to do with you?" routine.

Predictably, the day before my parents and their friends arrived, I was apprehensive. I drank too much, got up late, and was late leaving for the airport. Would they wait? What if they left for their motel without me? I cried with anxiety all the way to the airport. Rick tried his best to reassure me, and I was almost calm when we heard a bang and the car swerved. In tearful hysteria, I began raving, "Oh my God! Oh no! Not a flat tire! Not now! Oh my God! What are we going to *do*?"

"We'll have to get it fixed."

"Where, Rick? *Where*? We're miles from anywhere!"

The rest is a blur. In my high emotional state, I couldn't see the gas station just down the road, but I do recall Rick taking care of things. Somehow, we screeched into the airport merely minutes later than planned. I got out, kissed Rick good-bye, and raced into the arrivals lounge. When my parents stepped into view, I was breathlessly standing and waving at them. My bright pink cheeks made me appear happy and excited.

Miraculously, the storm blew off, the sun came out, and the rest of the week was tourist heaven. I thought I had made it. But then, Rick decided it would be a wonderful idea for him to return to pick me up the day before my parents' departure. He didn't have any idea I didn't want them to see him. I would have preferred that they had left before he appeared. Actually, I would have preferred to be sucked out to sea in a hurricane before these two links in my life connected. My only strategy was to be ready to fly out the door when he pulled up, and we could bid fond farewells over the roar of an engine.

It wasn't to be. Rick arrived a half day early in a sorry-looking truck loaded with beer. He was set to visit with "the parents." As he had none of his own, I'm sure he was enthused about his version of family day with plenty of beer. I hauled him down to the beach to swim, maneuvered him to the picnic tables, and kept harping about leaving, but he was determined to visit with the folks. He got drunk. I got drunker. When we finally left in late afternoon, I have no idea how he managed to drive or why no one stopped him. He seemed to think the whole day was just one cozy, fulfilling family event. So cozy, in fact, that he decided that while he drove, he'd like me to favor him with sex play. I was not impressed and not cooperative. I continued drinking.

"What? I came all the way down here just to be with your family and this is the thanks I get?"

"I didn't ask you to."

"And here I planned this really romantic surprise to be with you, and this is how you act?"

We rode in silence back to the clubhouse. I'd have a surprise for him all right when we got there. Yes indeed. When we pulled into the driveway, I marched straight back to the camper. I pulled out my passport and packed a suitcase. I started down the driveway with Rick chasing after me.

"Whaddya doing?"

"Leaving."

"Leaving? Why?"

"I've had enough!"

"Enough…of *what*?"

By this time, Bone was on the scene with Dixie at his elbow. (Why wasn't she at work?)

He was demanding answers to the same questions Rick was throwing at me, and I wasn't in any mood to explain.

"You won't be able to make it out there," Bone warned, gesturing at whatever lay beyond clubhouse territory. "You'll never find a man you'll ever love again. Nobody you can respect. Citizens out there ain't like us. After being with us, your life is ruined."

How much more ruined could a life get? His comments were ludicrous.

"You'll never find another guy who will put up with you like we do!" he called after me. Maybe he had a point, but I was still leaving.

"You sure about this?"

"I'm leaving."

"Okay, you're on your own." Bone threw up his arms and walked away, leaving Dixie with her eyebrows raised and mouth turned down, in near sadness.

As I turned my back on all of them and walked down the driveway, the sun dipped behind the trees and dusk followed me. Three miles stood between the edge of the driveway and the highway. I was on foot, dragging my meager possessions. It was growing dark. Hot, exhausted, and with the beer wearing off, I was feeling sick and shaky, but I made it and hitched a ride to one of the bars where I had once worked. After a few beers there, one of the customers I knew took me to the bar where I was currently employed. By that point, I was seriously drunk and without any intention of working. I was looking for pity and some cocaine to soothe my nerves. Instead, I was fired on the spot.

What would I do now? They let me sit in the dressing room for a bit. I found a sympathetic ear with one of the waitresses who was currently living with the night shift manager. I went home with them and crashed on their living room floor. After two days of sponging on their good graces, a note came from Rick. The biker network was very effective. He knew where I had gone and had found a new place for me.

The new place turned out to be a spare bedroom in the home of a married biker wannabe who hadn't yet made it into the club. I was happy to have a room and a door I could shut. After a visit to a second-hand store, I also had a bed to call my own. Rick visited and left some photos of us together, assuming I wanted them. Many of the ex–ol' ladies kept in touch with club members; I guessed they couldn't break ties. Rick's finding this situation for me was probably one of those excuses to allow myself to remain the same way. He was keeping tabs on me.

I had visions of living the perfect life. On the first night, I returned to the room, lonely but feeling independent. I don't remember if I made it back on the second night, but, by the third, I was threatened with eviction if I didn't keep the noise (?) down. To cool things out and relieve some of my loneliness, I got a job as a waitress at another strip club and started working double shifts. In my confused, miserable state, I missed Rick. At the same time, I hated myself for missing him. At work, I downed an assortment of sedatives, beer, and the occasional Long Island Iced Tea while I waited for Dixie, who had also moved to the same bar. She always brought news of Rick. One evening, I decided I had to make sure that Rick would never take me back. I was drunk, high, and in a very foul mood. If I could just insult him thoroughly enough, I'd never have to worry about throwing myself back into his arms. He'd have to reject me.

"Tell Rick...oh, excuse me...Flash...that I said he's a fucking asshole and I can't believe I stayed with him so long."

"You don't want me to say that." Dixie shook her head to make her message clear. I was making a dangerous move.

"Say it," I replied, bolstered by arrogant, drunken confidence.

She carried my message to Rick and reported the delivery back to me. I was temporarily satisfied. It lasted only two weeks before I hit the panic wall. I called Rick over to the room where I lived and begged him to take me back. Predictably, he told me he couldn't.

"Why?" As if I didn't know, I asked him through wild sobbing.

"The message you sent with Dixie," he said, quite calmly.

"Please! I didn't mean it!"

He shrugged. "It's too late. If you had come back the next day and apologized then, maybe things could be the same again." Of course, any woman in her right mind would want that.

I draped myself around him. We hugged and kissed in what I thought was a final farewell.

"I don't care where you go or what happens to you," he said. "I'll always be a part of your life." It was a fine speech, almost too prophetic.

So it was over. He left, and I cried for a very long time, working over possible plans to sabotage myself and reunite with him.

I moved out of my room and into a house with two other girls at work. One was Vicki, Mack's ex–ol' lady, who was my best friend. I brought along my used bed and set up a night table for myself with an overturned cardboard box. I decorated it with a towel, lamp, and several pictures of Rick. Always able to find trouble, I started dating a new guy named Carey. He was Rick's height. With his long, blond hair and moustache, he could have passed for his brother. At thirty-two, he still lived at home, but I overlooked his dependence because he had a job and a car. When Carey came to visit, I shoved the pictures of Rick underneath the night table. That location lasted three weeks before one of the girls moved and the rent became too much for two to handle.

Gail came to the rescue. Gail, Wart's former ol' lady, was trying to get her life together enough to get her kids back. How she envisioned that, I don't know; the strip joints where she worked were especially sleazy and she was deep into cocaine. She did, however, have a two-bedroom house and needed roommates to share the rent. Vicki and I moved in without hesitation. We had electricity but no phone. That was only a minor inconvenience because in an emergency, we could go next door to an affiliated gang's clubhouse. Their presence felt like security. If I got lonely and wanted to talk to my father, I'd walk the half mile to a pay phone to tell him how well I was doing.

Yes, indeed, I was doing well, or at least imagining it. I barely ate and lived mostly on pizza. In the morning, I'd wake and start drinking beer until I got to work. I'd continue and add shots and then cocaine to "straighten up." My periods had ceased, and I can't remember waking up without a hangover. When I got on the scales at work, it registered seventy-six pounds.

48

Thanksgiving arrived, and my roommates had plans elsewhere. I had never been so lonely, nor felt so sorry for myself. At the clubhouse next door, a party was shaping up. I could see it from my kitchen window while I waited for the oven to heat up for my frozen turkey TV dinner. That's how I saw Rick pull up in a car with his new ol' lady, Josey. Dixie had told me all about it. Rick had picked her up on a run to Chicago, right outside her high school. The girl was seventeen. According to Dixie, she was one tough piece of work; in fact, her nickname was Steel. From the stories Dixie heard, she considered me the enemy. Rick and Josey climbed out of the car, followed by Wolf. My puppy, Woofie! My baby! Unable to watch any longer, I took another beer from the fridge and retreated to the couch to cry. No sooner had I sat down than Dixie opened the front door and walked in.

"Sue, someone to see you!" She lifted my arm and started tugging me to the door. "Someone next door wants to see you!"

"Who?"

As soon as he saw me, Woofie came bounding over, knocking me to the ground and licking my face.

"Hey, Num." It was Rick. "How ya doin'?"

I kept my eyes to the ground while both of us petted Wolf, at different ends of the dog.

"I'm okay. You?"

"Yeah, not bad."

It seemed we were divorced parents, still attached to the poor baby caught in the middle. Rick searched for more communication.

"Do you want to come over for a beer?"

"Oh, okay. But just one."(Could I live up to that?)

We walked together to the bar, and Rick got a beer for me. For a few minutes, we were a family again. Rick walked away to join Josey, but not before saying, "Oh, by the way, happy birthday." He had remembered it was coming up on the first of December. Perhaps he still loved me. He had come to the party as a present to me.

"Wolf! Wolf! Here, boy!" A female voice broke my daydreams. Josey! How dare she call my Woofie to her? The dog looked desperately from one to the other, wondering how to react, but I helped him decide by bending down and kissing his nose.

"How's mummy's baby?" I babbled and patted him on his big doggy head.

His decision made, Woofie stayed with me. After a while, I realized I was there alone. I hadn't been invited to dinner. Even though Bone and Dixie were being quite decent, they were carefully distant with me. Too soon I had to leave and return to the dark little house next door to my TV dinner. It was one of the biggest family holidays of the year, and I didn't have anyone to share it. I threw the aluminum tray in the oven and cried myself dry. While the tinfoil bubbled up in the oven and the brown-gray sauce swelled in its tray, I came to a conclusion. There was only one person I could turn to. The dinner went untouched while I headed up the street to the pay phone. My dad loved me. He would let me come home.

I was back in Canada for Christmas. For a time, it seemed I was recovering. Home meant clean. It was drug and parasite free. My parents still ragged on me about choosing the right path. Frankly, I didn't have any idea why I ever behaved the way I did. I expected that everything would come up roses if I just waited long enough, and no one realized I really believed it.

All of my former friends had straightened up and were employed. Nobody was available for partying. I found a job at a nearby bar, which gave me a little money of my own, but time was dragging. I spent many hours sewing. Life became sane and safe. It flowed along that way until the night I stood face-to-face with a dancer from Clear Bay. What was she doing in Canada? And how had she managed to come into a bar where I was serving?

Coincidentally, she was dancing right next door. She was the ol' lady of the chapter president from another province and was in town for a visit. Why, I'll never know, but the significance of seeing her was huge. I couldn't shake the feeling of homesickness that I felt for the excitement of my old life. I'd watch *Miami Vice* on television just to feel the drama of such danger. In my head, life with my parents was nothing more than quiet desperation—a silent scream. Where was the reward to working and sewing and having no friends? I needed Florida. I could have made positive changes in Canada, but I rationalized that life could only be stimulating in Florida. As the clock struck midnight on New Year's Eve, and I sat alone in the bar, crying, I decided to return to the life pattern I understood best. Without anyone reliable to counsel me, I turned to the bar manager.

A sympathetic individual, he was eager to please. He agreed that was what I should do.

There was only one thing to take care of before my return to the United States. Once and for all, I needed to end my ability to get pregnant. It was probably one of the most responsible things I've ever done. I arranged for the surgery without much protest on the part of the doctors. My history was enough to convince them of the practicality of my decision.

The night before the surgery, I decided to party with my old boyfriend, Chase. He was working as a manager in a grocery store, which I saw as stability. Besides, with his strawberry blond hair and fondness for a good time, he was very appealing. We hit all the old haunts, drank, did some cocaine, flirted with each other, and concluded the night at two o'clock in the morning. I hadn't mentioned to him that I had to be in surgery at seven, nor did I share that I wasn't supposed to eat or drink after midnight.

Muttering as usual that I smelled like a brewery, my mother woke me in time to get to my appointment at the hospital. Would anyone know I had lied on the forms about whether I had eaten or had anything to drink? Panic set in. Was that a bad thing? Could it kill me? Oh well. Don't think. Don't feel. If I died, what difference would it make?

To my surprise, I woke from the surgery feeling wonderfully groggy. (How I loved anaesthesia.) I enjoyed two days of being pampered and sedated. On the third morning, with my abdomen too swollen for my regular clothes, my parents reluctantly took me to the airport. I sat in grinding pain throughout the flight, keeping my mind fixed on the thrill of touching down in Clear Bay. Perhaps I should have considered the landing an omen of things to come. It was snowing.

My friend Vicki was waiting in a borrowed car. After stopping to pick up a six-pack, we headed up the chilly, wet highway to Glade City. When we arrived, I was quite drunk, still in pain, and on the edge of belligerent. Good thing the couch in her trailer was already made up for me. I passed out immediately.

The next morning, I was hung over. Pain still clawed at my pelvis, but when a couple of party guys arrived wanting to know who would come with them to Bike Week, I was first in their van. Unfortunately, except for being told they had to leave early because of my drunken behavior, I have nothing more to report about the bike meet. Getting into the van is all I can recall. It was a situation often repeated. Strangely enough, I was better off with Rick. He at least controlled my drinking or drugging myself into oblivion.

As much as I hated it, I had to get a job, and it seemed the strip clubs were the only ones that would have me. Weeks went by and behold! A cute guy with long, blond hair and a curly moustache finally appeared one evening in paint overalls. He was drinking Budweiser. One thing led to another. We became an item. It helped that he had a job, a company car, and his mother's roof over his head. I moved in with them, but when his mother sold the house, my housepainter and I were suddenly both homeless. And, oh, did I mention he did drugs and beat me?

After we were both fired from our jobs for not showing up, our new dwelling was a garage that belonged to a family friend. We slept on a mattress on the dirt floor. The toilet was any nearby tree. It didn't matter. I cared more about drugs and alcohol than anything. My reality was beer cases for tables and beer cases for chairs. I had to bathe in the sink at the Laundromat. With his occasional work, my new man could afford us the necessities: beer and cigarettes. I found another job. Together, we could afford living in a cockroach-infested motel.

The doormen at my new bar carried guns—big black ones like the gangsters on television. The regular who dealt us the drugs was about as big a dealer as they get. I knew that because the real profit makers didn't do drugs themselves. This one was as sober as they came. Since I was warped enough to think of all of this as very exciting, my admiration of them earned me enough free white stuff to keep me afloat. I was even given a genuine offer to have Rick "taken care of" for me.

"Don't worry about the cops," I was promised. "They'd just think we was doing them a favor."

Ah, the world of privilege! Apparently, I only had to give them the blink of a bloodshot eye. Rick would be shark food. But of course, I couldn't do that. I still loved the jerk.

One night, someone put something in my mouth that I swallowed before tasting it or asking what it was. It had been a beer breakfast day as usual, followed into the afternoon and evening by shots, Long Island Iced Tea, and cocaine, but the unknown substance scared me. To calm myself, I took a few sedatives and drank coffee. That worried everyone at the bar because they had never seen me drink coffee. The boss sent me home.

And what a lucky mishap that was! I was still alive two days later and at least alert enough to read the newspaper. I was about to return to work, but an article caught my eye: there had been a bust just after I left. Several dancers were taken in for dealing cocaine. Two people were still being sought. I presumed one of them was me. For nearly a week, I jumped every time I heard a car pull up outside our motel unit. After a few more days passed, I gathered enough courage to return to work. Things had quieted down considerably, especially since both the night manager and the dealer had moved on to more comfortable grounds and had taken the gun show with them. It gave me an excuse to back off the drugs somewhat and try to stay sober. It was during this time that Rick appeared with Lennie. I was serving a customer when I saw them come into the bar and take a table against the wall—directly in my path when I went back to the bar.

"Hi," I said, trying to sound calm.

Rick bobbed his head solemnly.

"How are you?" I asked as I helped myself to sitting down.

"Good. You?"

"Oh, yeah. I'm great!"

"You look good," Rick lied. His eyes narrowed at my appearance.

"Probably because I've cut down on the drinking and stuff!" I answered proudly, not adding of course that I had been so close to death that I had to temporarily cut back.

"Maybe that's it," Rick mumbled.

"You guys gonna be here for a bit? I just have to go to the bathroom," I said cheerily. I really wanted to sneak off to the far end of the bar and down a beer.

"Yeah, I guess. Sure."

Happily, they were still there when I returned.

"So, how's my puppy?"

"Wolf? He's a dog, Num."

"Oh, I know. But he'll always be my baby."

Short, awkward silence. "Uh, Num, you seeing anybody?"

"Naw." A lie. I was still living with my derelict painter in the seedy motel. I considered us homeless, so I guess that was close enough to "not living" with someone.

"So, then, why don't you come back?"

"Come back?" My heart leaped. I wanted to. "What about Josey?"

"She left. Went back to Chicago."

"Oh." *Oh*! Wow! This was very good news for me. "Yeah. I guess. I mean, I'd like to."

"Okay then," Rick said, and leaned over and kissed me.

"Come home with her tonight." Rick motioned to Taffy, a dancer gyrating on stage. She was the ol' lady of one of the new probates.

I turned to Lennie and then back to Rick. He leaned over and kissed me again. Then he and Lennie got up and left.

So that was it? Deal done? Had he needed me or just wanted someone to fill a vacancy in his trailer? Did it matter? Not a bit. I left with Taffy that night without collecting any of my belongings from the motel. I didn't own anything of value anyway.

49

There is an expression that comes to mind when I reflect on my decision making: the definition of crazy is doing the same thing over and over, yet expecting different results. That's a fair summary of my return to Rick.

Rick was drunk when we arrived. His majesty, Bone, was still in command. The clubhouse was different, though. It was darker and dingier and in a different location. There were new members, but they were somehow fiercer, more threatening, and more restless. As soon as I walked in the front door, Rick wrapped his arm around my shoulders. Woofie bounded with delight around my legs. With my little family reunited, it was easy for me to be blinded by emotions. After a couple beers with Rick, I was escorted across the street to a house he shared with two other guys. We had a nice big bedroom, where I soon fell happily asleep.

"Num! Num!"

What was going on? Where was I anyway? Oh…right. I was back with Rick. Rick…Flash…in my face. My eyes began to focus in the dim light.

"Wha'? What time's it?"

"Five. C'mon! Get up!"

"Why?"

"We're having a contest. A dancing contest. And you're in it. You have to dance on the bar and show everyone!"

What in hell? "No! I'm sleeping!"

"C'mon…"

I made muffled sounds, like I had fallen back to sleep. Mercifully, he gave up. Five o'clock in the morning, and he was playing games. What had I expected?

In the late morning, I awoke to find Rick asleep beside me. I was feeling relieved and grateful for being home again. The early morning dancing contest was just a mild glitch in the scheme of things. After all, Rick had respected my wishes, hadn't he? I dressed for work and looked forward to returning later that night. Things would be fine.

But they weren't. I was due for my first reality check. Rick was drunk again, insisting I attend to our ice cube trays before I turned in for the night. He made quite an issue of it. I was to make sure our ice cube trays were filled before my head hit the pillow. But first, I had to fetch some ice cubes for him from our place and then run them back across the street to the clubhouse. Okay! Okay. I could do that. I found the trays already filled. I had no idea what his issue was, but I dumped half a tray into a cup, and ran them back across the street. I was finally able to get some sleep.

Two hours passed. I found myself being dragged out of bed into the kitchen.

"What did I tell you about the ice cube trays!" Rick was slapping my face before an open refrigerator. "Do these look full to you?"

"They were full!" I pleaded, dazed and confused. Weren't they? I was sure I had left them full.

"Don't lie to me, cunt!" Ugh. I had forgotten how much I hated that word. And I had forgotten how manic Rick was when he was drunk. I shut my mouth and curled into a defensive position on the floor, trying my best to stop the constant blows to my head. Over time, Rick had been given advice about not hitting me in the face to avoid clear evidence for the police. No one had warned him about blows to the head and brain damage. But then, a brain-damaged girl could hardly testify in an assault case now could she? I cowered in a corner for what seemed forever before the pounding stopped. Half the clubhouse had run over to see what all the screaming was about. They pulled Rick off me.

That was my initiation back into a world of organized chaos. I had learned the rules, but how they were translated depended on the mood or the moment. Rick was always his usual self the day after an attack. His secret shame would prevent any further immediate assaults on me—for at least several hours. Outwardly, he showed no remorse. During the months that ensued, the episodes blended one into the other. What was the use of struggling? Some force greater than me, some hypnotic lure, always drew me back. On it went, my mind never quite getting what needed to be done, that is, until one fateful day during a trip back to St. Helen's.

Rick was driving me to work when we were pulled over by the police. I was prepared to drive home alone. To my astonishment, the person being taken into custody was me. I was mystified. I hadn't done anything. The fact that I worked in a hotbed of illegal activity was lost on me. I was being arrested on a bench warrant, which meant I was going straight to jail, a "Do not pass go, do not collect $200" thing. The charge was nonpayment of fines. I could only connect it to the raid in Clear Bay, but somehow I didn't care. I was tired. The way I saw it, I was going to a nice, safe prison with clean bedding and three meals a day, where no one would hit me, call me names, or swear at me. It would be like going to a spa. I pretended to be upset and put on an award-winning show for Rick. I was secretly delighted and probably went over the top by crying, tugging at his shirt, and wailing, "Please, don't let them take me to jail. I'm scared!" As the squad car pulled away, I even managed to press a tear-stained face to the window and blink a tragic good-bye.

The act was too good. Rick raced back to the clubhouse to throw himself on Bone's mercy. I was out before I'd even got in. I didn't even make it into the holding cell. And so, I didn't get my lovely rest at the state spa, but I did get a court date the following month. Although I didn't know it at the time, that day would signal the end.

Bone had decided to make the court appearance into a club outing. Everyone would go. We prepared for my appearance at ten the next morning by leaving the night before on bikes and with one van. Things were looking like nothing more than a social gathering until I reached the courtroom. The $200 fine Rick had paid for me had gone missing in the system; therefore, I'd have to pay another $200 and, just for fun, a $250 fee as well. The proceedings went quickly, giving us the entire afternoon to drink at the bar up the street. When the dinner hour rolled around, we headed to the next bar. On the way, I saw a guy walking along who looked familiar. I turned back to be sure. That was a terrible mistake, one I paid dearly for. Rick was definitely not pleased. I guess I have to be grateful for being so drunk because when Rick began beating me in the parking lot at our next stop, I was too far gone to feel it. All the while he screamed about my look-ing at another guy, he was kicking and throwing me across the asphalt and into the fence. I was covered in blood. At the point of passing out, I heard a loud, male voice warning Rick that he had to stop or the police would come. That didn't even slow him down. In full rage by now, he started on my face, slamming me to the ground and yanking me up again. At some point, I found myself star-ing at a gun.

"What are you going to do now? Shoot me, you motherfucker? Well, go ahead. I don't care anymore!" I screamed at him.

I really don't know how I managed it, but I started to walk away.

The gun went off, and I fell to the ground. Before I could consider whether I had just died, several hands grabbed me and pitched me into the back of the van. Rick's own brothers couldn't believe their eyes. He had shot me with a twenty-two caliber pistol.

"What in hell got into Flash? She's messed up real bad here."

"Whad' she do anyway?"

"Aw, you never know with Num."

Voices buzzed around me. The van sped down the road. When we stopped again, the doors flew open and Bone and Diesel leaned in to see, presumably, if I were still alive. When even Bone's face showed concern and they produced a bottle of Jack Daniels, I got scared. Oh no…not that…that's what they used as an anesthetic when somebody had to be stitched up. The bullet had grazed my leg, but Diesel was holding me down, ready for Bone's primitive surgery on my head with his grubby hands.

"Your head's split clean open. Hold still now."

"Can't I go to a hospital?"

"No. No hospital, Num. You know the rules."

They doused my head with Jack Daniels in a kind of baptism, and then placed the bottle in my hand.

"Drink this," I was told.

I did, as much and as fast as I could. That's all I can remember until the next day when the doors of the van rolled open once again and Mack greeted me.

"How ya feeling?" he whispered. His eyes were filled with tenderness and some measure of fear. I must have looked awful.

"Don't worry, Num," he said gently. "We're going back to Glade City now."

"Where are we?"

"Never mind. It's not important. We're going home."

Home. What was that?

50

It wasn't long before Rick was standing over our bed. I opened my eyes to see that familiar expression he wore while he was checking the damage he had done. I rolled away from him and stared silently at the wall.

"You want a beer?" That was supposed to serve, I imagined, as an apology.

The invitation to speak had been given, and I responded. "Why? Why, Rick? Why did you do this? I didn't do anything!"

"That guy," he said lamely. "That guy in the parking lot. The way you were looking at him."

"That guy in the parking lot? I thought I knew him, that's all!" I hated myself for even trying to offer an explanation.

"Yeah, well…"

I rolled back to the wall.

"You wanna beer?"

"No." I had just turned down a beer. I left it to him to pick up on the seriousness of the situation.

"Well, okay." He was stroking my head. "You just rest for a while. I'll come and check on you later."

Who was he kidding with his Nurse Nelly act? I knew it was his way of admitting he was sorry, but why couldn't he just say it?

He did come back to check on me. I conceded to taking a beer and a couple of shots of scotch to help me sleep. The only good thing about this was that my beating meant there would be no work for me that night and no money for Rick. Besides, I had to get all the rest I could to build up the courage to look in the bathroom mirror the next day. When I did, even I was repelled by the image that stared back at me. Except for one small, pale spot on my chin, my face was so swollen and discolored that I hardly recognized myself. My nose was broken, both eyes were blackened, and my right cheekbone felt as if it had been snapped. Two deep cuts, crusted in blood, sat on my forehead like a second set of eyebrows. No wonder Rick had bolted outside as soon as he could. He had been in a wonderfully upbeat mood until he had a look at his latest fist-work. Then his happiness faded, and he made excuses to rush across the street to the clubhouse. On closer examination, I found scratches and bruises spattered the length of my arms and legs and a nasty wound on my thigh where the bullet had grazed me. The flesh was swollen and red, too sore to touch. I didn't know how would I be able to work in such awful condition, yet I had to go. My consolation was that anywhere was better than where I was.

I managed to shower and get dressed. Rick drove me to the back door of the bar. When the manager saw me, his jaw dropped.

"What happened?" He took my arm and helped me into the office, shaking his head and wincing at my appearance.

I threw him one of those "Oh, c'mon, you know" looks. Nodding, he tried to hug me, but I had to pull back in pain. Carefully then, he led me to his desk where I sat balancing myself upright until he went into the bar and returned with a bottle of beer and a double shot of something—for me. He didn't drink.

"You can't go out on the floor looking like that, Sue. Someone will definitely call the cops."

That again. Protect everyone except the victim. I rolled my eyes in frustration.

"Well, I can't just sit here! I have to make some money! If I go home empty-handed, I'll get it. Don't let me get beat up again!"

"Uh…How much do you need?"

I shrugged. "A hundred dollars?"

"Wait. Sit right there. I'll be back."

While I waited, the girls took turns coming in to visit me with drinks. It was like holding a wedding reception. People kept arriving to wish me well. Of course, no one was offering congratulations, but I was basking in the attention and the kind words—words that made me feel I was accepted and cared for. Emotionally and physically, I was quite broken, but being this beat up brought kindness.

All the warm, fuzzy goodness from the alcohol and the friendly support was reinforcing the wrong message for me, but that was soon adjusted by Sun. Sun was an older Seminole woman with six kids and a pack of troubles of her own. She was my favorite among the dancers. She set down a beer and a shot of very strong bourbon and stood watching me for a long while before speaking. When she did, her voice was cold.

"We been talking, me and the other girls."

"Yeah?" Oh, goody, maybe they were going to pitch in and put me up somewhere for a couple of nights!

"Yeah. An' we come to a decision."

I lifted my chin hopefully, waiting for a smile that didn't appear.

"We decided. If you're not gonna help yourself, then we're not gonna help you anymore either!"

The breath went out of my lungs. Sun threw the results of a collection on the desk and walked out of the office. A hundred dollars in tens and twenties: this was not the payoff I had expected for my injuries. The realization that I wouldn't have any further sympathy or donations for my special charity was beginning to sink in. Sun's words, sharp as they were, told an awful truth. Continue like this, and there would come a morning when I simply wouldn't wake up.

It was my one moment of sanity.

When I returned home that night, I was calmer and more sober than I had been in a very long time. Rick gave me a long, sad, loving hug. I think he knew. It was time.

The next night, I made a collect call from the manager's office to Canada. My parents had recently divorced, but I called my father first, seeking the old, familiar bond of father-daughter love. Maybe he'd let me stay with him.

I could hear the operator asking if he would take my collect call. My heart fluttered in fear that he would say no. After all, by this time, he had every right to.

"Yes," he said.

I started to cry. Perhaps it was relief. Perhaps it was because my parents had been right all along.

"I miss you. I want to come home. Is it okay? Can I?"

I didn't want the third-degree about whether anything was wrong or whether I was in some trouble. I just wanted an open invitation. Hearing anything else would have devastated me.

"Yes, yes. Of course, you can. When?"

"As soon as possible. I guess."

"Do you have any money?"

"No." I bit my lip.

"How will you get here?"

"I...uh...can you send me a ticket?" The tears burst again. I couldn't hold them back, even though I truly wanted to sound casual and in control of myself.

"Tsk, it's always the same with you, isn't it Susan?" he sighed.

Like a spoiled child, I wanted this to go my way. I wanted my dad falling all over himself to welcome me back, showering me with affection and the means to return. When I was on Rick's turf, things went his way. With my parents, I expected to be the manipulator. (My views of love were really quite underdeveloped.)

"Forget it then! I shouldn't have even asked! I just thought...I missed you. I don't have to come home. I'll just stay..."

"That's not what I meant," he said impatiently.

I was silent, suddenly embarrassed for my martyrdom.

"Where do you want me to send the ticket?"

Thank God! I was swept away with relief. I was going home. Away from Rick! I gave him the address at the bar and thanked him profusely.

My escape would not be announced. There would be heavy secrecy around this mission. The next night, Dad was to call my manager to give him the date and time of my flight. He would allow enough time for the ticket to reach me by courier. It would be locked in the safe in the office.

My first order of business while I healed was finding someone who could help me with money and a ride to the airport. For that, I'd need a relationship of sorts and not with someone who knew the other ol' ladies. I found my solution in Jim, a lonely, balding, compassionate, middle-aged guy who wore middle-aged glasses and middle-aged clothes. The night before my flight, he'd let me stay with him. The next day, he'd give me bus fare and a ride to the station, from where I'd go on to the Clear Bay airport. My heart lightened. It was over. I was almost home.

51

Two weeks later, I slipped away from Rick while he was in the shower. Shoving what little I owned into an old, ratty suitcase, I ran out the door as quickly as I could. Up the street at the convenience store, I called a taxi. I hid in the store until it came.

When I arrived at the bar to pick up the plane ticket from my dad, Jim was already waiting for me to take me out to dinner. That was a good plan. I'd be out of the bar when the other ol' ladies arrived. Rick would still be wondering why I hadn't been standing waiting with a towel when he stepped out of the shower. Following a pleasant meal at a restaurant, Jim took me back to his place, where I slept on the couch. It felt strange to be treated with such respect.

Jim woke me with coffee at six. The bus was leaving for Clear Bay in a half hour, and I still needed to buy a ticket. We arrived on time. Not only did Jim pay the fare, but, before he left, he also gave me a hundred dollars, kissed me on the cheek, and wished me luck. There were really people like that! As I waited for the bus, my mind began filling with hope and happy thoughts. My family would fawn all over me. I'd get a real job, some nice clothes, and go out and socialize. Things would be perfect in Canada. I'd have friends, and everyone would love me.

Then, abruptly, someone called my name over the PA system, requesting me to report back to the ticket counter.

"Phone call." The lady behind the counter handed me the receiver.

Now, who would be calling me here?

"Hello?"

"What the fuck do you think you're doing you ungrateful bitch?" Rick! My world came crashing in at the sound of his voice.

"I...uh..." I started to cry. Just then, I heard the announcement for the bus. That changed everything. I stood for a moment with the receiver spewing foul language into empty air, glanced out the window, and said, "Gotta go." I ran out the door to the safety of the bus. When it pulled out of the station, I was on it and ready for my new life. The closer we got to Clear Bay, the more excited I got. No more getting beaten up, being called names, or working in a sleazy strip club. All I had to do was retrieve my little suitcase and catch a cab to the airport. I was nearly free.

When we pulled into the bus station, I was horrified to see Rick standing in the parking lot, hands on hips, with Lennie standing stupidly at his side. My whole body went into shock. Every muscle trembled.

Where are police officers when you need them? The bus didn't have a back door. The windows were too narrow to climb out, so I tried my best to shadow a large man off the bus. I directed myself quickly to the open luggage compartment at the side of the bus, and I was reaching for my case when a hand clamped my arm.

"Which one's yours?" It was Lennie, the errand boy.

At that moment, a deep resignation washed over me. I stood with my shoulders drooping while Rick strode up. There seemed nowhere to run.

"What're you doing to me, Num?"

I shrugged and stared at the ground.

Almost hypnotically calm, he asked, "You leaving me? Where ya going?"

"Home," I replied. "Canada."

"*Why?*"

The question hung between us. When I finally raised my eyes to meet his, I saw bewilderment. Truly, on some level of consciousness, he must have known the answer to his own question.

"C'mon," he said suddenly and escorted me back to the car.

Lennie tossed my suitcase in the trunk, started the car, and wheeled out of the parking lot. I trusted they were taking me back to Glade City, a captured escapee. In the back seat, I sat submissively, knowing it would be a long ride, but I didn't care. I didn't care about anything anymore. After a short while though, the car stopped behind a bar. Rick called me out. We stood in the heat for what seemed like hours while he grilled me about my motives. My only answers were uh-huh, nope, and yep, and the occasional "I don't know." He could do with me what he wanted. What was the use?

The next thing I knew, I was back in the car. We were returning to the Clear Bay airport. Lennie parked in an obscure spot in a parking garage, so far from anyone else that I was sure this was it. They were finally going to put me out of my misery and leave my body to be found by the maintenance crew. Instead, Rick rifled through my suitcase, emptied my wallet of Jim's hundred dollars, confiscated my phone numbers, and set me free with a few items of clothing and my passport. I think that's what surprised me most. He let me go.

I ran to the elevator. My singular thought was to get inside the terminal. My flight was at two o'clock, and I'd be on it after all. Everything was a blur until I took my window seat and watched Clear Bay drop away as the plane lifted. And finally, I wept. Was this the right thing to do? In my old life with Rick, I knew what to expect. I knew the pattern. It was easy and predictable, and, in some strange way, safe. In my new life, I would have to do my own thinking, make my own decisions, and pay my own way. I wasn't sure I'd be able to do it. I wondered if I had made yet another mistake.

When we landed in Canada, the pilot announced that the temperature outside was eight degrees celsius.

"What is that?" I asked the person in the seat next to me.

"Don't know," he said. "I think it's warm."

Warm, if you have a winter coat, which I didn't. Oh well. Soon both my parents would be waiting for me with outstretched arms.

It was over. I had been released from my invisible prison, or so I thought. In reality, my journey had just begun.

52

"The greatest discovery of any generation is that a human being can alter his life by altering his attitude."

William James, psychologist and philosopher

There are some people who kick up and rebel, yet still manage to find a normal life. They seem to know what is right and safe, but, after years of addiction to alcohol, drugs, and an abusive lifestyle, I couldn't pretend I was okay or that I even knew how to function as an individual. I returned to Canada disgraced, with nothing except a shabby suitcase. Coming home wasn't a triumph. I was admitting defeat and carrying all the emotional and physical scars I had collected on the way. There were no banners flying for me. There weren't any flowers or "Welcome Home, Sue" signs. My divorced parents stood in the airport lounge looking prepared for more disappointment. They managed smiles, but, nevertheless, they were weary.

"So," my mother said flatly, by way of greeting, "you made it, did you?"

"Aren't you even glad to see me?" I hung back a bit to show my uncertainty, eager to beat them at the usual guilt session.

"Oh, of course we are, love!" Mom reached out and gave me a warm hug.

My father acknowledged me likewise. We headed out of the terminal, pausing just inside the doors.

"Don't you have a coat?" asked my mother, already consumed with worry.

"It's only eight degrees," my father added, to emphasize my obvious oversight.

"Oh," I offered lamely, "the pilot said it was, but what's that in real degrees?"

"About forty-five degrees Fahrenheit. You just double the Celsius temperature and add thirty," he replied.

I was home. The instructions had already started. Dad was always delivering some sort of lesson: how to live, how to think, how to drink in order to avoid disaster. I never listened.

"Never mind. We'll just have to get you a coat," Mom said and steered all of us out the door while she continued to organize. "Maybe Sarah has something lying around that she could give you."

It was dark outside when we arrived at Dad's apartment. As soon as we got inside, he set my bag down in his living room and launched the interrogation.

"You can tell us now. Why did you want to come home?"

"I missed you!"

"Susan, there's got to be something more than *that!* What happened?"

"I just missed you."

"Something must have happened."

"No."

My mother studied the proceedings like a player on the sidelines of a familiar game. They were both curious, and, by the looks of it, they were also becoming suspicious.

Dad picked up on the obvious. "Do you have any money?"

"No." Rick had already taken care of that when he emptied my wallet.

"Well then. What are you planning to do?"

"Get a job."

"A job. Oh? Just like that?"

My answers were grating on him, but I couldn't offer more. It had only been a two-beer day, paid for by the guy on the plane next to me. I was growing nervous and regretful. It was simpler living with Rick. Being worthless with him was standard. With my parents, it represented a very wide gap between us.

"Okay," I volunteered. "I guess I hadn't thought about that. I suppose it won't be so easy."

I didn't even offer the old, "But I'll try."

"Hadn't thought about it," he echoed. "I guess not!"

"Stop, Brad! Leave her alone. She's probably hungry and tired."

My mother saw that the situation was leading nowhere.

"Susan, would you like to go out to get a drink or something? Just you and me?" my mother asked.

A drink or something? Absolutely, but I didn't want to appear too eager. "Mm, I don't know…I guess."

"All right, let's do that," she said soothingly. "Do you mind, Brad? Is there someplace around here you could suggest?"

"No, no. That's fine. Go ahead. Try that place, Dingo's, at the far end of the mall."

"How about that?" Mom turned to me suddenly very upbeat, as if she were trying to appease a cranky toddler.

"Yeah, I guess." Remembering Dad's point and that I would be staying with him, I quickly added, "I can check it out to see if it's somewhere I can work." Even more eagerly, I said, "If it isn't, is there somewhere else we could go? Maybe I could find something right away."

Oh, that was a good one. I felt suddenly much better at the prospect of having a job. Then again, maybe it was the thought of a waiting beer that was fueling my sudden ambition.

And so began my new life. It was just like I had never left.

The next day, Sarah appeared with an old winter coat for me. It was suede with a fake fur collar, but it was still nice, and I was appreciative. Her presence at the apartment, though, did nothing except confirm my failures. She had married a firefighter. They had already bought a house. (I was certain it was darling and surrounded by a white picket fence.) Sarah was glowing in her second trimester of pregnancy. Her life, in contrast to mine, should have given me incentive to get myself together and make everyone proud. But then, I guess it wasn't a surprise that no magic took place. Little did I realize it at that point, but I was facing two more years of trying to destroy myself before being jolted into reality.

I got a job at Dingo's the very next day. It started that same evening. Without money to buy the required uniform, I stopped by a local discount department store and found a black skirt for ten dollars and a white blouse on sale for eight. I left them waiting for me on the rack and returned to the apartment. As soon as he opened the door, I gave Dad the good news. Quite willingly, he let me borrow a bit of money. I bought the clothes on the way to my new job, changing into them in the mall washroom.

That first night was a huge success. I arrived perfectly on time, sailed through the training, and even eavesdropped on a complimentary conversation about me.

"Can't believe it! She caught on so quick!"

"Yeah, she's gonna be great. We're so lucky!"

Lucky. My doing well had nothing to do with them. My efficiency was all about me. The quicker I caught on, the faster I became. The faster I worked, the more tables I could serve and the more money I would make in tips. This was not about them; it was definitely all about me.

The only drawback was my tacky dialect. In all the years I had spent away from Canada, I hadn't realized that I had adopted a twang. Asking, "Hi! What can I get for you?" translated into, "Hay, whut ken I git fer y'all?" It amused the customers to no end, but it scared me because it might blow my cover. I feared if I spoke too much, my life story would come tumbling out. Everyone within earshot of the awful truths would race for the exit. I needed to stay anonymous, a nonperson. I certainly didn't want my secrets exposed. There were huge adjustments to make.

I was suffering culture shock. It became apparent one night while I watched a couple fawning over each other. The young woman and her boyfriend were seated at the bar when she expressed a wish for some potato chips. His next step was foreign to me. I had only to watch in amazement while he actually got up, purchased the chips, and happily returned to her with them. Is that how real people treated each other? I had so much to learn. I had to keep quiet in order to disguise my ignorance.

That first night was so promising. Not only had I made $120 in tips, but when the bartender asked all the waiters and waitresses what they wanted after closing, I ordered only one light beer. I was fiercely proud of myself...yes indeed, so proud that I went back to the apartment and drank a six-pack. The next morning, I repaid my dad and announced I had full-time shifts for the rest of the week. He left for work smiling, and I was relieved.

53

My new sense of pride and accomplishment would never last. Of course it wouldn't. After a couple nights, I started ordering three or four beers at last call. Predictably, with my inhibitions lowered by the booze, I began socializing in all the wrong ways, including going to after-hours parties with the regulars. Many were former classmates of mine from high school. I couldn't relate to them, though. They were all employed. From what I saw, they were mature and stable. They laughed, joked, and even discussed news events. They were informed and responsible adults. They had friends and someone who cared for them. They never got into trouble because they only had a few drinks before going home. Not me.

I was afraid they would find out. How could I explain it: that I was really a low-life strip club waitress, a biker's ol' lady who hadn't a clue what was happening in the outside world? We had nothing in common to talk about. I was lonely, so I did the thing I knew best. I partied with them and drank enormous amounts of alcohol. If someone had it, I'd snort cocaine as well. Surely my willingness to party would make me appear cool and, therefore, acceptable. Once I got started though, there weren't enough drugs or alcohol to keep me happy.

Inevitably, being the blackout drinker that I was, I'd wake up the next day with bruises and cuts all over me and not able to recall anything about the previous night. After every episode of my self-induced amnesia, I'd walk around on eggshells, waiting for someone to make a comment about my behavior. By last call, if I hadn't heard anything negative, I'd be relieved enough to start the process all over again. Oddly, without Rick beating me up, my life should have been improving, but it was getting worse. I was abusing my own health; apparently, I didn't require any help to do that. The bike club still existed in my emotions. Every morning, their estimation of me spoke from the mirror.

"Worthless piece of shit!"

"You'll never amount to anything."

"No one will want you. You're lucky you have us!"

Months passed. I couldn't handle living beneath everyone else's standards any longer. I wanted to go back home to Rick, where I belonged. One afternoon, my courage bolstered by enough drinks, I picked up the phone and dialed the clubhouse.

"H'lo?" A woman's voice, a pleasant one at that. Ol' ladies weren't allowed to answer the phone. Did I have the wrong number?

"H…hello? Who's this?" I asked.

"Who's this?" she replied, not quite as pleasantly this time.

"It's…uh…" Quick! What name should I use? Num, it had to be. After the Lilac Pond incident, the name was famous all up and down the eastern seaboard. "Num! It's Num. Is Flash there?"

"How are ya? It's Peg!" Peg, Mack's most recent ol' lady, was still there.

"Peg! I'm good. What's with you answering the phone? You surprised me!"

"Yeah, they changed the rules. We're allowed now."

"Cool," I replied, growing a little impatient for her to tell me if talking to Rick would be possible.

"Num, I suppose you don't know about Wolf."

Uh oh. I had done a good job not thinking about my Woofie. I missed him.

"No. I haven't talked to anyone in quite a while."

"Oh, I'm sorry to have to tell you, but he…well…he kicked the bucket a while ago. Heartworms."

"I didn't know. I'm sorry you had to be the one to tell me." I wanted to sound so detached, so unemotional, but inside my head I was hysterical. "Is Flash there?"

"Yeah, oops, forgot. I'll get him."

In the space of time it took for Rick to be summoned to the phone, I became a babbling wreck.

"Yeah?" It was Rick, with his familiar, gravelly voice. "That you, Num?"

"Yes, yes. It's me," I cried into the receiver, hardly able to catch my breath I was weeping so hard.

"What's wrong?" His voice was gentle.

"Woofie. Peg just told me about Woofie," I wailed.

"I didn't want to call. I knew you'd be all upset. Fucking stupid Peg shouldn't have told you either! Stupid bitch!"

"Oh well, she didn't mean…"

"He was really old for a dog his size," Rick offered. "He had a good life."

"I guess…" sniff, "yeah…" sniff.

Unable to console me, he tried changing the topic. "What's happening in your world, Pebbly-Pooh?"

Pebbly-Pooh. That name, from another time, and it had slipped so easily back to his lips. It drew me momentarily away from my sadness. Here was the Rick I loved, trying to cheer me up.

"Uh, nothing much. I…um…just wanted to tell you I'm sorry!"

"Sorry? For what!"

"For leaving you. I never…" The tears welled up again. "I never should have done that. You were right all along. I can't make it on my own. Please, I need to come home." I was sobbing, begging, and inconsolable.

Maybe someone had come into the room or maybe Rick was just frustrated with our never-ending struggles. Abruptly, I was Num again.

"Listen. Listen to me, Num! You can make it! You have to try. You can do anything you want. I know you can. Are you there? Are you listening to me?"

"Yeah." I was listening, and I was also hearing that he didn't want me to return. "I need you. I need to come home to you."

The silence at the other end lasted an eternity. "No, Num. What you need is your family, the people who love you."

"But…"

Returning to him was not an option. The topic was finished. Wanting only to distract me, cheer me up, he tried again, "Tell me what you're doing up there."

"Um…well…I have a job I really like…I'm a waitress." I felt like a kid calling to complain that I hated camp and I wanted to come home, but the secure adult at the other end of the line was purposefully ignoring my unhappiness.

"Great, Num. Good for you. Do you have a new boyfriend?" Such a strange question, such detachment! What to tell him? Sure, I sort of had a boyfriend…nothing serious because no one would ever want me, including him. We just mostly went to parties, and I'd give him money. A boyfriend? I guess you could call him that.

"Yeah, kinda. I guess. How about you?" Did I want to know?

"Yeah!" His response was so quick and so enthusiastic it shocked me. "I got a new ol' lady. She's got two kids! Me! With kids! Can you *imagine*?"

Well, yes, I could imagine. I had imagined that picture many times over except, front and center, they were our kids…our babies.

"Huh? Yeah. That's funny. Do you like her?"

"Yeah, I guess she's okay. It's money. You know."

"Yeah, for sure. But, Rick? Can I ask you one more question?"

"What?"

"Do you…Do you ever beat on her like you used to with me?"

"Naw, she's not worth it."

An awkward silence separated us while we each tried to sort out our thoughts. He had moved on with his life and accepted it as it came. As for me, I was stagnated. Apparently, I owned the problem.

Rick said, "You okay?"

"Yeah. I guess."

"Okay, well then…keep in touch, Num."

"I will." Then before we hung up, I added quickly, "I love you."

It would be the last time I'd get to say it to him. We never spoke again.

"I love you too, Num."

Click.

That was it. My life was over. I cried so long and so deeply that my face and body ached.

54

After my final conversation with Rick, things spiralled rapidly downhill. My drinking and drug use increased and, along with it, my self-loathing. I didn't care anymore. Trying to fit in had only set me apart as the outcast, the loser everyone got to stare at. I didn't have any friends, my family believed something was wrong with me, and now Rick had officially rejected me. My family loved me, but that didn't seem to count. I couldn't find my own way in the world, and I wanted out.

My escape was the usual path. I drove myself harder and faster into a routine: work the evening shift followed by partying until four or five in the morning, followed by sleeping until three in the afternoon. I went back to work to repeat the endless cycle. To achieve a state of oblivion and the release of pain I craved, I needed both drugs and alcohol. I didn't realize what a final solution I had until one evening, with bottle in hand, I bent over a counter to snort a line of cocaine. When I lifted my head, a sobering moment of recognition replaced the usual rush of euphoria and energy. My heart was beating so hard and so fast that I thought it would leap out of my chest. I could die like this. At first, the thought panicked me, but then I understood that death this way would be a good thing.

From that point on, I was in conscious self-destruct mode. With any luck, I could overload my system so that, one day, I just wouldn't wake up. They'd call it an accidental overdose. It would spare my parents the grief of my suicide. Then again, maybe I could get murdered walking home at two o'clock in the morning staggering along the sidewalk, inviting the ultimate crime. That would also render me a victim.

The alcohol and drugs dragged me farther down, but I didn't care. Nothing was left for me anyway. My boyfriend cared more for my cash handouts. He didn't want me. Nobody did.

One day, after I had lost my job and even the ambition to get up in the morning, I gazed at the ceiling and called out, "Why won't you let me die? Please, just let me get hit by a bus on my way to the beer store!"

I had already tried to commit suicide by swallowing a handful of sedatives and chasing them with beer, yet, despite myself, I survived. I couldn't do anything right. That's why I needed to die by accident. Getting run over or stabbed would do quite nicely. It would have to be something fitting, something expected of my lifestyle, but not self-induced. An accident would be kinder for my parents and just easier for them to handle.

55

In 1990, I was thirty years old and unemployable. Sadly, every day, I woke up, still alive. Something had to change. If death refused to take me, then I'd try for help. I'll line up the order here as a sampling of my efforts:

1. I made an appointment with the family doctor. With all the courage I could muster, I gave him a very close approximation to how much I really drank. Hmm, I was "depressed" he said, and needed therapy. And by the way, "Here's a prescription for some antidepressants."

Ah, gee, and here I thought I was a drunk and a drug addict. No? The good doctor didn't agree with my presumptuous diagnosis.

2. At the alcohol and drug center downtown, I filled out a questionnaire, all 300 boxes. While I was busy with that, a delivery driver, someone I knew as a teen, arrived with a package. He recognized me and said, "Hey, looks like you're in the right place!" He knew? All those years ago at the burger joint, he knew…and so did everyone else? Then why couldn't the counselor who interviewed me come to the same conclusion? Young, fresh out of university with her brand-new degree, she concluded that I needed to "modify" my behavior. (Uh, ya think!) Yes. And how to do that? Well, the next time I felt like reaching for a beer, I should just munch a few potato chips instead. Maybe I should hijack a potato chip truck. That should work.

3. I asked my dad if he thought I might be an alcoholic. There, I had said the word. That was a step forward.

"No. No, I don't," he replied. "You don't drink in the morning, and alcoholics do."

He may have been trying to help, but what he didn't take into consideration was that I didn't drink in the morning because I was *passed out* every morning. But because I loved him and respected his judgment, I decided he was right. Something else was wrong with me.

The very next night after Dad's diagnosis, I watched a television interview with a movie star who was being interviewed about her manic depression. Her symptoms sounded suspiciously like my own, including uncontrollable mood swings, self-hate, and an inability to hold a job. So, that was it. I was manic-depressive. It made sense. Just having the label was a comfort. But then one day as I lay curled in my familiar posture on the couch, I began wondering why I was in this predicament. I used to work. I used to be able to hold a job. What had happened? Rick said I could do anything I put my mind to, so I decided to try. The classifieds in the paper had an ad for wait staff: part-time evening and weekends. Not only that, it was a country and western bar. It suited me just fine. I got the job.

It only took the first night for me to find an after-hours party. On the second night, I showed up hung over and barely able to stand. Even so, it worked out just fine because that night after last call, I met my new warden—a friend of some of the band members. His name was Gary, and he had spent some time in Texas. He understood the culture I had recently left. At last! Someone who could understand (tolerate) me. Needless to say, I attached immediately. It was a bonus to discover that he owned a house, drove a decent vehicle, and dressed well. An evening in his hot tub clinched the matter. I moved in and, as usual, stopped showing up for work.

After about a week, I got another job closer to Gary's neighborhood. I was behind the bar pouring beer when a familiar face appeared. It was one of Rick's old buddies who I thought was fairly decent because he was the only one who ever defended me or at least tried. Soon, more of the old gang from Gilbert's began appearing, people I hadn't seen in nearly a decade. I could quickly pick up where I left off. It didn't take long before I woke up one morning and didn't recognize my surroundings. After gathering my belongings, I ran out to find a street sign to give me some direction home. Lucky me! Why, I was only a few blocks from where I lived with Gary. He'd be at work, so I could sneak in and get showered and changed. But instead, two green, plastic garbage bags sat on the porch with my stuff sticking out of them. I'd been kicked out! I'd proven everyone right again. What a loser! Frustrated and filled with despair, I sat down on the cold, concrete stairs and cried. I'm not sure how long I had been there with my face in my lap when Gary appeared.

"I think you should leave," was his greeting.

I begged, I promised it wouldn't happen again. I carried on with excuses, more promises, and unending remorse while he stared into space, obviously unmoved. Seeing his reaction, I simply had to give up. Trying for as much dignity as I could muster with flushed cheeks and swollen eyes, I collected the bags and dragged them to the driveway. Halfway to the road, Gary caught up to me.

"Hey, wait. Where're you going?"

I shrugged.

"Back to your boyfriend?" he said mockingly.

"No," I answered calmly. "It wasn't about a boyfriend. I spent the night with people I hadn't seen in nearly ten years. I just got carried away talking about old times."

"Yeah?" His tone sounded like an invitation.

"Yeah!"

"If that's true, maybe I can give you another chance. But if it ever happens again..."

"Oh, it *won't!*" I gratefully promised never to repeat such thoughtless behavior.

The next day, I opened the front door at work and was immediately escorted out the back. I was told I was talented but unreliable. I needed help and could apply again when I got it. That was it. The door clicked shut, leaving me, quite suitably, in the alley.

Gary helped me gain perspective on the situation. It was a matter of working in the wrong place. I drank too much because I worked in bars. That was quite a revelation. For months, while I sat on the couch every afternoon talking to the beer bottles I emptied, none of them ever told me that.

"How is it that something as small as you has such power over someone as big as me?" I'd wonder aloud and never received an answer.

I knew I had a problem. It wasn't the beer. It wasn't me. It was where I worked! I vowed to quit the bar and get a normal job. Problem solved. Following my momentous decision, I groomed myself nicely and put on my very best dress. I was going to the unemployment office to line up with regular human beings, the kind who kept reasonable hours and controlled themselves. I would join their ranks and disguise myself among them, even though I felt I didn't deserve the chance. Gary and I were both thrilled when I found a seven-dollar-an-hour job in a women's clothing store. A whole year passed without any drugs, only three hangovers, and otherwise minimal drinking. And then I crashed.

One beautiful morning in May, I decided to toast myself with a beer. I had been doing well, and, besides, it was only nine thirty. I wasn't expected to work until noon. I never got there. I can only remember making two calls: one to the taxi company to deliver a case of beer and one to quit my job. The second call was the right thing to do. The drinking had actually started at work. I hid beer in the back room under piles of clothes so I could have a few sips between customers. It's not that I considered myself clever. I knew what I was doing wasn't right. I was always afraid people would smell the evidence on my breath. That's why I was decent enough to call and quit. I explained to my supervisor that I was really screwed up and needed help. That task completed, I helped myself to several more drinks to drown my conflicted feelings: sorrow about losing my job and celebration for my sense of responsibility.

The next morning, I could barely lift my head from the pillow for the pounding pain inside my skull. I was afraid if I moved I'd be violently ill, although I managed to reach for a bottle of beer on the floor beside the bed and guzzle a third of it. It was warm, but it didn't matter. A whole year of approximate sobriety was ruined. I was back to being a lowlife.

In an instant, my life flashed before me. I knew I had to stop drinking. Slowly, feeling dangerously shaky, I pulled myself to the edge of the bed, stood up, and walked to the sink with the bottle. I tipped it upside down into the drain and emptied it. That was the last time I ever drank.

56

I'm often asked how I came to such an abrupt halt with the drinking. Truthfully, I don't know, but I suspect it had much to do with what my father told me the night before I quit. By his recollection, not mine, I called him. I had walked away from my job and was on the verge of being kicked out of Gary's house. During our conversation, I assured him that, because he was always there for me, I'd always be there for him whatever happened. I'd take care of him. I'd do whatever was required.

He remembered clearly how he responded to my sincere offer. "No, you won't, Sue. In a crisis, you'll do what you always do. Go out and get drunk."

He expected nothing of me because I was unreliable. The statement itself was quite sobering. Perhaps his estimation of my character bound me to prove him wrong.

That day, when I was alone and the beer was gone, the only observation was my own.

"Now what?" I asked myself.

Alcoholics Anonymous? Yes, I'd call Alcoholics Anonymous (AA). The thick fog in my brain and my unsteady legs were not much help. My brain translated finding the telephone number by going out to buy a newspaper to look for an AA advertisement. I could hardly stand up straight, let alone walk. The smallest movement jarred my delicate stomach. I wanted to hurl at every step. After repeatedly forcing one foot in front of the other, I made it to the store and back. I had to lie down with exhaustion before I even opened the paper. When I did, nothing jumped out at me until the classified section revealed an ad: "Are drugs and alcohol ruining your life? Do you feel you have no place to turn? Call today."

A helping hand was reaching out to me from the daily paper. My heart thumped with hope while I dialed the number. Someone answered on the first ring.

"Hello, Phoenix House."

"Yeah...uh...I..." And here the crying began. I was surrendering my most closely guarded truths—the ones I could barely admit to myself. I told the lady my problems. I had no job, no money, no friends...no choices. Her reaction was kind and gentle enough to give me the confidence to agree to an appointment the following day.

Gary would be so proud of me for trying to clean up my act. Until his return in the late afternoon, I stayed in bed where I could nurse my hangover and have hours to think. In that space of time, I concluded that there were certain facts I knew for sure:

First, my life was out of control. Another year had passed. I was now thirty-one years old and had nothing. I hadn't achieved anything worthwhile. Second, I didn't have any friends. My family was fed up. I had steadily driven everyone away. Third, my health was deteriorating. I couldn't choke out a sentence without coughing. I had to rely on an inhaler prescribed by a breathing specialist. Sometimes I was so depressed I had to struggle out of bed, and, when I did, there were bouts when I was so nasty I even scared myself. Fourth, I had intelligence, neglected and forgotten while I struggled to maintain even the most mediocre of minimum-wage jobs. I was wasting my talents. Fifth, I would never be able to fix any of these problems unless I quit drinking first.

My determination grew to quit, maybe not forever…but just until I got my life on track.

Gary was skeptical. I think his exact words to my plans were "when pigs fly!" He was happy, though, to keep me sober as long as possible. Just so I could get over the rough patch for the next several hours, he took me to the store. We bought some "near beer," the 0.5 percent alcohol stuff that tastes like brew. It helped me get through the night.

The next morning, Gary went to work. I boarded a bus to the Phoenix House Counseling Center. I was nervous but feeling relieved at the same time. The place was easy enough to find, but then my misgivings started. What if they laughed at me, turned me away, or didn't want to help? While I was standing outside, considering whether I could face these possibilities and on the verge of leaving, a scruffy-looking guy approached. He was carrying a tray of take-out coffee. Instinctively, I turned away from him and studied the sidewalk. He talked to me anyway.

"Hi! You going in?" It was an invitation. He was already holding the door open for me.

"Me? Oh…I…um…no."

"They're pretty good in there," he coaxed. "You look like you could use some help. Like you're kinda lost."

He had my full attention.

"Is it that obvious?"

"Only to somebody who's been there. You wanna smoke?" He closed the door partially and waited for my answer.

"Don't you have to take the coffee inside or something?"

"Naw, it can wait," he said, and let the door swing shut.

Imagine. Just when my courage was about to fail me, this stranger had stepped up to reassure me. I was very close to leaving every good intention at that doorstep when he appeared and spoke. Here was an angel with rough clothes and a scraggy beard telling me his story of how Phoenix House had helped him. I could relate. We went inside, and he introduced me to his counselor, Pete. They sat and listened while, perfectly comfortable with them, I poured out my story. Pete, in a bright yellow short-sleeved shirt, had tattooed arms and three hoop earrings in one ear. He was a sincere listener, as was the guy who had guided me in and now sat sipping his coffee and nodding while I told both of them my history.

When I was finished, Pete was direct and said very simply, "We can help you."

The center arranged for people like me to enter rehab clinics. With my permission, he'd rush my application. I agreed and signed all the forms he offered. Something good was happening. These people understood my desperation. Not only were they willing, but they could also help.

Barely a week later, I was on a plane with three other guys and a counselor bound for a state 3,000 miles away from my home. My father was worried I had been victimized by some hoax, but I went anyway, drawn almost hypnotically to the thought of a cure.

It was after midnight when we arrived at the clinic where I was given a small private room. The nurse would check on me in the morning and introduce me to twelve other patients, all men. Some were high-profile professionals. For the first several days, I never uttered a word, afraid someone in charge would recognize how socially deviant I was compared to the others and, for that, kick me out. Their stories seemed so dissimilar to mine, so tame, I was sure I didn't belong. By the second week, I was ready to quit.

I was sent to women's meetings. Every day, I listened to their stories, and every day I convinced myself that I had nothing in common with them. One particular afternoon, I was dropped off at a women's support group in town. I really didn't want to go. All I ever did was stand in a corner by myself anyway. This time promised to be no different than the others. The speaker was a woman who was talking about how messed up her life was and how she drank too much wine and embarrassed her kids. How could I possibly identify with some suburban mom who tippled a little wine before her kids came home from school? If I opened my mouth about my episodes, the room would clear. I was certain of that. After the meeting I ran outside, expecting my ride to be waiting, but it wasn't. I took it as a sign that I wasn't supposed to be in this situation. I didn't fit. I'd have to get to a main road, stick out my thumb, and hitchhike back to Rick, where I belonged. And yet, another intervention prevented me from sabotaging myself; my ride showed up. Back to being the obedient child, I got into the car and let myself be taken back to the clinic.

When evening rolled around, I went to another meeting across the street at the hospital. On my way in, I took a ticket stub for the draw they held at the end of every meeting and found myself a seat at the back. A man spoke about losing his car and nearly his family to his drinking problem. Again, his story was not even close to my awful stuff. I was starting to get anxious for it all to end so I could leave. Finally, the meeting was concluded and they held the draw. The ticket they pulled was mine. I had won a book about recovery. As I walked to the front to claim it, I was in tears. I thanked them and ran back across to my room clutching my prize, crying uncontrollably the whole way.

The book was the first thing I had ever won in my life. Something, some invisible force, had been rescuing me, keeping me alive all these years for this moment.

"You're not going to let me leave, are you?" I asked the trees outside my window.

"No, Sue, we're not," they seemed to reply.

Whatever I wanted didn't matter. My path had been chosen. I understood what my father had been trying to tell me for so many years.

"Just go with the flow."

I needed to stop fighting. It was over. All I could do was cry. Two of my fellow patients heard me from the hallway. Worried after they saw the way I left the meeting, they burst in to help. That they cared when I hadn't even bothered to speak to them in the two weeks we had been in recovery together was more than I could comprehend. People I didn't even know cared.

For the first time in ages, I slept soundly that night. In the morning, I woke up in exactly the same position I was in when my head touched the pillow. The covers hadn't even been disturbed. It was the first day of the new me. I decided to start listening—not for differences, but for similarities with people around me—my sameness.

I started contributing in group sessions and spoke with my counselor for the first time instead of letting her speak while I remained silent. By changing my habits and releasing some fears, I made discoveries so astounding I wondered why nobody had told me about them before.

It's okay to be who I am and not what others expect me to be. *It's okay* to have and to express my feelings, including anger. *It's okay* to be imperfect.

Because I had spent so many years in denial practicing my "don't think, don't feel" mantra, I had lost the capacity to identify my feelings. That stunning realization got me a homework assignment. I was given a page illustrated with a variety of cartoon facial expressions. Each time I thought I was experiencing an emotion, I had to use my page to identify which one it was and report back at my next session. As it turned out, I was feeling a lot of confusion and frustration, enough to lead me to the conclusion that everything I thought I knew about being a real person was false.

This was going to be a long journey, but I kept making discoveries. Take for instance the session in which we had to list ten reasons why someone would want to be our friend. One of the guys said he'd make a good friend because he was funny and made good mashed potatoes. Another said he had a pool in his yard. After ten minutes of trying to think of why someone would want to be friends with me, I had nothing. Except for the tears splashing on it, my page was a blank. The exercise was measuring something called self-esteem, and it appeared that I had none. Mental note: normal people have this self-esteem thing. Find out what it is and get some.

Everyone suddenly seemed supportive, not that they weren't before; it's just that I was convinced I didn't deserve their trust, their praise, or their concern. Now I was beginning to understand genuine approval. To top things off, my district manager from my job back home sent me a letter. I don't know how she knew where to find me, but she wasn't accepting my resignation. If my work ethic was so strong when I was messed up, she was really looking forward to what I could accomplish when I was better. She even went so far as to pay me sick benefits for my six weeks at rehab. A new life was dawning for me. Not only would I have a little money in the bank when I returned, I'd have a job waiting for me.

The old Sue wanted to believe that things could be so different, that people might not *like* my new self. Maybe the new me wouldn't like them…or any number of disasters could occur, but…hey, who cared? It wouldn't be the end of the world if someone didn't like me! Life would go on. And so would I. Wow! Had I just passed another milestone? Yes, I believe I had!

57

I decided to take the first week back at home to settle in by signing up for a self-esteem improvement course at the YWCA. There I learned that self-esteem is feeling that you're effective as a person, able to cope with life's challenges, and believing you're worthy of happiness. By that account, I was sure missing out on the self-esteem factor; I was not even close to being an effective daughter, sister, partner, or you name it. I certainly had no idea how to cope with life's challenges except to dismiss them in my "don't think, don't feel" motto. Counting those flaws and the crimes I had committed against myself and anyone who tried to love me, I did not deserve to be happy. Was there a reversal to this trend in my life? I found the answer by resolving to understand this self-esteem business and make my life as normal as those I saw around me. I also wanted good relationships with family, friends, and my partner. I wanted to be able to communicate, to cope with life's ups and downs, and to recognize and process my feelings in a positive direction.

My counselor at the clinic had suggested that, when I returned home, I should find a friend, preferably a woman, with whom I could identify. When I finished laughing, she altered her advice to my finding a woman whose conduct and self-assurance I *admired*. The task was easier than I expected. At one of the support sessions I attended, I was drawn to Cathy. She was well-spoken and elegantly dressed, the lady I wanted to be. I gathered up the courage to chat with her. To my grateful surprise, we exchanged phone numbers. We began each call with minor conversations that flowed like this:

"Hi, Cathy. It's Sue."

"Oh, hi. How are you?"

"I'm fine."

"How did your day go?"

"Okay. Yeah, it was okay."

"Good. I had an interesting experience today at work…"

She'd continue with the story while I listened. After weeks, I began engaging in conversation and opening up about my life, delighted she hadn't given up on me. We became the best of friends. Cathy was my sounding board, my emotional support, and the person who offered the voice of reason during my bouts of self-doubt. She also agreed to go to school with me. We dubbed the adventure our "how to be a real person" training. I signed up for everything: group skills, interpersonal skills, human relationships, psychology, and sociology—anything that had to do with human interaction. One course at a time, I started to grasp what it meant to be a real person.

The day I learned "I am not responsible for other people's feelings, and they are not responsible for mine" was an eye-opener. Because I had always been committed to the notion that I was somehow accountable for other people's unhappiness, I was dumbfounded. How had I developed a belief that had caused me so much misery? My search to answer that question led me to a self-help book about families. It was a difficult read for me because I had to face my own dysfunctions. What I discovered was that my perfectionist mother, without meaning to and certainly without being aware of it, had passed along the message that you always needed to work hard in order to measure up. There had never been a suggestion that I had truly measured up. I had carried the burden of not being good enough for thirty-one years. Compound that belief with allowing abusive relationships to rule my life, and it was no wonder I had remained convinced of my worthlessness for so long.

More enlightening was the knowledge that my mother's perfectionism was all about her, not me. My childhood had revolved around her approval, which I seldom received because I operated on a different level. I wasn't wrong, just different. I'd have to reconnect with who I really was, and I understood, really understood, for the first time that Rick didn't have any right to beat me. I didn't deserve punishment. I was a good person. I just never knew it.

It was my value system, my way of thinking, that was destroying me. It had left me emotionally unstable and ill-equipped to cope with life's challenges. It wasn't the drugs or alcohol. They were only symptoms of my muddled beliefs, hiding the truth.

At school, I was older than the majority of the other students. My goals were more urgent. I was there to learn about functioning as a human being. I had to listen, I had to learn, and I had to put into practice everything I was taught. My ambition would tolerate no compromise. Knowledge was giving me permission to become a functioning adult. It was so liberating! I practiced conversing with people and processing information correctly. I was careful to recognize what I was responsible for and what I was not. I learned that the only person in the world I can control is me, including all of my thoughts and actions. That knot in my stomach became my guide. Whenever it tightened, I had to decide what I was doing that wasn't right. Slowly and steadily, I started to heal.

I had always blamed my parents for my unhappiness, but it became clear to me that it wasn't their fault. As human beings, they did the best they could to raise their children with the values they understood. With that awareness, I had to forgive them and take responsibility for my own behavior. I couldn't change the past, but I could manage my own present and plan rationally for my future.

Children learn what they live and live what they learn. I was obliged, for my emotional health, to break that cycle.

I am thankful to have found success and peace of mind. Even those I used to call real people can have issues and poor coping skills or lack a solid foundation in self-esteem. That's why I've made it my goal to share my story and knowledge with as many people as I can and show them that there are ways to find a happier, more productive life. None of us has to stay locked in the prison of our own or someone else's creation. We only have to look inward and identify how we prevent personal success by our thinking and actions.

Don't get me wrong. My life, like anyone else's, isn't perfect. Five years into my recovery, the worst blow I could imagine struck my life. My father died. My trusted safety net was gone forever. I never felt more desperate or alone. Another five years after that, I had a breast cancer scare. We can expect life to toss us unexpected challenges as a nudge to rise above circumstances.

Let this book be your challenge to stop standing in your own way. Free your potential from its invisible prison.

Where to Get Help

National Association for Self-Esteem
PO Box 597
Fulton, MD 20759-0597
www.healthyselfesteem.org

National Coalition against Domestic Violence
PO Box 18749
Denver, CO 80218
(303) 839-1852
Hotline: (800) 799-7233
www.ncadv.org

Alcoholics Anonymous
A.A. World Services, Inc.
PO Box 459
New York, NY 10163
(212) 870-3400
www.alcoholics-anonymous.org

National Mental Health Association
2001 Beauregard Street, 12th Floor
Alexandria, VA 22311
(800) 969-6642
www.nmha.org

National Association of Addiction Treatment Providers
313 West Liberty Street, Suite 129
Lancaster, PA 17606-2748
(717) 392-8480
www.naatp.org

About Susan

Susan Armstrong is a professional speaker, trainer, and author who books more than one hundred paid speaking engagements each year. During the last ten years, Susan has spoken to 20,000 people, helping them overcome their own barriers to personal and professional success in both the public and private sectors. Susan's clients include Fortune 100 companies as well as associations and nonprofit organizations.

Susan is a coauthor of the book *Professionally Speaking* and has contributed to such industry magazines as *Chemical News* and *Society for Human Resource Management*. Portions of Susan's story have also been featured on the Discovery Channel's *Health on the Line* series and the Life Television Network's *Skin Deep* series.

On a private note, Susan is happily married with two grown stepsons. She has recently taken up scuba diving to overcome another of her demons, claustrophobia. Oddly enough, she finds it relaxing to be in sixty feet of water with only a limited amount of air.

A Note from Carol

I liked Sue's character right from the very beginning. Of all the submissions I was editing for a professional speakers' collection of experiences, hers was the most genuine because it was fearless in its honesty about learning the hard way. When asked to share her biggest mistake, she didn't flinch. She gladly related her decision to remain onstage before a large audience while her microphone (hastily clipped under her dress to her panty hose), began sliding down her leg. Her startled audience watched her wiggle the microphone back into position, completely clueless as to why the guest speaker was gyrating on stage. And yet, she remained at the podium to finish her speech. What does she admit to learning after that episode? Not to take herself too seriously.

That introduction to Sue and her determined style occurred three years ago. Until then, we had never met; we worked by way of e-mail. Now I know that her humor and stubborn optimism (that innate British "carry on regardless" outlook) are the hallmarks of her survival. Not only has she risen above the mistakes of choosing wrong goals, an abusive partner, and an addicted lifestyle, but she's fought self-doubt, heartbreak, and, yes, a battle with cancer as well...and won.

We have worked together on this book without misgivings or conflict. Her main objective in engaging me to help write her story was to alert young women to the trap of romance with the exciting bad boy and never to surrender their self-esteem. She wanted the tale simply told and in her own voice. I believe we have accomplished that goal. All that remains is for others to read the story and reflect on it. When they do, they will recognize some of their own strengths in Sue and, hopefully, will act on them.

Carol Clarke, coauthor.

Keynotes

Whether Susan is speaking for an audience of fifteen people or a conference of 1,500, she can captivate and motivate the audience with her original, entertaining style. It's what makes her such a sought-after speaker for business professionals interested in overcoming their own personal and professional barriers to success. For additional information about Susan or to have Susan speak for your group, please call us, e-mail us, or visit our Web site at:

Stop Standing in Your Own Way
(a division of Susan Armstrong, *Training & Development*)

Email: info@stopstandinginyourownway.com
Toll-Free (North America) (877) 368-9200

www.stopstandinginyourownway.com

978-0-595-38277-4
0-595-38277-0

Printed in the United States
143316LV00001B/7/A